LYAUTEY

By ANDRÉ MAUROIS

MARSHAL LYAUTEY

From the painting by Philip A. de Laszlo,
in the Versailles Museum

LYAUTEY

BY

ANDRÉ MAUROIS

Translated by
HAMISH MILES

"... *the royalist who has given an empire to the Republic.*"
—PRINCESS MARTHE BIBESCO

D. APPLETON AND COMPANY
NEW YORK   MCMXXXI

TRANSLATOR'S NOTE

THE published sources upon which André Maurois
has drawn for his study of Marshal Lyautey are
indicated in the footnotes. The quotations from
official reports and letters are taken from unpub-
lished documents in the possession of the Marshal
and placed by him at M. Maurois's disposal.

At the author's suggestion I have myself added
a few notes on matters which may be less familiar
to English or American readers than to French;
these are distinguished by the square brackets [ ]
enclosing them.

H. M.

ILLUSTRATIONS

I

PATRIARCHAL authority has been waning since the War, but about the middle of last century its strength in the French provinces was at its height. The rigidity and austerity of family discipline would nowadays be a matter of extreme surprise. The father was paramount, and remained so to his dying day.

It would have been particularly interesting to observe this patriarchal power as it existed in a family living in the neighbourhood of Besançon about the year 1854, where the submission of the sons was emphasized by their social rank no less than by their age. Its head was Pierre Lyautey, aged ninety-five, at one time holding high administrative rank in the Imperial Armies; of his three sons, the eldest was a divisional artillery general and a senator of the Second Empire, the second an artillery brigadier-general, and the third a comptroller-general, but he treated all three as children.

One evening after family prayers, when the Ancestor had already gone up to his room, the burgraves of the second generation made a bid for emancipation. One sister had taken her seat at the

1

piano, the civil servant had sung a song, and at that moment the door opened. "What's all this noise? What's going on here?" said the father. "It's that rascal Charles, I'm certain. He'll never be serious. . . . Charles, go up to bed instantly." And without a word the comptroller rose.

Outside the family circle the peasants of "the Comté" invested the four generals of the Lyautey family with an equal and collective respect. "A fine stock," they said. On the eve of his death the Ancestor, almost a centenarian, climbed a ladder to lop the branch of a cherry-tree. The eldest son, General Hubert Lyautey, was handsome and charming like his father. He had become a lieutenant at the battle of Wagram, a chevalier of the Legion of Honour at the Kremlin, and had then served four régimes, with a tinge of favour towards the Orleans monarchy.

His son, Just Lyautey, entered the Ecole Polytechnique, became an engineer in the department of Public Works, and was sent to Nancy. Entrusted with the construction of the Nancy-Strasbourg section of the new canal joining the Marne and the Rhine, he had frequent occasion to visit Crévic, which lay alongside the new waterway. The family domain of Crévic was the property of a Norman gentleman, the Vicomte de Grimoult de

Villemotte. A younger son, owning no land in Normandy itself, he had in 1830 married Mademoiselle de la Lance, sprung from the lesser nobility of Lorraine and heiress to the estate of Crévic. And there he settled. Going over to see the canal excavations, he met the engineer, and remarked to his wife when he came home: "Well, I wish I could see our daughter married to a man of worth like that, instead of one of those conceited titled popinjays who swarm round her!"

Those were the days when a marriage desired by the parents was a marriage concluded. Just Lyautey married Laurence de Grimoult de Villemotte, and their eldest son (the Lyautey we know), christened Hubert like his grandfather, was born at Nancy in 1854. Not long after his birth his life was imperilled by an accident. During May, 1856, the baptism of the Prince Imperial was being celebrated with festivities in the Place Stanislas, and little Hubert, then eighteen months old, was being held up by his nurse to see the review from the residence of Madame de la Lance, his great-grandmother. He was placed on the railing of the window. The metal trellis-work had rusted. The baby fell head first on to the pavement, and would have been killed had not the shoulder of a cuirassier broken his fall. He dented his forehead.

After a few weeks he was believed to have re-
covered, but a couple of years later the doctors
realized that the spinal column had been affected.
The child, suffering great pain, was operated upon
by Professor Velpeau, and spent two years in bed
encased in a construction of plaster-of-paris. It
was not until he was six that he could walk, with
the aid of crutches; not until the age of ten did
he resume a normal life, and even then only with
endless precautions, avoiding nearly all physical
exercise and wearing a sort of mental frame which
he retained until he was twelve. To this prolonged immobility Hubert Lyautey owed his taste
for reading and study; and to that also he owed
his later fondness for activity and bodily elegance,
for he was resolved, once on his feet again, to show
that he too sprang of "the fine stock." Into his
need for domination, for being everywhere the first
and the foremost, there would always enter in some
degree the memory of this childish disability. It
was illness likewise that fostered his perfect knowledge, his all-embracing, idolizing love of the family
world which surrounded his invalid cot.

Astonishingly rich and varied that world was.
The whole history of France was woven into the
child's life. Grandpapa Lyautey often stopped at
Nancy with his son the engineer, and when dress-

ing in the morning would show the boy the scar
he had on his thigh from a Cossack's lance. The
forefinger of his right hand was missing, because
his finger had been frostbitten when he was serving
his last cannon with his own hands in Russia. On
New Year's Day he gave his grandson big boxes
of lead soldiers, whole battles in fact. "When my
grandfather came to Crévic he used to set out the
soldiers on the billiard-table himself, and 'do the
battle of Wagram,' with particular attention to a
large body of artillery of which he had been part."

But the child's favourite amusement was "playing at countries." In a corner of the park a sand-
heap had been placed for him, wherein he outlined
roads and rivers, and built bridges and houses. At
Nancy he was provided with a large board, on
which he again made the country, building towns
and villages of cardboard and tracing lines of railway. In the country, when he played with the
village children of Crévic, it was he, notwithstanding his metal corselet, who took command. For
a long time his memories retained his control of
the "Crévic army" and the plan of his tactics
against neighbouring hamlets.

Like his grandfather, his great-uncles infused
the house with the tradition of the Empire. Antoine Lyautey had fought at Waterloo, the recol-

lection of which remained so painful to him that
although he was for ever re-reading the Napoleonic
campaigns in M. Thiers's volumes, he always
skipped the pages on the defeat: to read them
caused him pain. The war of 1870 crushed him.
After his death a volume of Thiers was found on
his desk, open at the page—"Jena."

In Paris, General Lyautey, the senator of the
Second Empire, lived in the Rue de la Chaise, facing the garden of the Abbaye-aux-Bois. Close
beside his study window, over a mahogany writing-
desk, there hung in symbolic grouping, "Napoleon
Crossing the St. Bernard," a lithograph of the Duc
d'Orléans, and a photograph of Napoleon III.
The walls displayed oil-paintings in series of the
July Monarchy uniforms, a few weapons, the General's pistols. And whilst the latter sat writing
at his desk, little Hubert squatted there, well-
behaved, reading, turning over pictures, and
watching his grandfather.

"Every Tuesday there was a family dinner at
the Rue de la Chaise. It was a regular institu-
tion. It was a pleasure to be there, amongst all
one's cousins, but the evening reunion was a solemn
affair. One sat in the great drawing-room, the
women in a circle with their sewing, and the conversation flowed steadily forward with no diver-

sion, no flash of illumination, touching on the whooping-cough, measles and teething of all the children of the family. My grandmother kept all these matters under meticulous survey, or perhaps there was some expansiveness in family self-congratulation. Everyone overflowed with goodwill. That was what we called the 'Rue de la Chaise spirit.' "

In the eyes of all the children of the family, the "great day" of the Lyautey grandparents was that of their golden wedding, which was celebrated in 1866 at the Château of Montrambert in the Jura, where they spent every summer with one of their daughters, Madame Ménans. Couple by couple, a long procession wended its way to the chapel as if for a wedding. Hubert and his brother Raoul wore short black jackets, white waistcoats, cravats of blue moiré, and light grey trousers, their first long ones. The General and his brothers wore morning clothes with the medallions of the Grand-Officier, the cravat of Commander, and the ribbon of Ste. Hélène. This took place after the victorious campaigns in the Crimea and Italy, and in the minds of the children the memory of this festivity remained linked with the picture of the unconquered France of the days before Sedan, the France of the family Generals.

It can now be imagined what the son of Just

Lyautey found on the paternal side of his family: a heredity of administrators and methodical military men, "the utmost simplicity in tastes and habits, fewness of needs, rigid austerity in morals, a very deep religious faith and the strictest observance, fervid devotion to every conjugal and family and social duty, assiduity and exactness in work, a taste for cultivation of things of the mind, moderation in all things, a horror of showiness, outward display and distinctions. . . . On the other hand, except to a small extent in music, no aptitude for the arts, no interest in furnishing or arrangement. (The furniture of the room could be changed without my father noticing it.) The sense of order and economy, habits of reckoning. Service to the State regarded as one of the primary duties and a duty strictly fulfilled." When three generations have scrupulously observed such a code, the fourth, barring a reaction, is deeply imprinted with their mark.

*   *   *   *   *

But if there was a Rue de la Chaise spirit, there was also a Crévic spirit, a very different one. Monsieur de Villemotte, father of Madame Just Lyautey, was a man of elegance, a fine horseman, lively, full of dash and go. "The brilliant Villemotte,"

they called him at Nancy; and his wife, known
to the children as "Maman Louise," had his own
quickness in riposte and his own charming ease
of manner. His town apartment at Nancy was
reached by a great stone staircase with a wrought-
iron bannister, "one of those vast and handsome
staircases of the eighteenth century so frequently
found at Nancy. . . . There was no constraint,
everything was cheerful, smiling, sunny. In the
morning she made her own chocolate, pounding
it in the silver bowl with a little ribbed wooden
pestle, letting it simmer on the fire, and toasting
slices of bread with a long double-pronged fork
with a black horn handle. Sometimes she entrusted
this to me, and there was quite an art in holding
the bread to the flame so that it was done 'just
right' without being singed. . . . When our parents went to the big dinner-parties she gave, we
dined at home alone, but we were allowed to come
for a moment after dinner; we used to sit quietly
in the drawing-room waiting for the end of the
meal, whilst the candelabra and the Carcel lamps,
clicking their springs, were lit. I can still hear
the scrape of the chairs that told us the company
were leaving the table. . . .

"Every morning after breakfast she called at our
house after her shopping. And I still hear her ring

of the bell. Up we leapt, my brother and I, from the table where we did our lessons, and waited. She always came by way of the kitchen, stopping for a moment to say good-morning to the servants and to see that everything was in order, and then came into our room. It was like a burst of light. My mother arrived, lessons were stopped, and there was a stocktaking of the twenty-four hours. Had we been good? Were we too warm? Had we coughed? And I can hear her quick, well-pitched voice, just a little abrupt; and with an effort I can still hear it so distinctly that it pains me to the point of agony that I cannot fix that dear, dear voice which to-day sounds only in the ears of my brother and myself.

"What pretty movements she had—with her arms especially, when she rested her chin on her hand, or turned the pages of an album, or crossed her hands on her lap! On full-dress occasions I never saw her *décolletée,* but only slightly open in front, no more than any Nancy lady of her age, elaborately dressed in the evening, but always in a high-cut gown, or one slightly open at the neck, long-waisted, with those charming little caps set on the crown of the head, in fine crochet lace, with pearl beads or sequins. Except at Crévic, where she would wear gowns of woollen stuff or frilled lawn, I see her only in silk, sometimes watered silk, or in jaconet muslin; one of those gowns I can see again now, with large white checks; another was pearly grey with bows on the shoulders; another too, black, with mauve flowers and a long Watteau fold; and when she went out of doors in summer-time, a light scarf of black lace drooped— how gracefully!—over her arms and waist. And I nestled lovingly against these dresses, which still rustle softly in my ears."

The annual move to Crévic was the great event of the children's life. A pantechnicon was chartered, into which were loaded the piano, the packing-cases, the trunks; and then the family started off with grandmamma in a barouche hired from the Antoine establishment. In 1860, the year when Hubert Lyautey was so ill, he had to be conveyed in his slung cot on a carriage with eight springs.

At Crévic Madame de Villemotte spent a great part of the time in the park, with a grey linen apron, her pruning shears, and, on sunny days, a large flowered linen coif in peasant style, chivvying the gardener, inspecting the paths and the washerwoman at the washing-place, making the round of the kitchen-garden. "There she would take us, counting up her fruit, selling her mirabel plums, peeping into the ice-house under its straw covering; or else she would go round to the poultry-yard, where old Nanette was so expert in wringing a fowl's neck and terrified us by throwing its head to us.

"After luncheon and before dinner, we gathered under the three Japanese trees which were called the 'summacks' over by the hothouse. Maman Louise was sitting there in a folding chair. There she took coffee and received visitors, afterwards making a round of the hothouse, where we watched the ripening of the Frankenthal, a magnificent black grape hailing from the banks of the Rhine, the first bunch of which we always laid before the image of the Blessed Virgin, or else we admired the plants, cacti or aloes, which I little thought that later, throughout so many years of my life, I should see in their proper soil, gigantic growths, in strange lands."

But great as the influence of his grandmother was over young Hubert Lyautey, that of his mother's sister, Berthe de Grimoult de Villemotte, was even greater. "She was heart and soul a Grimoult, and thoroughbred to the finger-tips. Of her blood, her name, her rank, she was supremely proud. . . . Though not active in politics, she was a royalist. It was a matter of blood, not of reason, with her. She was profoundly Catholic too, and practising, but liberal. . . . She had an open mind and great sureness of taste, and was always glad to discuss matters of religion no less than those of art or intellect; she read St. Teresa, Madame Swetchine, St. Francis de Sales, and Father Lacordaire, but preferred them in fine editions. Her religious library comprised the humble, dog-eared prayer-books of her grandmothers, cherished like relics, but she took pleasure in having her countless devotional books bound at Gruel's and stamped with her arms."

Hubert Lyautey was enchanted by this charming woman, who read St. Teresa but preferred her in fine editions.

II

WE must bear in mind the graciousness of
this childhood, the boy's pride and happiness in his two families, and his heredity as a man
of the Borders—Franche-Comté on his father's
side, Lorraine on his mother's. A Frenchman,
certainly, but one cherishing a local patriotism
woven into the stuff of his national sentiment, and
judging certain traits of Paris with the sober detachment of a man from the Eastern provinces.
All his life long, irony would be foreign, even
hateful, to him. In his eyes the Midi would always be "a land conquered by *us*." On days of
festival it was to be the red and yellow flag of Lorraine that waved over the home of his old age.

In matters of politics he has himself analysed
the heritage of his ancestry. No single one of his
forbears had been an active politician. "On my
father's side, they knew nothing but the service
of the State, and private life: on my mother's,
military service until the fall of the monarchy, and
thereafter private life and the life of fashion."
Their opinion had been royalist, with a dominating Orleans tendency in his paternal family, and

14

a Legitimist one on the maternal side, but always without violence.[1]

If this young man came under any influence, it was rather that of women—doubtless by reason of his long illness. And two women especially, from childhood days, reached his intelligence through his sensibility. One was his father's second sister, Madame Ménans. She was a militant Catholic, a Royalist tirelessly engaged in the Legitimist cause in the Franche-Comté, staunch to the Jesuits, to Pius IX and the Ultramontanes; and she had come to venerate the Comte de Chambord. Of the second woman we have already spoken—Berthe de Grimoult de Villemotte, who became Madame Saulnier de Fabert in 1860 and was likewise of Royalist opinions. It is necessary to appreciate the strength of family doctrines such as these, in order to understand not only the history of France between 1870 and 1890, with its violent political battles, but also the private drama of Hubert Lyautey's mind during those years. To secure acceptance, the new régime had to overcome a high barrier of hostile feeling in a great number of

---

[1] [The Royalist camp in France during this period was divided. The Legitimists supported the claims of the elder branch of the Bourbon family, as represented by the Comte de Chambord. The Orleanists maintained the rights of the Orleans branch, descended from Philippe, younger brother of Louis XIV, as represented by the Comte de Paris, grandson of King Louis-Philippe.]

15

French people. In 1889, at one of the last family
dinners she attended, grandmamma Lyautey (the
wife of the General) gave utterance to a sincere
and astounding remark; she was then ninety-two
years old, and her children, grandchildren and
great-grandchildren numbered sixty. "My children," she said, "I thank God that among all of
you, for all your diversity, there is not one Republican."

It will be curious to see how the child with this
upbringing was brought into active partnership
with nearly all the statesmen of the Third Republic, and into choosing some of them as his friends;
and in this he was instinctively loyal to the tradition of his father's family, where the sense of service had always overcome factious bitterness.

In his sense of duty, therefore, as in his restless
desire to be taking action, constructing, commanding, he was a Lyautey; in his elegance, his taste for
beautiful things, he was a Grimoult—a Grimoult
likewise in his skill in understanding the common
people, and his aristocratic liberalism, the mark
of a man sure enough of his own breeding not
to be afraid of compromising himself; a Lyautey
also in his capacity for work, his need for the post
of command. (That evening at Thorey, it was a
Grimoult who was eager to read to me the charm-

ing portrait of his grandmother, but a Lyautey
who found the page of text painstakingly type-
written and in its proper place in the cupboard of
files.)

        *   *   *   *   *

He was educated at the Lycée of Nancy, amidst
a group of friends like himself, intelligent and
imaginative boys, aflame with political and religious ardours. His closest school-friend was
Antonin de Margerie, a son of Amédée de Margerie, professor of the faculty at Nancy, a man
who enjoyed a great reputation in Catholic circles.
By 1866 Hubert Lyautey had collaborated with
young Margerie in compiling a Legitimist profession of faith—"Why we are Royalists . . ." They
wrote it out in their best handwriting, on paper
which they had headed with a sketch of the arms
of France. "We cannot be Bonapartists, because
of the murder of Louis XVI. We cannot be Republicans, because no man of probity can belong
to that faction. So we can only be Legitimists."
And their programme followed. Lyautey was
then twelve, Margerie eleven. They burned with
piety. They knew by heart countless religious
verses of Lamartine's and had no love for Victor
Hugo.

There was at this time in Nancy a whole group

of youthful friends of the same age and with the same background, who met every Thursday. They played an "Army" game of their own, had picked on a chief whom, despite the Royalism of the majority, amongst them, they called "the Emperor." Lyautey felt ill at ease in a subordinate place, after his leadership amongst the village boys of Crévic; and Margerie also, with a few others, were anxious to raise their friend to power. "Hubert," they said, "you are the one to be Emperor—you must be." And that was just what Lyautey thought. The boys used to meet in a courtyard where they had made a platform with a few packing-cases. One day Lyautey ascended it with a brace of toy pistols in his hands, laid them in front of him on the packing-case platform, and carried out a *coup d'état*. He was acclaimed by the rest. The holder of the title was deposed. In his parent's circle the story of young Lyautey's *coup d'état* quickly went the rounds, and was a great success. The old gentleman now always called him "the Emperor." But his grandmother, a Legitimist, did not acknowledge usurpations, and was stern with her grandson. A couple of days later he entered the drawing-room of an elderly friend, formerly a sous-préfect of the July Monarchy, and was met with the laughing greeting:

"Bravo, Louis-Philippe!"—"Don't make a joke of it," said Madame de Villemotte, with a look of annoyance and seriousness, "In my opinion Hubert has behaved like a usurper."

When his father was appointed chief engineer at Dijon and left Nancy, Lyautey still kept Margerie as his closest friend. He saw him again at Nancy during the holidays, and they made plans for the future together. The war of 1870 and its disasters inspired them with the desire to play a part in the revival and reconstruction of their country. The unconquered France of the Lyautey generals was no more. Another had to be refashioned. What would it be? Frenchmen could not tell. In 1871 Lyautey decided to enter the Ecole Polytechnique,[1] like his namesakes there before him, but he had no wish to spend his whole life as either an engineer or an officer. His dream was of a political career, at first regional, based upon Lorraine, and then national. Later he was to note in his diary: "My oldest mistress is that unbridled ambition of my middle teens." Yet it was not only ambition; in the same diary will be found something no less heartfelt: "In these days of anxious waiting through which we are passing,

---

[1] Polytechnique trains engineers and artillery officers. The examinations are more difficult.

men of spirit, even if they are but young people, have another path to follow than the path of pleasure and heedlessness." That generation of defeat was more ardent than frivolous.

Lyautey became a pupil of the school in the Rue des Postes in 1872. Father du Lac, its director, advised that as he had three years before him he should enter for the Saint-Cyr [1] examination in his first year, simply to inure himself to examinations. At the Rue des Postes the liberal, almost Gallican, Catholicism of the Lyauteys conflicted with the Roman spirit of the Fathers. Father du Lac, who had taken a particular fancy to him, did not restrain him from discussing it, and in the course of one of their talks the young man answered the Father with Montalambert's remark: "I shall die a penitent Catholic and an impenitent liberal."

At the end of the year he was accepted for Saint-Cyr, and Father du Lac advised him to profit by his fortune. He thus gained an advance of a year or two, and by passing next into the still existing Staff College, he would form part of a special corps comprising a number of Polytechnique pupils, which in his father's view was essential. Besides, the uniform was tempting to the young man; he had long been an invalid, and was de-

---

[1] Saint-Cyr = West Point but only for infantry and cavalry officers.

lighted to be able to show himself one no longer, handling arms and foils, riding his horse. He agreed.

Saint-Cyr disappointed him slightly. Enthusiasm was what he needed. Placid instructors put him through routine exercises: "nothing to elevate or transport the soul." He was exasperated by a certain pettiness of authority. On the day of his entry to Saint-Cyr, when uniforms were being allotted, he was given too close-fitting a tunic. "Does that jacket fit you all right?" asked a non-commissioned officer.—"Yes, but the neck is too tight."—And he was answered: "When you're asked a question in the army, you begin by holding your tongue."—For a long time that remark remained with him as the symbol of an erroneous soldierly attitude, entirely the contrary of what he would have liked to find in the army.

One meeting was to transmute his monotonous life there. In the course of a reading to the pupils at the Rue des Postes, one of the Fathers had introduced them to a few fragments from the pen of Captain Albert de Mun, and had told them something of that man, an apostle, who had founded working-men's clubs and was spending his life in their midst. Lyautey's interest was kindled by these few sentences. During his first year at Saint-

Cyr, he received an invitation to attend a Sunday address by Captain de Mun, went with some companions, and was completely won over. This cuirassier with his white epaulettes, aide-de-camp to General de Martimprey, Governor of Paris, and supported on the platform by bishops and leaders of the Catholic party, expounded a doctrine and a programme calculated to rouse the enthusiasm of the young. It was one's duty, he declared, "to win the minds of the people by example and by the practice of self-devotion." The road to which he pointed, that of social reform through Catholicism, was precisely the one which Lyautey during his adolescent fervour had been so eager to follow. Here at last was an officer, a senior, giving him a more uplifting reason for existence than the handling of weapons or the company school.

On the following Sunday, accompanied by three fellow cadets, he rang nervously at Captain de Mun's door. He received them instantly, himself a little intimidated by these young men who told him that their lives were at his disposal. "What use do you wish to make of us? Give us the command—we shall obey."—"But what can I do with you?" he answered. "You belong to Saint-Cyr! You are not free. . . . I must think it over." And he summoned them back the next Sunday. When they arrived, full of grave concern, he told them: "I have thought things out . . . and found a means. Some students from the Polytechnique came here after you last week. I am going to ask you to found in each of your schools a small group for social and religious action. . . . No outward or demonstrative propaganda. None of your comrades should know of the existence of your group. Act by way of example, of the respect you show for your own ideal, of your staunchness, of your self-denial." It showed a true understanding of youthful minds to set before them the lure of a mystery and the sternness of a lofty asceticism. Throughout the whole of their life at Saint-Cyr the members of the group were true to their oath.

Captain de Mun had nominated as leader of the Saint-Cyr group Sergeant Prosper Keller, son of the deputy for Belfort who headed the Alsatian protest in the Bordeaux Assembly. The Polytechnique group were headed by Antonin de Margerie, who was more and more closely bound up with the life of his Nancy friend.

When Keller and Lyautey entered their second year they were called upon to recruit a like-minded group amongst their contemporaries at Saint-Cyr. Margerie and his friends were doing likewise at the Polytechnique. These were years of hope, of

anxious seeking, of moral perfecting. Their journal kept by Lyautey at Saint-Cyr is courageously
sincere: "A bad month. Too much talk, no action.
Chattering, commonplaces, complaining for complaining's sake, childishness, sulkiness. Little self-
examination for all my saying I was doing so. I
have given myself the semblance of reflection and
have reflected very little. Grimaces, childishness."
He complains of his excitement and his outbursts
of violence. "Lord, a little calm, night, repose, a
few hours to myself, of self-examination and peaceable thought! A little kneeling in prayer, head in
hands!" Weariness and ambition, faith and doubt,
the craving for action to escape from weariness and
doubt—all of Lyautey is already there in that adolescent. A few pages further on one finds—"Act,
act, act." And again: "I remain a solitary in
spite of friendships, an idler in spite of a consuming activity." And at holiday-time, after a retreat at the Grande-Chartreuse: "Resolved: to
read the Gospels and the *Imitatio Christi*. Never
to neglect my public duties. Above all, no proudness of heart in all this."

On leaving Saint-Cyr Lyautey had entered the
Staff School in Paris. He was being introduced
to social life, and made full use of it. On Sundays
his chief pleasure was going to concerts with his

friend Margerie, but he reserved a considerable part of his leisure time for the working-class club in Montmartre to which Albert de Mun had attached him.

Lyautey found the Staff School no more agreeable than he had Saint-Cyr, perhaps even less. The old house, on the point of vanishing, was dominated by a narrow and out-of-date system of instruction. There was only one teacher who had the art of animating the youthful—Captain Niox, then just beginning his career, who taught geography. In the other classes, dreary grinds aimed at nothing but memory; Lyautey was bored.

I go [he says in his journal at this period], and boredom follows me, incurable. For a year now, and even going further back so long as I have known myself, it has insinuated itself everywhere, poisoning every joy, fettering every study. . . . This eternal *tædium,* this disgust, this boredom in fact, is the very thing, always the same, that Lucretius speaks of—*Sedet atra cura.*

And forthwith—for a deep faith existed alongside a restless pride in this youth—he sought to master himself, and filled his notebook with sacred texts: "Woe unto you, Pharisees! for ye love the uppermost seats in the synagogues, and greetings in the markets!" At his father's house in Versailles, where he was at that time at the head of

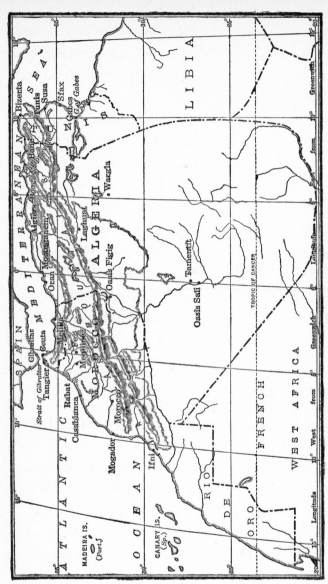

NORTH AFRICAN COLONIES OF FRANCE

the engineers' service, Lyautey was able during those years 1875-1877 to observe the last struggles of the monarchist deputies to retain power; he met them round the family table. It was the time of May 16th,[1] the Fourtou and Rochebouet ministries, passionate arguments on the possibility of a *coup d'état*. The young officer was all eagerness to see the return of the Comte de Chambord to Paris as Henri V. His father would be content with the maintenance of the ordered régime represented by Marshal MacMahon and the Duc de Broglie, and although having no fondness for the Republican label, he would gladly have seen the Republic endure in this reassuring form.

*　　*　　*　　*　　*

When his school training was over, Lieutenant Lyautey served for a time in a cavalry regiment at Châteaudun. During the severe winter of 1879 the spinal pains from which he had suffered as a child returned in the form of acute rheumatism, and he was obliged to take six months' leave. He spent the time at Versailles with his parents. It so happened that he there met Margerie again, and another youth, slightly younger, Joseph de la

---

[1] [Referring to the dissolution of the Chamber by the Senate in 1877, a turning-point in the battle between the monarchical Right and the republican Left.]

Bouillerie, son of MacMahon's minister, who had also belonged to the Albert de Mun group at Saint-Cyr. The three officers were inseparable, and were soon known to the whole town as "the three Musketeers." They spent several intoxicating months together. All three were handsome in person, elegant, constantly invited out, and smiled upon by the ladies; and they made a pleasant place for themselves in the society (quite distinct from Parisian society) then living at Versailles. In Lyautey's independent apartment in the Rue d'Anjou (his parents' gift) they held endless "palavers." "Faith, aspirations, the aim of life" —they regarded existence as a splendid battle in which they would engage together. Their religion was a thing of romance and passion. They hoped for everything from life, and especially for Lyautey, whom they regarded as their spearhead. What would his future be? He conceived it as political rather than military. This brand-new Republic hardly looked very stable. Who could tell?

When Lyautey's health was restored again, the former Staff corps had just been abolished and its officers scattered amongst different services; Lyautey was attached to the cavalry and set out with his regiment of hussars for Algeria. There he spent two years; they seemed short. His last six months he spent in almost complete isolation in a southern outpost, where he read a great deal. In particular he resolved that it was his duty to be better acquainted with his religion, and he began a study of the Gospels, comparing them and making his own exegesis. One should picture this lieutenant of twenty-five, alone with a handful of soldiers in the desert, lying outstretched on a divan and covering endless sheets of fine Arab paper with synoptic tables of St. Mark and St. Luke. The outcome of his labours startled him. He felt a profound uneasiness. He was alone. He could consult nobody. He sent for the books of Renan, which left him interested but unmoved. He ceased to practise with regularity, but once again he felt his life to be aimless and his zealous self-devotion unused.

Nevertheless, his seriousness and his scrupulous attention to duty made him an excellent officer. Before leaving Algeria he received his captaincy.

III

HE returned to France in 1882 as a captain in the 4th Regiment of Chasseurs, and in the following year, as his aunt, Madame Saulnier de Fabert, had to go to Rome, he requested a few months' leave and accompanied her. He was anxious to go through Austria and make a pilgrimage to Gorizia, where the Comte de Chambord was living in exile. On this twofold journey he set out with a great desire to find confirmation of the political and religious convictions which had been those of his family.

Austria he found congenial: "the people *gemütlich,* people of our own kind, of our own Lorraine, good *sauerkraut,* and on the walls the Emperor Francis Joseph, sacred pictures, and 'Napoleon in bivouac at Austerlitz'!" At Gorizia he experienced, as fully as he had imagined it, the emotion for which he had prepared himself by twenty years of exalted feeling: "I have just left Him. The emotion is such, the stamp so powerful, that I cannot yet recover consciousness of my personality, which was surrendered, merged in Him, during those hours of grace. The King of France!—

I have seen him, touched him, heard him. . . ."

This letter was addressed to Antonin de Margerie; Lyautey described to his friends this private audience, in the course of which he had offered the Comte de Chambord the devotion of the trio of officers whom the Comte, prompted by M. de la Bouillerie, referred to as "his three Musketeers."

The conversation? A reminder to begin with of my La Bouillerie friendships, of yours, of the pact joining all three of us, about which he seems to be well-informed; my work, what I am going to see and do in Italy; Algeria; and finally politics. We shall talk about this, for no nuances must be overlooked. Here I confine myself to showing you that there was marked interest in my journey to Rome, and, to my extreme surprise, in the unfavourable attitude of Leo XIII, in my possible desire for an audience, in the word which would be sent to the Princess Massimo to smooth the way for me; and here are the words with which the audience concluded: "The Pope must be made aware that there is still a Royalist youth in France, active, and full of faith, and that I have behind me something more than old staff-officers. It is essential that he should ascertain this. You must see him or speak to him frankly." You may guess how I was thrilled! I certainly pitched my imagination very high, but I had the impression of an investiture, that of the Royal Word which it was my lot to transmit.

That evening, on returning to his room, he tried to fix the images and feelings of those six hours:

First and foremost the impression of life, personality and authority which emanates from him. How far he is from being the congealed and obsolete Buddha that some people imagine. He carries his sixty-two years with youthfulness and cheerful vivacity. Were he not the King, how charming he would be as a man, whom one can easily picture at the club, at the play, in a drawing-room, conspicuous by his power of charm and by the lively aptness of his repartee—so very French, so very Parisian even! I was dumbfounded by his up-to-date knowledge of persons and things; he talked of my colonel, of generals, of men of fashion, as if he had seen them all yesterday. . . . But here I stop. I shall make you a complete note from all this, when my head is rested; I shall hold it back, not sending it to you, however trusty the messenger, but so as to bring it to you myself. . . . Now, quickly to bed for a few hours' sleep before taking my train, which I almost wish I could miss so as to see *Him* again.

*   *   *   *   *

Rome was to bring Lyautey a great emotion and a great surprise. On Easter Sunday he was present at the Pontifical Mass in the Sistine Chapel.

Leo XIII is exactly like his portraits; his pallor and thinness are transparent, and still more striking with his white cassock, but he has the look of a saint: superbly solemn and dignified, and I can imagine nothing to compare with the gesture of his benediction. As always since 1870, it was a Mass without any pomp, except for the eight Swiss Guards waiting at the entrance of the chapel in their archæological uniform designed by Michael Angelo—doublet, breeches and stockings striped yellow and black, helmets on their heads, the halberd before them, and the large two-handled sword at the side. Robert O'Gorman was there, looking superb beneath his helmet and its white plume falling back like a Russian horse-guard's. We numbered only a couple of hundred, the women in black mantillas, the men in dress-coats and white ties. The Holy Father entered by the small door at the end, underneath the "Last Judgment," which I was just beginning to look at, but from that moment my eyes were all for him. He was preceded by eight noblemen in waiting, amongst them his nephew Count Camillo Pecci, and surrounded by his familiar prelates. Leaving his huge red mantle at the doorway, he stood out against the dark background of the entrance like an apparition, in his white diaphanous vestment. He walked draggingly up to the altar, scarcely a body, but erect and smiling, and holding out his open hand in blessing. . . . The organ throbbed, every prayer of the Mass could be heard, clear and cadenced, in every corner of the chapel, and the *Corpus domini nostri* in particular, repeated a hundred times over, was spoken with a gentle gravity and a penetrating expression which the years will certainly never

33

efface from my ear. A very fine, tall figure, truly Christian, truly ascetic, truly moving, and the sight of him was enough to rechristianize Rome for me.

On Saturday, March 31st, he had his private audience, and found himself "cowed at being the bearer of certain words and at being honoured with lofty pronouncements. . . ."—"I send you these words and my impressions all fresh, just on emerging, in a note for yourself only. I sum them up by saying that I leave this audience profoundly troubled, with a sense of having lost my bearings. . . ." The secret note explained to his friends what had already been hinted to Captain Lyautey in the conversations at Gorizia: the Pope was a Republican. . . .

During the twelve days since my Papal audience, every word of which remains graven in my memory, all the conversation I have had with those who have been in contact with Leo XIII, with all who are preoccupied and concerned with this question, confirm what I have heard—something which I would so gladly have been uncertain of having heard correctly: not only is the Pope not a Legitimist, but he dissuades one from remaining a Legitimist. That is the starting-point. Probably his visit as Nuncio to Brussels has some connection with this. There he was the friend and confidant of Leopold, that perfect parliamentarian, son-in-law of Louis-

Philippe. This tendency of his, so far as we are concerned, would at first have remained rather Orleanist, but as the question does not arise with the Comte de Chambord still alive, and as in any case events have moved on, I return to what I wrote to you immediately after my audience—for France, it is towards the Republic that he is heading, and wishes also to head us.

Lyautey made a long inspection of the museums and antiquities of Rome, and made a very intelligent study of the society of the new Italian monarchy, the relations between the monarchy and the Vatican, and the army. A diplomat or an historian who could have read the letters which this unknown captain was then sending to his friends, would have been surprised by this young man's mental penetration and force of expression. Stendhal would have been delighted with such a dissection of the "Black" Society, that of the families loyal to the Vatican—Orsinis, Altieris, Colonnas.

The Roman strikes me as very *adaptable*. I don't see in him those enthusiasms or cleavages of principle which create in France a hitherto unbridgeable gulf between Royalist and Republican. Frequently a husband is Black, his wife White, and the children Grey (for there are Grey circles too), and everything goes on all right. It is the triumph of the *combinazione*, their own word, their answer to everything."

LYAUTEY

He spent the whole of April in Rome, a little anxious at finding a new-born hostility against France, arising from the annexation of Tunis.

*   *   *   *   *

This journey to Rome did not produce the effect on Lyautey which he expected, and which his innermost heart desired. He had knelt before Leo XIII with a sincere, a desperate, desire of faith. He came home unappeased. On his return to France he rejoined his regiment at Epinal, and a few months later, after the annual manœuvres, was picked out as a General-Staff officer by General L'Hotte, the famous horseman, who was at that time inspector-general of cavalry at Commercy. There Lyautey found himself very much isolated, lacking companions to associate with outside his duties with his superior officer. Once again he began to read widely, still attracted by the problem of philosophy and religion; now it was Herbert Spencer, Auguste Comte, and Strauss's *Life of Jesus,* which he covered with his notes. His religion was fleeing him. It was a time of intense moral suffering. He fought as best he could. He went as far as Paris in order to consult the Abbé Huvelin, who bade him read certain Christian exegetists. But these disappointed Lyautey, and failed to restore his peace. It was not that he had turned hostile to the Church, as happens to so many young men after a crisis of this nature; indeed, he retained affection and a fond respect for the beliefs which had formed the matrix of his family life, and for a form of idealism which was still in his eyes the loftiest. He was no longer certain of dogmatic truth, but he envied the believer.

Politically he was slowly evolving. Until the death of the Comte de Chambord he had remained an ardent Legitimist. When the Comte died, Lyautey was stationed at Epinal and was unable to attend the funeral at Gorizia. The organizers of the working-class clubs dined together every Wednesday, and from Epinal Lyautey travelled frequently to join them. A few weeks after the burial of the Comte de Chambord, he met Albert de Mun and La Tour du Pin on their return from Gorizia. Over their table they faced the great question: what next? Were they to rally to the House of Orleans? Were they to hail the Comte de Paris at Eu? Were they to take the independent line and steer perhaps towards a Christian and conservative Republic? Opinion varied. At one of the succeeding Wednesdays Albert de Mun, who had visited Eu, described his experience. "He

certainly made us very welcome," he said. . . .
"He spoke to us of social questions and the workers in our movement as one who has studied them
and takes great interest in them. . . . But it isn't
the same thing. . . . He shakes your hand. . . .
You dine in a black tie. . . ." (At Gorizia no one
approached the Comte de Chambord without kissing his hand, and one always dined in a white tie.)
The young Royalist officers did not go to the
Château of Eu. Lyautey, however, remained a
Monarchist, and if he was shortly to show himself
a passionate opponent of Boulanger,[1] that was
partly because of his inborn hatred of disorder,
but even more because Boulanger had counter-
signed the decree for the expulsion of the Princes.

*   *   *   *   *

Lyautey's rally to the Republic was one of fact,
not of doctrine, and took place, like that of many
French conservatives, between 1887 and 1891, at
once for general and personal reasons.

At the end of 1887 Captain Lyautey was commanding a squadron at Saint-Germain. He commanded it well. Into the routine and monotony
of barrack life, this fisher of souls, the disciple of
Albert de Mun, strove to introduce humane feel-

---

[1] [The General who was on the point of upsetting the Republican
status in the early months of 1889.]

ing. That Grimoult in him which had been so fond of the fine houses of Nancy had never been able to take for granted the ugliness of War Ministry buildings, the hideous uniformity of their architecture, their tarry smell, the broad strips of black coal-tar at the foot of their whitewashed walls. He would have liked to make the barracks a kind of home or club for his troopers. And he made the attempt:

My aim is to give them distraction in their quarters as well as instruction and fatigues, to set up, in fact, a sort of home for these children (and children they really are) whom we have in our hands, and to escape from the absurdity of the present state of affairs, in which after five o'clock in the evening every man who is not sufficiently stupefied to go to bed is condemned to the street-corner or the canteen.

Accordingly he arranged a large room supplied with tables, a library, lamps, where the men found books, games, a billiard-table, writing-paper. A committee of eight members, under the presidency of the senior non-commissioned officer, administered the club under the captain's supervision. In the army of 1887 this organization was something quite new, and regarded by many as revolutionary.

But to command a squadron, even a model one, to choose the furniture of a refectory, and to satisfy the decisions of a committee presided over by a non-commissioned officer was scanty nourishment for the activity of a man of thirty-four who had dreamed of a boundless future. Somewhat discouraged, Captain Lyautey could see stretching before him the endless, dusty road of his career, and was beginning to ask himself whither all this was leading him, and how on earth he was to escape from it. But just about this time, when the demons of boredom and ambition were vexing him more determinedly than ever, he discovered the existence of worlds totally different from that Legitimist, pious, provincial sphere in which he had hitherto breathed so naturally. This discovery had come by stages, and one might say by accident, if it were not that life brings to every man, and usually several times, the chance of finding amongst the infinite variety of creatures just those men of whom he is in the most urgent need.

At Le Pecq, near Saint-Germain, lived a certain M. de Guerle, a gentleman of standing who had been in part responsible for the education of the Comte de Paris, and then, after 1870, had been a préfet under Thiers and held an important post in the exchequer at Nancy. There Lyautey had been entertained as his guest. He was a man of

culture, a friend of the Broglies and M. d'Haussonville. He had resigned his official post in consequence of the expulsion of the Princes, and had
taken an administrative post in a bank. Settling
at Le Pecq, and being a great bibliophile, he entertained there every Sunday writers and social
personages—the d'Haussonvilles, Eugène-Melchior de Vogüé, the Baignères, Brunetière, Coppée,
Mme. Arvède Barine. . . . Learning that Lyautey, with whose family he was well acquainted, was
in the neighbouring garrison, he invited the young
captain, whose measure was then taken. Vogüé
was surprised and delighted at finding an officer
of Chasseurs who knew almost by heart his book
on the Russian novel, and made a friend of Lyautey. Brunetière at first cast an uneasy eye on the
boots and spurs of this soldier who talked of Vigny
and Lamartine and seemed to have read them, and
then came to respect the young man too. Soon
people were quarrelling for him. Deserting the
drawing-rooms where they danced, he became the
habitual guest, first, of his dear Eugène-Melchior
de Vogüé, his *"patron";* of the Baignères, where
alongside famous men of letters he found young
men like Henri de Régnier, Jacques-Emile
Blanche, Marcel Proust, and also the three daughters of Hérédia, and their father, who was made

to recite his still unprinted sonnets. Before long
he was one of the regular guests at the famous
dinners of Mme. Aubernon, and the mistress of the
house observed to him that he was its first officer.

There was then something surprising in the type
of lettered soldier. It had always been Lyautey's
ideal. Frequently, as he looked at a charming
copy of a portrait by Angelo Bronzino, belonging
to his mother and representing a young esquire
some twenty years old, with his sword by his side
and one hand on a book, he had let his thoughts
turn back to the days when a soldier could be pas-
sionately devoted to study and yet escape ridicule:

How often have I looked at him and conversed
with him, that charming witness, so grave and
pensive, of a vanished age! How often have I
relived with him that true, that real life, when there
was stabbing in plenty at the street corners, when
battle was here, there and everywhere, where every
spring was taut and every faculty vibrant! He
has his sword. He is "a noble cavalier, courteous
and bold"; he is a soldier, as every gentleman is; he
has just been fighting, no doubt, at the head of his
men against the troops of the Emperor Charles V,
who is threatening the city. It is just that after
plenty of cut-and-thrust he likes to read Dante; he
has perhaps composed a few sonnets himself; without a doubt he has conversed of the affairs of the
republic and chatted of art with his painter and his
comrades. Things then were quite simple; man

and citizen dwelt always beneath the coat that covered them. . . . But in our day a soldier is not entitled to move beyond the horizon traced for him by theory and profession. . . . Men laugh in his face if, once out of the saddle, he finds any pleasure in his old books, and the least they can do is to regard him as having a screw loose somewhere.

But now, in those hitherto unfamiliar circles whose intelligence was proving so sympathetic, Lyautey found himself welcomed not only as a pleasant friend but as a new and rare being. He was enthusiastic and brilliant. He held surprising views on soldiers and their handling, on the evolution of the army, the dogmatism of the Ecole de Guerre, the formalism and routine habits of the staffs. He spoke out boldly of these things, to the point even of rashness, at a time when many an officer was afraid of his own shadow. He was listened to with pleasure. He himself felt more at ease in these circles of comparative liberty and novelty than in the "quite irreproachable" houses he had hitherto frequented.

In these sceptical and markedly liberal drawing-rooms he did not conceal his Royalist sympathies, still less his distaste for the left-wing régimes. He was chaffed about it, and he parried gaily. But when he moved again in that intransigent society which had been, and still remained, his own, he could not help feeling that the spirit of his friends was rather narrow, and somewhat remote from life. Around them everything was shifting; the France of the provinces and the peasantry was reassured by the seriousness of Carnot, as it had been by that of Thiers. Patiently, in spite of early checks, Pope Leo XIII was pursuing the plan which he had sketched before Lyautey in 1883. Several times Cardinal Lavigerie, by order, had had secret interviews with President Carnot and his ministers. In 1890 he invited under his roof, at the Archbishop's Palace in Algiers, the staff of the Mediterranean squadron, and proposed as a toast "the Union of all good citizens in acceptance of the régime." Admiral Duperré, a former aide-de-camp of the Prince Imperial, only just responded, but the band of the Collège Saint-Eugène played the Marseillaise. It was a great event.

Lyautey's former party was beginning to break up. The deputy Piou proposed the formation of a constitutional Right, which meant an acceptance of the Republic whilst avoiding the use of the word. The Comte d'Haussonville protested. Leo XIII issued an encyclical urging adherence to the Republic; and this "rallying cry" still met with many opponents amongst Catholics. Lyautey was now

one of those who desired it. Hungering after fruitful action, he deemed these wars of Frenchmen
against Frenchmen merely sterile. His personal
experience inclined him towards the liberals.
Whom had he found opposing him in that very
modest but sincere work he had fostered at Saint-
Germain? His political friends, who had warned
him against this "revolutionary" interpretation of
his part as an officer. Who had encouraged him?
Liberals like Vogüé; republicans like Ernest La-
visse, whom Vogüé had brought to show him this
model squadron. In order to be strong, Lyautey
required to feel that he was liked and approved of.
Almost despite himself, he moved towards those
who lent him help and support. He remained convinced that monarchy in the absolute is a superior
form of government to democracy, but in his eyes
the Royalists of 1891 were too clumsy, and France
too much divided.

And with this we reach the occasion which definitely settled Lyautey's direction, and indeed the
course of his future. Every great life is born of
the meeting of a great character and a great hazard.
The incident which was fated to uproot Lyautey
from regimental routine and to determine his future seemed in its origins very small to produce
such consequence. In 1891 Vogüé, more and more

impressed by the methods of Captain Lyautey and his conception of the new army, asked him to prepare a few notes which would help him, Vogüé himself, to write an article on this subject destined for the *Revue des Deux Mondes.* In a short time Lyautey brought him his work, some fifty pages, bearing the title, "On the Social Functions of the Officer under Universal Military Service." Vogüé read it and was greatly astonished. In his young friend he had certainly seen an officer who united with the knowledge and practice of his profession a high degree of general culture and the gift of expressing his ideas; but he had no grounds for supposing that Captain Lyautey was a writer. When he saw Lyautey again he said: "The article is written. It will appear as it stands." An Officer actually serving could not publish anything without authorization, and the essay therefore appeared unsigned; but notwithstanding the determination, and indeed the interest, of the author in his wish for anonymity, his name was revealed by an indiscretion after a few weeks. There was a great uproar.

For an officer in the year 1891 these were novel, not to say bold, ideas. A true conservative is always a reformer; but many conservatives were then far from any comprehension of this political

truth, and were indignant in their comments on
Lyautey's ideas, speaking of this "socialist" officer,
this "revolutionary," and making it plain to him
that his advancement would have been better served
by silence. But to compensate for that he was
approached by certain figures from the other camp,
such as Henri Bérenger, the president of the Association des Etudiants, Paul Desjardins, the Lazard
brothers, Victor Bérard, Max Leclerc, and the
Pasteur Wagner. Many requested to be introduced to him and to see his squadron. Republican
politicians like Charles Roux, Edouard Aynard,
Jonnart and Paul Deschanel, noticed his article
and congratulated him. And in this way Lyautey,
whose family links with the party of resistance
were so strong, now suddenly found himself carried to the head of one section of the party of
progress. At the age of thirty-seven he retained
the enthusiasm of his adolescence. He had been
estranged from the Right by the fact that, apart
from the circle of Albert de Mun, the Right was
then devoid of generous feeling. He had long
been seeking an idea to which he could devote
himself. He adopted the notion of Union.

Furthermore, there appeared at almost the same
date some other pamphlets which appealed to open-
minded men and were inspired by feelings not far

removed from those of Lyautey. These were Max Leclerc's "Le Rôle Social des Universités," and Paul Desjardins' "Le Devoir Présent." Desjardins had met Lyautey at Vogüé's, and a friendship sprang up between them. It became the custom of a small group to meet at Paul Desjardins', formed of Max Leclerc, Arthur Fontaine, the Abbé Ackermann, chaplain of the Collège Stanislas, the Pasteur Wagner and André Lebon, with Lyautey. Each of them brought friends; Lyautey, his intimates, Antonin de Margerie, then a captain at the Ministry of War, Jean de Larminat, an engineer of the Ouest railways, of which he was later to become manager. After a few meetings they decided to form themselves into an association, uniting Frenchmen of all parties and all formations in the cause of common action, setting aside whatever divided them so as to retain only such things as united them. Each founder brought his suggestions for the constitution.

The text of the first manifesto was as follows:

We are a meeting-ground, not an association. We have a spirit, not a doctrine. That spirit is one of solidarity, justice, freedom, respect for the human person. Widely though our beliefs may differ, far removed though our own spheres may seem from each other, we share the common conviction that all modes of life are not of equal

validity; we fight against moral nihilism, whatever
name it may bear; we believe in the necessity and
the efficacy of effort. . . . We are persuaded that
the rifts in our crumbling society are more facti-
tious and less unbridgeable than they appear, and
that in a common search for social peace and national unity it is possible for men of good faith to
come together, freed from all sectarian or party
spirit. . . . The fact of adherence to our meeting-
ground implies nothing beyond recognition of these
principles and consent to this programme. Each
of us, on his own responsibility, continues to be
active in his own sphere of life, but with a zeal
heightened by the sense of co-operation. We
firmly believe that our attempt corresponds to a
pressing need. And moreover, we regard it as a
duty—that is to say, that no difficulties can release
us therefrom.

There was something noble in this tone. The
question now was of giving the group a name.
And here it was that the first differences began
to show. Paul Desjardins proposed the "Union
of *Moral* Action"; Lyautey and some of his
friends were firm for the "Union of *Social* Action."
The divergence of conceptions lay precisely in
those two words. The Desjardins formula carried the day. Later it was transformed into the
"Union of Truth," the name under which the association still exists to-day.

Whatever Lyautey's sympathy for his new

friends, he was not very long in feeling ill at ease. His Legitimist and Catholic framework found difficulty in adapting itself to Tolstoyan doctrines with a Republican vocabulary. A body of soldiers to train for a definite mission, a country to restore or to create—those were the things for which he would have been eager. But the fields which his profession offered him were narrow, and closely watched over.

In 1893 he was promoted Commandant at Gray, and a few months later, Chief of Staff to the 7th cavalry division at Meaux.

IV

THE most painful human tragedies are rarely visible on the surface, and about nearly all human beings we are mistaken. To all but a few intimates, Lyautey, on nearing his fortieth year, must have appeared as a happy man, and one who in his fashion had succeeded. He was a commandant of Chasseurs, and a divisional Chief of Staff; he was affectionately welcomed in the fashionable world, and in the literary world too, where his article had given him a small halo of his own. He knew how he was esteemed in the circle, so novel to him, of the Union of Moral Action. A certain and straightforward path was leading him quietly towards the five stripes, and then to the gold-embroidered stars.

In point of fact, he was sickened by the comfortable barrenness of this life. Would he still have to drag on this mechanical existence for five-and-twenty years from the colonel's stripes to the general's stars? Were the ardour and faith of his twenties to yield, when his forties were ending, to the worries of a courtier? Was it his own fault, or that of his circumstances? That background of his was respectable and kindly, "but loaded with prejudice, clichés, and formulas; where the whole of our adolescence and youth, under the pretext of safeguarding and correction, was kept at arm's length from life, from the rough contacts that give enlightenment and stiffening; where everything was combined to restrain us and make us church-wardens of small churches; where the human and intellectual horizon was deliberately drawn in so tightly round us. . . . And during these past ten years what personal efforts were needed, what scandals roused, to free ourselves from those swaddling-clothes! A heavy responsibility lies on the generation of 'people of our class' whose sons are born to the life of 1870 to 1880. We were really placed in a glasshouse. . . . No, it is not our fault." [1]

He was right: it was not his fault. It was the fault of society, of the military bureaucracy, those machines revolving in the void. And how Lyautey hated offices! Indeed, to touch the root of his unrest, how unsuited he was to the servitude of army life! "Discipline provides the main force of armies. . . ." And of all men he was one of the least disciplined. Above all, he felt himself to be "an animal of action"; so far, he knew this only in a

---

[1] From a letter to Antonin de Margerie.

vague way, but he guessed at it from the overwhelming boredom he felt at these routine tasks, these petty intrigues about promotions and decorations, that lack of enthusiasm and collective effort. Even the Union of Moral Action—how fundamentally vain the enterprise seemed to him! Good intentions, without a doubt—an idealism that gave him a moment's warmth—but no results. Words, words, words. . . . Surely life ought to hold other possibilities than this dreamy round.

In the month of August, 1894 (Carnot had been assassinated in June, and the newspapers were full of the anarchist trials), Commandant Lyautey was at the manœuvres in Brie, when a telegram informed him that he was appointed to Tonking. He had had no presentiment of this move. It was General de Boisdeffre, chief of the General Staff, who wished to do him a good turn; noticing that the essay on the social function of the officers had created a sense of displeasure and hostility amongst certain of Lyautey's superior officers, he had thought that the young commandant would be all the better for a "change of air," and had put him down for a staff post with the troops of Indo-China. He was more than happy to accept, and he set off. He had no regrets—and no high hopes.

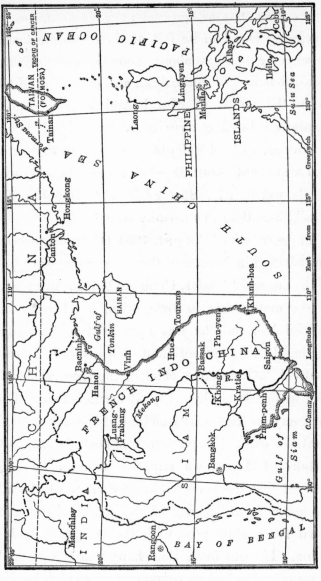

FRENCH INDO-CHINA

The heroic days of Indo-Chinese history, those of
Garnier and Rivière, who captured a town with a
handful of men, seemed to be over. Hanoi and
Saigon were now garrison towns like Saint-Germain and Versailles. The expedition would doubtless prove merely an incident in his career, he
would spend a few years in Tonking, and then
return to command some regiment in a provincial
town. Life was finished, and spoilt. A pity. . . .
He had believed himself capable of big things.

Lyautey embarked at Marseilles, and within a
few days of sailing he had struck up acquaintance
with colonial officials returning to their posts, and
with these unknown men he discovered a bond of
brotherhood. Their talk was of a life of action, of
a making of towns, of new countries which could
be moulded at will. What was happening? It
suddenly seemed to Lyautey that he was breathing
a healthier air. "How many regrets the contact
with all these men of will and initiative and toil
called up—regrets for the ten lost years of France's
life, years of trials undergone, of submission to the
rod, of the accepted clichés of family or administration! These conversations between men of pure
action make one feel as far distant from the falsity
of literary salons and dinner-parties of Paris as

from the mummified existence of our unemployed,
routine-ridden, swaddled army! And it is a resur-
rection."

❊   *   *   *   *

He went ashore in Egypt, and at Singapore,
and he was there filled with admiration for certain
aspects of the British Empire. But instinctively he
had little love for the English. Those were the
days when England had just taken Egypt out of
France's hands, when Fashoda was hatching, when
a French officer still habitually saw in the Englishman his hereditary enemy. But in Lyautey there
was something that gave back an answering chord
at their contact. Like them he had a feeling for
style, the sense of caste, a liking for rather wild
flights of fancy going hand in hand with a love
of tradition. Revolutionary Conservatives—such
are the grave English. In the flowery, well-de-
signed barracks of Singapore Lyautey was stirred
when he recognized the realization of what he had
vainly striven to do for his French soldiers. "So
they are not Utopias. Somewhere there do exist
the cheerful, inviting, open quarters that offer a
complete mode of life, where duty bears a smile.
Where men are men, and not a pen of down-at-
heel convicts for ever sweeping dreary courtyards

under the slanging of the sergeant-major. . . .
But what would our French sergeant-majors say?
What would the Engineers say at the appearance
of these erections which have *shunned* uniformity,
which are deliberately not laid out symmetrically,
not aligned in accordance with a specimen model,
but are scattered as at the Trianon, with no pre-
occupation with rule and line, for the pleasing of
the eye?"

On board ship throughout the long voyage he
was working—for this apparent dilettante was a
man of method. In preparation for his landing in
Egypt he had made a study of Arabic art and
archæology. And now he was writing splendid
letters to his friends in France, in a style of chivalrous culture that recalls at once Stendhal and the
Prince de Ligne.

At Saigon he established relations with the Governor-General, M. de Lanessan. The two men
took to each other at once. The Commandant
found Lanessan both intelligent and amiable. And
Lyautey himself has always had the gift of con-
quering a human being when he so wished. He
showed his brilliance and his versatility, he was a
good listener, and was a pleased listener in any
case, for Lanessan, during their joint journey
from Saigon to Hanoi, laid before him a doctrine

of colonial administration which came to Lyautey as a revelation.

"In every country," said Lanessan, "there are existing frameworks. The great mistake for European people coming there as conquerors is to destroy these frameworks. Bereft of its armature, the country falls into anarchy. One must govern *with* the mandarin and not *against* the mandarin. The European cannot substitute himself numerically; but he can control. Therefore, don't disturb any tradition, don't change any custom. In every society there exists a ruling class, born to rule, without which nothing can be done. Enlist that class in our interests."

Such a doctrine went straight to Lyautey's heart, first of all on his aristocratic side; "and besides, this system is distasteful to the military mind, which is a powerful argument for its good sense." Around him on board ship officials would criticize Lanessan's methods. "No doubt," they said, "our government finds a superficial facility there, but the native organization remains upright; it is with us to-day, but to-morrow perhaps will be against us. Furthermore, by supporting the mandarin, we are not the liberators of the people, in the French tradition, but the props of their oppressors." These are not negligible objections, and at the present time in 1931 their consequences became plainer. But in Algeria Lyautey had seen the other school in actual practice, that of kicking down the mandarin. "It may satisfy your corporals, but it doesn't lead far." He arrived at Hanoi having convinced Lanessan that he was a man of parts and that something might perhaps be made of him.

*　　*　　*　　*　　*

The first days in Tonking were a disappointment. Once again he found a bureaucracy, and intrigues, and gossiping worse perhaps than he had seen in Paris. "Personal questions take precedence of all. The majority, military or civilian, does not care a damn for the colony. Everything that is said is repeated and exploited in two or three hours. People whisper, looking behind the bamboo leaves to see that nobody is listening." But Lyautey was attached to a branch of the General Staff, and immediately he engaged upon the entrancing study of the history, the politics, and the negotiations of Indo-China. Throughout all the northern part of the country there remained unconquered districts which were terrorized by great pirate chiefs, aided by the Chinese from the frontiers. "I find it thrilling indeed to foresee the moves of the Chinese Marshal Sou in Kuang-tung, the policy to be followed with regard to the great pirate chiefs Luong-Tam-Sy and Ba-Ky must more than explain to General B—— why the 18th regiment of Dragoons have sent in an incomplete establishment return."

Almost immediately, by an unhoped-for stroke of luck (for in every hierarchy a senior's misfortune is a junior's luck), the Chief-of-Staff fell ill, and Commandant Lyautey, a newcomer to the country, found himself ten days after arrival chief-of-staff of the troops of Indo-China. "So there is a very pretty stroke of fortune, throwing me right into the middle of all the affairs of this country, which to some extent satisfies my passion for power—though less, to be sure, than if I were Prime Minister. . . ." A revealing phrase, in which there suddenly appears, breaking through the mask, the true Lyautey. "The passion for power . . . less than if I were Prime Minister. . . ." A creature of action and one who requires for his happiness an enormous allowance of actual facts, decisions, and human material to put in the mill.

And now he was going down to his office every morning at half-past seven; he left it only in the evening, and then often to work at home. "It is such a change from France to feel that instead of working in the void, making plans for transport which will transport nothing, and preparing conventional manœuvres, one is doing something immediate and real. What has emerged from my desk in the past three weeks? Instructions for the winter campaign of four military territories; the steps to be taken for freeing a certain Madame C——, who had been abducted by pirates and was set free the day before yesterday; a plan for the commissariat of the frontier posts, which will come into force on the first of January; a whole series of diplomatic notes and arrangements to be exchanged with Marshal Sou and the Mandarin Trong; a similar note for Pekin, and so on in that vein; that is to say, the most varied work, the most immediately practicable, and dealing with men of open mind, devoid of formulas."

He was beginning to be aware that he was both liked and successful in this country; and for his happiness he had a deep need of being liked and being successful. But he did not think that he could carve out a real career in Tonking. "What a pity not to have come here ten years earlier! Every single one of these little lieutenants commanding a post or a survey party develops in six months more initiative, will, endurance, personality than an officer in France can in the whole of his career. And what a gain in maturity, what confidence in oneself, what close grappling with reality, with the practical, with the fruitful!" How he envied those men who at thirty-five had already a past made up of action, and who did not scold at life *because they were never bored.* In the memories of each one of them lived some corner of a country cleared, or a map drawn, in fact an achievement, and not that absurd occupation which Lyautey himself had been drudging over for twenty years.

But the decisive touch was yet to come. It came a few weeks later with the visit of the great man of the Indo-Chinese army, Commander of the territory where fighting was going on—Colonel Galliéni. The Colonel was forty-four. He had already made his name in Senegal and the Sudan. "He has just arrived to spend a week here and has left me with a tremendous impression of being a person of lucidity, both exact and broad-minded; and besides, he patted me on the back for my article—to which I was not unresponsive." It was curious, this immediate linking-up between Galliéni and Lyautey. From certain points of view it would be impossible to imagine two men more different: Galliéni brought up at La Flèche,[1] in a

---

[1] A military school for sons of N.C.O.'s; very democratic.

very Republican mould, extremely simple in his
way of life, and rather dry; Lyautey the traditionalist, the aristocrat, the enthusiast. When later he
was to hear Galliéni remarking of Captain de
Grandmaison: "It's odd—he's of noble birth, he's
been educated by the Jesuits, and yet he's intelligent"—something within Lyautey was to rise in
astonished protest. But they were united by something stronger than what divided them. Their uniting link was a common trend of mind, a common
taste for useful activity and reality. They had a
common habit of flinging themselves into the present moment instantly and with all their strength, of
staking everything on one card and giving it its
highest possible value. Their link, to go deeper
still, was the secret motive force of all action—*a
prodigious capacity for boredom.* Galliéni was
married, the father of two children, and had been
in the Colonies for twenty years. "It's no good, he
can't get on without it, and after six months in
France it was his wife herself who said to him: 'I
can see that you are bored—off you go again!'"
In his conversations with Lyautey one feels the contact with a nature like that of some great yawning
wild beast, always ready to spring. "I have lived,
I have spent my time, I have enjoyed myself.
Isn't it enough on this unhappy earth—to imagine

that one is amusing oneself and doing things that are useful? This existence has only one drawback, that one gets into the way of it and that you find any other becoming intolerable." This aroma of the zest for action whetted Lyautey's appetite.

In the conversation of this "exact and broad-minded person" he caught glimpses of a great doctrine that suited him exactly, a theory of civilization by conquest which, from Cæsar to Galliéni, by way of Bugeaud, has hardly changed at all. To Galliéni military success was an essential, but it was *nothing* unless combined with a simultaneous work of organization—roads, telegraphs, markets, crops —so that with the pacification there flowed forward, like a pool of oil, a great belt of civilization. "These are your true military boundaries. That is Bugeaud at his best." Galliéni detected a disciple in this eager listener. He asked him to dinner:

"I suppose you have brought out all the very latest documents for your work as Chief-of-Staff?"

"Certainly, Colonel."

"You can show me all that after dinner. It would interest me."

Lyautey went to his quarters to fetch the recent "Active Service" publication, the latest edition of the "Staff Recommendations," the latest "Course of General Tactics" from the Staff School.

"That's capital," said Galliéni, "just give them to me." And without a word he took a piece of brown paper, carefully wrapped up the three books, tied the parcel up with string, and concluded:

"These breviaries would only get you into trouble here. You'll learn your job on the spot, by handling men and matters."

It was a great delight for the young and independent Commandant, rebuffed by the "mandarins," to find a commanding officer with this scorn for official lore.

*   *   *   *   *

About this time the Governor, M. de Lanessan, was suddenly recalled to France on account of an unimportant difference with the Ministry. Commandant Lyautey was shocked and indignant. He had become attached to this man. But the personal question did not matter. The serious matter, as he saw it, was that in this country where French power was still so weak, where the fight against piracy was not yet over, where the Governor-General ought to stand for a vast moral authority, the prestige of his function and confidence in France should be thus undermined by a harsh recall. The incident went to form an idea in Lyautey which was to remain one of his most compelling—

namely, the absolute value of stability of power. Permanence is in itself a strength. It is curious to reflect that the episode of which he was then the witness formed, as it were, a prefiguration of what was one day to be his own destiny.

After Lanessan's departure and the return of the Chief-of-Staff, Galliéni claimed Lyautey's services again, and to the latter's great delight, it was decided that he should accompany the commander of the Second Territory on a tour of inspection. The journey was a great moment in Lyautey's life. For the first time he saw what the life of a Founder of Empire was, a life of difficulties, but a marvellously full one. The game of "playing at countries" began again, but this time it was not in a corner of the Crévic billiard-room. On the bare soil avenues were outlined, and houses were already rising, based on a rectilinear, American plan. There was no administrative formality. Orders were given to demolish the old native hovels with pickaxes, and the inhabitants themselves were rebuilding with zest. An arbitrary method; but the towns were shooting up, already healthier and cleaner places. For Lyautey himself it was a keen delight to see this type of absolute chief in action, "soldier and administrator, a countryman and a brain-worker," and to live with a man who although

he wore gold bands on his cuffs, "did not imagine
that he was tied down to the Interior Services
Regulations, and developed his personality un-
fettered." To the Staff offices at Hanoi Galliéni
seemed a mountebank and a hothead; the "corporals," as Lyautey said, held him in horror. But
alongside him stood enthusiastic officers who blessed
him for having made their lives fruitful, for having
"delivered them from the morbid depression and
burdensome existence of the outposts." The man
was a leader and inspirer, and had disciples who
found their own happiness through him.

It was a hard journey. Frequently he had to lie
down undressed, rolled in a blanket, on a mat in
the corner of a platted hut. Sometimes Galliéni
and Lyautey had only one between them; and then,
nearly all night long, Lyautey would be intoxicated
with stories of the Sudan and lie there envying the
richness of his chief's life. He made himself absorb
Galliéni's methods: to bite directly upon reality;
to take as little account as possible of the circulars,
the vague and abstract orders of men living far
from the actual scene; to pay as much attention to
a sergeant's opinion as to a captain's, because nobody is more competent than the man who is handling the raw material.

A concrete case. For a whole year Galliéni was requesting credits for the building of sheds to protect his stores, but they were refused and the foodstuffs were meanwhile rotting. But along the Chinese frontier there were clandestine gambling-houses which drained away the money of the native inhabitants. Galliéni did not hesitate. He was supposed to feign ignorance of the existence of these houses, but he imposed a very heavy tax upon them, with the proceeds of which he built his sheds. One fine day he received word from the financial officials that he would receive his credits in six months' time. Galliéni replied that this was needless, that the sheds were built, and that the protection of the provision against rain was saving the French Government a million francs. The head of the department was furious: "I would rather see a million francs' worth of stores destroyed," he retorted, "than think they had been saved by irregular means." Officialdom was peeved, but the stores were saved. Lyautey hearkened, pondered, and moulded himself.

* * * * *

Pirates had killed one French employee and abducted another; an expedition became necessary to clean up the frontier zones.

Galliéni asked for Lyautey, the brand-new colonel officer, as his Chief-of-Staff. Lyautey was both delighted and touched. He had grasped his chief's tactics: there were to be no direct attacks on these bands who bolted irretrievably into the swamps and forests; converging columns would try to hem them in; and then, as soon as one region was cleaned up, there would be a line of outposts, armed villages; and so the native himself, through the prosperity of the country, would have an interest in defending himself against the Chinese pirates. "Piracy," said Galliéni, "is not a necessary historical fact. It is the result of an economic condition. It can be fought by prosperity."

A campaign on tracks where the interwoven lianas hung over faery ravines, bathed in moonlight. Extraordinary villages, perched high on isolated crags to be reached only by ladders a hundred and fifty feet in length. Defensive nests, the only habitable spots in this region infested by brigands. It was rough going, and Lyautey was delighted. "You are certainly a man of the jungle, Lyautey," said the Colonel. "I am," he reflected; "and why did I come to them so late? Why not ten years ago? I would have given a century of Saint-Germain and Meaux for ten years of this bolder life! But the age for dreaming is over, and there's nothing left but to live as a sightseer."

Meanwhile, as Chief-of-Staff, he was responsible for transport and commissariat. To find 3000 pounds of rice daily in a stripped country was far from easy, and one morning at the end of the first week of the expedition, he was told that the supply of rations had collapsed. If he did not find his rice before the following night the expedition would break down. Galliéni had heard this threatening report from his own hut, alongside Lyautey's, and then heard his new subordinate giving orders in an attempt to repair the damage. He did not say a word himself; not a muscle of his face moved. Lyautey observed him, and learned a lesson in commanding. Perhaps there was a certain affectation in this demeanour, but there are moments when the man must vanish into the leader. Before setting out Galliéni had said to him: "I don't want to know anything about details. I want to keep my brain free to conceive and direct. It must be understood that no difficulty is to be referred to myself. The *end* is my sole concern; the *means* are your business. . . . I have taken your measure. I believe that things will go well, and if they don't, I shall drop you. I never let my own feelings count once a question of duty is involved. Take that as said." And that evening, while Galliéni turned a deaf ear and read a volume of philosophy, Lyautey was rather nervously thinking that if the column did not have its rations next morning he would indeed have his "measure" taken. Next day he secured 8000 pounds of rice.

The assault of the pirates' lair was made up a sheer face of cliff. Sixteen hundred feet. They had to climb pulling themselves up. "Get your foot over to your left, sir," cried the gymnastic sergeant, "there's a hole there. Let go with your hand. You'll find another tuft eighteen inches down." And this went on whilst the pirates were firing on the climbers from the other end of the precipice. Here Lyautey heard the whistle of bullets for the first time, and standing erect on a narrow ledge from which one false step might send him spinning into space, he inwardly exclaimed with a strange intoxication—"This is better than Meaux!" He entered the conquered stronghold, had a flag run up on top of it and a bugle-call sounded, and then sent his Colonel a note: *"We're there."*

Unfortunately, although the fortress was captured, the brigands had contrived to escape. The column found them only after a long pursuit, and the final engagement was difficult. There were only supplies for three more days, and this in a region where it was impossible to replenish them. On the eve of the fight Galliéni issued his orders, and then appeared to be quite unconcerned. He had imposed an unaltering rule on himself, that even on active service he should indulge for an hour every evening in what he called his "brain bath"— a talk with an intelligent friend on non-military topics, or some reading. As he only talked to Lyautey about Mill, the Commandant could not help reverting to the risks of the next day. Galliéni cut him short. "Leave all that alone now! The orders are given; everything needful has been done; how will it help you to reason things out? You need to keep your brain-cells in as good a state as I do. Let's talk about John Stuart Mill." That was another lesson. Lyautey was to remember it later, when Fez was besieged.

The outcome of this campaign was that, in a region where the pirates had abducted one hundred and ten women in a year, where life was impossible except in fortified caves on the tops of cliffs, and roots were the sole nourishment, the fertile valleys became once more habitable. . . . *Pax Romana.* These French officers were doing again what Cæsar's legions had done. Is colonial policy just

or unjust? In other places it may be unjust, but
in this form and in these unhappy regions, doubt
is hardly possible. The war against piracy is a
police function. Order replaces disorder, peace replaces war. The life of farm and family rises in
lieu of brigandage and rape. And these would
seem to be a positive good.

*　　*　　*　　*　　*

Returning to Hanoi, Lyautey became one of the
prime favourites of the colony, in the social no less
than the military sphere. With his love of beautiful objects, he contrived to fashion for himself a
comfortable and amusing interior in a military
building, a whole series of large rooms, a blend of
the pagoda and the opium smoke-room. The Commander-in-Chief was always glad to come to play
whist at Lyautey's, amongst the purple hangings
and the odorous incense-burners. In the room next
door a Chinese orchestra played soft airs. A few
connoisseurs smoked opium. Lyautey refrained,
but he liked the little lamps of tooled silver, the
precious pipes of ivory and ebony.

So the Grimoult tastes in him were satisfied,
whilst the scion of the Lyautey generals drew up
accurate reports and minute plans of campaign.
The time he had spent at Tonking was brief, but he

was a man quick to grasp things. One of his notes
for the Governor was a lesson in history:

It should not be overlooked that the pirate is a
plant which will grow only in certain soils, and that
the surest method is to make the soil uncongenial
to him. . . . Pirates do not exist in completely
organized regions; on the other hand, there do exist
some, under different names, in countries like Turkey, Greece or Southern Italy, which possess only
an incomplete system of communications, a rudi-
mentary system of administration, or a sparsely
scattered population. . . . Supposing that a piece
of land overrun by rank weeds has to be brought
under tillage, it is not enough to extirpate these
weeds; that will only mean starting again next day;
but it is essential that, where the ground has been
ploughed up, the conquered soil should be isolated,
fenced, and then sowed with the good grain which
alone will make it impervious to the tares. Simi-
larly with regard to territory given over to
brigandage: armed occupation, with or without
fighting, is as the ploughshare; the establishment of
a military cordon fences it and isolates it definitely,
if an internal frontier is in question; and finally the
organization and reconstitution of the population,
its arming, the setting-up of markets and various
cultivations, the driving of roads, are all as the
sowing of the good grain, and render the conquered
region impervious to brigandage.

After these general views, in which the essentials
of the "Lyautey doctrine" can already be discerned,

came a detailed plan, in which he showed how they could advance right up to the Chinese frontier, re-opening roads and markets, restoring villages to life, recreating life. This plan of campaign was approved. Lieutenant-Colonel Vallière was appointed to carry it out, and was given as his adjutant Commandant Lyautey, who had conceived it. This was his first large military undertaking. It was successful. He went up as far as China, negotiated with the lords of the frontier, and won their respect. He thus became a great figure in the land, the more so as Galliéni had just been summoned to Madagascar, where things were going ill with French fortunes. But the departure of Galliéni discouraged Lyautey. With the remaining officers he did not feel at his ease. Certain of them he liked, and to others he knew that he was unjust; but his reactions differed too widely from theirs. He felt that he alarmed them. Sometimes he had thoughts of abandoning the soldier's life for the life of large-scale business or of politics. To Max Leclerc he wrote:

As the army is unwilling that I should drive my way forward, and as I feel more than ever in the grip of the need for action, with plenty of elbow-room, I have serious thoughts of returning to France in the summer of 1897, and then the plan I imagine would be this: to find a wife who would bring me, with her other qualities, an ample independence of means, to refashion for myself a centre of campaign and social action, and henceforward to look out for an electoral seat for 1898. At forty-three one can still do something in parliamentary life, and I shall try to steer towards the colonial cause and become a candidate for governor's rank. Simply that. Investigate this plan of campaign. Decidedly the army, with its hampering ill-wills, is a blind alley.

What chiefly horrified him was the idea of returning to France and reverting to ordinary garrison life.

Decidedly, I am a creature of action. I had always thought so; facts have finally confirmed it; and after twenty years of chafing that gnawed my spirit I at last seemed to have action within my grasp. I believed that auspicious circumstances were at last putting me in the saddle for a Cecil Rhodes career, and that I might possibly in this mortal life leave my mark upon a work of enduring fruitfulness. I believed that I was perhaps to be one of those men in whom other men believe, a man in whose eyes thousands of other eyes seek order, whose voice and pen open up roads, make lands alive with people, and raise up cities. I lulled myself with these ideas, and if they escape me it is going to be a harsh disappointment. For I feel more than ever, *that bereft of productive, compelling and immediate action I am eating myself away, corroding,* and that my functions remain unused. I am at the opposite pole from the anony-

mous, indirect agent, from the pure bureaucrat.
. . . I can conceive command only in the direct
and personal form of presence on the spot, of cease-
less inspection, of the starting-up of a piece of work
by my words, by a personal power of winning men
over, by the visual and oral transmission of faith
and enthusiasm. All last winter, on the banks of
the Claire, under fire or at the outposts, I have felt
all too well that I was leaving a trail of life and
activity; I have felt all too well that where I had
been, where I had spoken there was stimulus enough
to last for weeks. I tell you this in full certainty,
because there can be nothing misleading in it, and
my direct agents brought me evidence of it in their
eyes and their zest.

And now the mail brings us word of Galliéni's
departure for Madagascar. Why didn't the Havas
Agency telegraph this to us? I would have cabled
to him that I was ready, and sent all this to the
deuce—except for returning to it later on, with
him. And now to-day, he's gone. Too late. A
pity! I have such a yearning to feel again an intense life, personal responsibility, command, and
bare-chested struggle.

V

COLONIAL Minister to Governor-General of Indo-China:

If you do not consider it inconvenient instruct Commandant Lyautey proceed Madagascar requested by Galliéni.

Governor-General to Ministry:

Absolutely require Lyautey until some time January. Can Galliéni reserve post until then?

Galliéni to Colonies:

Keeping Lyautey's post until March.

At one moment he had been tempted to remain at Tonking. The general Commander-in-Chief had offered him colonel's rank, along with the Third Territory, where the fighting was going on. To be the man who would reopen the Claire river, and to work with officers whose sympathy he had won, was indeed all the kingdoms of this world offered by a starry Tempter from the heights of the rocks. But before this he had written to Galliéni: "Wherever you are, whatever you want to do with me, I shall be at your orders everywhere and at all times, at the first sign." Galliéni was giving the sign; he was the chief. Lyautey hurried off.

The long sea voyage from Tonking to Madagascar left him leisure for serious reflection on the two full and rich years which he had just passed through. Before this experience of colonial life, he had had the painful impression in France of a country grown old, divided against itself, enfeebled by a century of Napoleonism, over-centralization and dread of responsibilities, and, above all, by a taste for a mental habit, which Lyautey, the romantic and enthusiast, had always detested—irony. He had now regained his confidence in the individual Frenchman. "I cannot count the number of officers, officials, missionaries, engineers, consuls, and colonists who, simply as common human beings, are superior in energy, disinterestedness and capabilities to anything that England or Germany can set up against us."

He wondered whether there were not grounds for further hopes, whether the colonies could not become a sort of social school for the metropolis, as it were an apprenticeship of active life, whence leaders and administrators would return capable of giving the old country a new life. "And if that came to pass! If our neighbours, who are already counting on our disappearance and already regard us, not without reason, as a negligible factor, were one fine day to see unmistakably that we were resuscitated! Then perhaps there would be no more need of the anomalous Russian alliance, and we could again set to work towards an *integral Europe,* in all its historic logic, which was prepared by the slow travail of centuries and which the fratricide of 1870 smashed before it was brought into being." Here was the idea of a Franco-German entente, an idea cherished by Lyautey, who has always admired Germany's social sense, her taste for collective effort and devotion to the State.

He was beginning to be convinced that he had a mission to fulfil. "The essential thing is to know what one wants and where one is going. Well, I know that: to make social duty paramount over all others, the duty of snatching this country from decomposition and ruin. Not by any change of constitutional formulas, an empiric and ephemeral remedy, but by a violent reaction upon morals, upon energies, upon quietude." Not by any constitutional change. . . . As regards that he was henceforth to have neither reservations nor *arrière-pensées.* He had felt as much contempt for a Boulanger as admiration for a Galliéni. He did not believe in the magician in politics any more than in military action. He had seen that success is won by slow and patient activities of detail, by a perfection of preparation. And now he would conceive of no other methods.

Arrival at Madagascar, however, interrupted his general ideas. Here was a new world to be understood and absorbed, a new activity to which his intelligence and his powers must be given over. It is curious to note his immediate concern on landing about the resources of the country, the possibilities of cultivation, stock-raising and construction. The island had been annexed in 1896. But the Hova ministers (the feudal race), dismissed from power, had fled to the jungles and had massacred French explorers. Galliéni, on being appointed Resident-General, had deported Queen Ranavalo, shot two ministers, and tried to build up groups of vassal races in resistance to the Hovas. It was a policy quite opposed to that which he had followed in Indo-China, but in action as in science, theories must alter shape with facts or events. The experiment did not seem to be advancing very well. The vassal races had vassal minds. Several Hova chiefs were still waging war successfully. Lyautey no doubt was going to be entrusted with the subjection of one of them. It would be a troublesome job in this country which seemed to have "the colour and fertility of brick."

Galliéni came to meet his lieutenant with a fine escort intended to impress a half-rebellious people —"red spahis, a standard bearer, in fact an extremely smart Governor-General's turn-out." Lyautey, a connoisseur of pomp, admired this. On arrival at Tamatave he had found a telegram from the great chief: *"Willkommen.* Come up *maoulen."* (*Maoulen* is an Annamite word meaning *quickly.*) And *maoulen* he had come, with a slight touch of fever, curious to know what activity Galliéni would suggest for his appetite. At Antananarivo he was told what his ration would be: it was one-third of the island in military occupation.

* * * * *

This region was made untenable by a great Hova rebel, a former royal governor, Rabezavana by name. Lyautey immediately applied the methods which had succeeded in Tonking; no linear columns, but converging detachments, the first of which brought him in 1200 oxen and 400 fleeing peasants. These fugitives he reassured, and tried to repopulate the district. Three weeks later he had 800 peasants at work in the rebel zone. Add to this that he had 100,000 of them behind him under his civil command, plus a small army of marine in-

fantry, Senegalese, Malagasy sharp-shooters, some
artillerymen, "and all this with more or less absolute power, and everything to be done, to be
organized, and built up. No, really, I can't see
myself any longer commanding a cavalry regiment
or living on the gossip of the Paris drawing-rooms."

The struggle against Rabezavana lasted for a
month, during which the converging columns
stripped the rebel of his herds and his stocks of
provisions. Before long the Intelligence service
informed Lyautey that Rabezavana was cornered,
that his partisans were deserting him and that he
was going to surrender. And one morning, crip-
pled with fever, but still erect, thanks to an injec-
tion of quinine, Lyautey awaited Rabezavana's
submission at the outposts. The Algerian sharpshooters, Malagasies, and Sengalese, who had been
fighting for a year against this invisible enemy, had
furbished up their uniforms and put on their
medals. The vanquished chief arrived on horseback, followed by his warriors, all armed with rifles.
They rode down between the two files of French
troops, dismounted, and then, flinging their rifles
in a heap, lay prostrate, the chief at Lyautey's
feet. Then Rabezavana drew from his finger a
ring of polished uncut coral mounted in gold, and
said to Lyautey, "This is the ring of my authority.

I no longer rule. Take it, so that every one can see now that you are the ruler." Lyautey slipped the ring on to his finger. It was the signal for a great acclamation. The Galliéni method had worked.

Next day he followed its application to its end. The captive was expecting to be deported, or perhaps put to death. Lyautey staked boldly; he would let him go free and place him at the head of the region which he had formerly ruled as Governor-Royal, where all the inhabitants knew him and respected him, and where he would be able to direct the work of reconciliation. "He pinched himself to see if he were not dreaming. He came to dinner with us. We found a bottle of champagne in the depths of our boxes and he did honour to it, recovering his demeanour of a high, civilized, Hova official, accustomed to mix in the best society, when he appeared duly dressed at table. He extracted his wife from his baggage, and she joined us with the coffee; the entente was sealed. To-morrow I am beginning a tour with him during which I shall have his ring on my finger, but in which he will act as my *ad latus* and go-between in reinstating this hapless populace to their homes and restoring this devastated country. And I shall see for certain whether I have been wrong."

* * * * *

During the whole of 1897 Lyautey led this life of the soldier-administrator. As the absolute master of an ever-widening territory, he held undivided responsibility, but also uncontrolled powers. The Proconsul. He only saw Galliéni occasionally, but the two men exchanged letters. Amongst the leading lights of Madagascar, Lyautey was almost the only one who understood Galliéni. The devotees of the Resident-General were the lesser throng of junior officers, non-commissioned officers, ordinary soldiers, natives, and colonists. The ministerial bureaucrats fought him from Paris. Lyautey had but one desire—to see his chief hold out, and to hold out with his chief. "Nothing is done save by holding on. What a joy it is to give oneself to a work and to see it advancing! What a justification for living, when in France one is for ever doing unfinished things! I look upon the General as the most wonderful example of the man of action, the organizer, that we can put up against the Anglo-Saxon in these closing years of the century. Madagascar *versus* South Africa, Galliéni *versus* Cecil Rhodes—a fine match to play out!"

Then came the winter of 1897-98, which Lyautey spent entirely in touring his region, to push on "the big creative effort. Everything had to be done there, and there for the first time (and how often since!) I knew the joy of the *urbs condita,* when the little town of Ankazobe was made to rise from the soil, a town of which I had myself traced out the plan on the ground, and which now, with fatherly feeling, I saw rising house by house, street by street, tree by tree." It was the "country game" once more.

By now there was beginning to form around him what he had himself found around Galliéni—admirers, a team. Senior officers and junior officers worked without a break. Lyautey was happy. "How I enjoy this life! Wasn't I created and brought into the world for it! After twenty years of routine professional life in France, after so often knowing the anguish of passing destiny by, I have for three years now felt myself sailing with a fair wind behind me, sure of myself, sure of what I am doing, controlling my own life, controlling people and things. I felt that I was born to create, and I am creating; to rule, and I am ruling; to stir up ideas and schemes and tasks, and I stir them up by the spadeful. I was not born to undergo a passive discipline; and Heaven knows this is not so with Galliéni, subordination to whom is an intimate collaboration, having nothing of the relation of schoolboy and master, like those of all subordinates with all the senior officers of France! It is splendid to lie down at night after ransacking a mail which brings word all in one day that an advance of one day's march has been made on the Menavan, that a reconnaissance has reached the fixed objective, that two villages have been repopulated, that another six kilometres of road have been completed, that 6000 francs of unexpected tax-revenues have been brought in, that an attempt with potatoes somewhere has been successful, that a new merchant has started business, that a market has been reopened—how well one sleeps on all that! Yet every day brings also its meed of bad news, of things that are breaking down or not being done. Well, that even becomes a necessity to one. Cares and concerns are the indispensable conditions of action, blessed, divine action, the thing one can no longer dispense with! . . . And now, to end up, you're going to give me a present. I have just found a scrap of verse in Shelley which I want to make my motto:

The soul's joy lies in doing.

Have that engraved on a signet-ring for me and send it out." [1]

Some of Lyautey's friends in the Union of

---

[1] Letter to his sister.

Moral Action, opposed in principle to all colonial conquest, were astonished at his relish therein. He replied that, with the best will in the world, it was impossible to apply the term of warlike conquest to this substitution of relative peace for a state of permanent brigandage.

I wish you could be with me [he wrote to Paul Desjardins] in this strange countryside. . . . The storm has passed, and the village nestling beneath amazing crags is completely visible in the moonlight, in the elbow of a stream bordered by the loveliest trees you can imagine. This is peace. The women with their heavy necklets and the naked children have come out from their huts, and the chief has just brought me a humble offering of rice and chickens and eggs. The captain whom I have installed as suzerain of this borderland has taken possession of his people. Yes, I really believe it is peace, and to-morrow I am going to my advanced posts, which are ready for attack, full of hope that the peace will be contagious. You could not believe what a fine, complete delight there is in feeling the stout club in one's hand, and not using it. The strong are gentle. Antiquity has proclaimed it, and truth is verifying it. Come—goodnight, my dear friend!

Two years earlier, returning from a journey he had been making in Annam, he had said of a Resident there: "He is very intelligent; but he will never do anything, because he has not that grain of love without which no great human work is carried through."

Lyautey had never been able to act without love. That was why, notwithstanding the weaknesses deriving from his function rather than his character, he was great. "Practical undertakings," says Alain, "succeed only by merit of the spirit, by merit, I mean, of that other field, be it great or small, where the spirit is cultivated as the primary value." And it was in the fields of the spirit that this soldier had cultivated action.

His seven years in Tonking and Madagascar had taught him much, and on his lesson Lyautey shortly after this wrote an article which complemented his essay on the social rôle of the officer. It was entitled "The Colonial Rôle of the Army," and in it he defined the Galliéni-Lyautey method in brief and precise axioms. "Military occupation consists not so much of military operations as of an organization on the march."— "Military command and territorial command ought to be joined in the same hands. When the high military officer is also the territorial administrator, his thoughts, when he captures a brigand's den, are of the trading-post he will set up there after his success—and his capture will be on different lines." Re-reading his Montesquieu about this time, he underlined this passage on the methods of Alexander the Great: *"Alexander resisted those who wished him to treat the Greeks as masters and the Persians as slaves. He left the vanquished races not only their manners, but also their civil law, and often even the kings and governors whom he had found. He respected ancient traditions, and it was in order to preserve everything that he strove to conquer everything."*

VI

HE returned to France for the first time in 1899, accompanying Galliéni, who was coming to keep an eye on Madagascar's interests and to seek money for his colony. He found a country both anxious and rent asunder. It was the period of the conflict with England on the Upper Nile. From Madagascar during the preceding year Lyautey had followed the Dreyfus Affair, the discovery of the Henry forgery, and the Zola trial. Regarding the Affair his feelings were painful and complex, for his natural sympathies—like his compeers, the majority of his army friends—were in one camp, whilst his own intelligence and many of the men with whom he was in intellectual friendship were in the other. In October, 1898, Vogüé had written to him:

One's first wish was to believe—as we nearly all believed—in a conspiracy against the Army, against the ultimate bulwark of order. To-day we have to bow to the evidence: little by little our General Staff has been dragged down by the deplorable moral standards engendered by the milieu, by a false conception of the military status, and has itself become entangled in a network of lies, com-

91

promising acts, indescribable clumsiness. It is bound to be now a ruined stronghold, powerless against the scientific attack of the anti-social forces leagued against that ruin. All are, or will be, swept away, one after the other, and nothing will then be left.

Your letter is on my table [Lyautey had replied]. I have read it and re-read it, and read it to General Galliéni. It accords with all that we are feeling. . . . From before my departure from France, as you well know, I had good reason for retaining only a moderate trust in certain conduct of the personnel of the Rue Saint-Dominique and the General Staff, coteries for mutual admiration, worshippers of clichés and formulas, the clever boys of the class-room bringing to the War Ministry, and close to the High Command, the petty meannesses of school, truckling to the form-master, always on the look-out for a good mark, cramped in personality and independence of mind. And that is why, four years ago, as soon as I set foot on board ship, I felt as if I were escaping from a gaol. And that is why, three months later, with my first column, I had the sensation of plunging into a fountain of Youth.

But if he condemned the action of one party, he was deeply shocked by the attitude of the other. To one friend in the Union of Moral Action, a Dreyfusard who had accused him of being "just like the rest of them," he wrote:

You say "the question was very simple." Yes—
was simple. But even if the General Staff people
have made it singularly complicated, do you suppose that the mob, exciting itself and gambling
behind your own sincerity, has not injected a
powerful poison into it? From a distance it all
looks as if you had started off like madmen, without foreseeing the consequences, without reflecting
that the very life of our country was at stake, and
that the whole world was on the watch for the hour
which very nearly struck, the hour for which we
here are prepared with the anguish of a patriotic
feeling all too well fostered with facts. And note
too, that while I receive this unfair letter of yours,
I receive also letters from "the other side" which
regard me as a Dreyfusard. To this I am resigned,
and find a noble and lofty consolation in these
double blows. . . . I cannot forgive either your
friends or the others for the reciprocal outrages
with which they have once again cleft France
asunder. And vainly do I seek the spirit of our
beloved *Union* in its early days, when we were all
so eager with the same single concern—to extract
the common denominator from the sectarian and
philosophic and social and professional labels—
those labels which pen us up at the gateway of life
and seem to separate us from each other by
watertight compartments—and to extract common
grounds for life and action, to extract everything
that makes for unity. And to-day, like any Inquisition, like all the excommunicators of every
age, you are hurling an interdict against this class
or that corporate body, and it is by this right that

you label me because I am a soldier, notwithstanding all our talks in the old days—you label *me!*

What revolts me is the declaration from your pen that there are two sides, and two sides only. "What a sorry business!" I should say with you—but in a different sense. But I check myself. My approaching return to France (at the end of April or May), to which I was looking forward keenly, is now simply a nightmare. I no longer know to whom I shall turn. Amidst all this turbulence I can't see my place. But this anticipation drives me back upon myself, sets me face to face with my conscience; and I am resigned to being alone. It was Luther, I think, who said: "Happy are those who can, at a moment of their lives, be solitary." I shall be so, but not without pangs. For over four years I had been cherishing the joys of return, to your group more than to any others. It was there that I thought my pulse would beat fastest and most warmly, that my ideal, matured by perspective and exile, would be best understood. And I nevertheless sign myself—Your inseparably . . .

This return of a man divided against himself to a land divided against itself was, as he said, a nightmare. He arrived in Paris on May 26th, a few days before the Auteuil scandal, the Déroulède trial, the Haute-Cour. Galliéni, with whom he had returned, had bidden him make it his watchword to keep aloof from any demonstrations, and to make it his sole task to make their joint work in Madagascar known and understood. On arriving in Paris, Lyautey introduced the chief of whom he was so proud to the circles in which he himself had lived before leaving for the colonies. It was a curious contact, that of the bluff, weather-beaten Galliéni with the conservative friends of his adjutant. "How do you come to know all these people?" asked Galliéni in surprise. But he was quick to realize that he could make good use of this new type of mandarin to make public opinion favourable to his schemes, and he used them very adroitly.

*   *   *   *   *

In May, 1900, Galliéni set off for Madagascar again, taking Lyautey, now promoted to colonel's rank, along with him. He had secured his loan, made certain of the establishment at Diego-Suarez of a naval base and a fortified camp, the setting-up of which was entrusted to Colonel Joffre, and arranged all the concerns of his colony. This time Galliéni entrusted Lyautey with the command of the southern third of the island, a great part of which had still to be conquered, pacified and organized. The headquarters of his command were at Fianarantsoa, capital of the Betsileo, but being continually with his columns or making journeys, he was hardly ever in residence there. In two years the task assigned to him was completed. He returned to France early in 1902, to take up the command of a regiment as colonel.

This return was no less difficult than the last. For several years Lyautey had been a free man, liberated by distance from the chains of caste, and almost from all hierarchy. He felt it irksome to find himself again condemned to seek his place in a rigid society: "Shall I confess it? I am really frightened when I contemplate my return to France. I shall try to stay there as little as possible and to find refuge under the wing of family affection, and of a few friends like yourself with whom it will be possible to open one's heart completely."

He had hoped, as was quite natural, that he would obtain a post where he could carry on the mission for which he now felt himself so well prepared. He was appointed colonel of the 14th Hussars at Alençon, and was advised to "lie low." One of his letters to Max Leclerc shows what his feelings were at this time:

My dear friend, you tell me very affectionately that you cannot easily resign yourself to the thought of my bitterness and discouragement. You have given too many proofs of your stable and faithful friendship for me to refrain from opening my heart to you. For eight years of my life, from thirty-

nine to forty-seven—that is to say, through my
fullest maturity—I have given myself up body and
soul to an idea and a work—the work of the
colonies, the overseas policy of France. The posts
I have filled, and the men with whom I have been
associated, have enabled me, whilst actively carrying out this work in detail, to have a bird's-eye view
of it, to grasp its general outline, and to understand its inner workings under conditions of which
few others can have had the benefit. You will
understand when I say that in this my faculties
and temperament have found factors of action and
adaptation which my previous career had not furnished. The confidence which I so quickly won
from every one, the increasingly important posts
which were entrusted to me, had given me the illu-
sion that my real path lay here henceforth, and I
even confess that I had made myself conspicuous
and that I did not think it would occur to anybody
to employ me in anything else. . . . Not for one
moment throughout this long term had I conceived
the possibility of being diverted from the task on
which all my work and all my thoughts had con-
verged, the work on which I had accumulated
notes, documents and experiences. . . . I fully
granted that one day I should return to France,
but I assumed that, as I was indisputably a Colonial, it would be in order to take part in a different
capacity in the same work either in an office of
the Colonial Ministry, or in the Ministry of War,
and that even if, for form's sake, I were given a
regiment to command, I should continue, like so
many others, to participate in the councils where

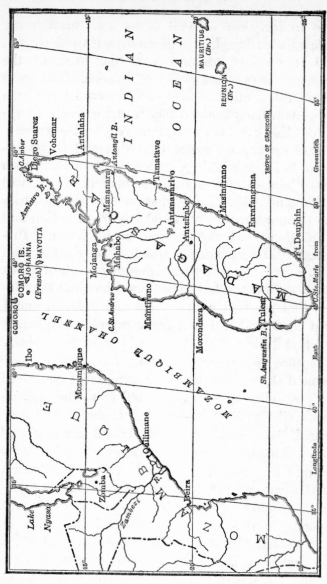

MADAGASCAR

colonial affairs are thrashed out. . . . In a word, that I should not be abruptly thrown right outside of everything I know, everything that has been my unique concern for ten years past, to be relegated right away into the most mechanical, the most routine of tasks. . . .

The objection that I am bound to command a regiment will not hold water, because, as General Galliéni himself has made perfectly clear in several official documents sent to the Ministry, I have carried on not Staff functions, but an effective post of command, held over a prolonged period, much higher than the command of a regiment, or even of a brigade, the appreciable equivalent to that of a division, and have done so *on active service,* which, according to all the regulations and precedents, decides the question. It is merely through sheer folly inspired by ill-will that anybody could claim that after commanding 4000 rifles and 150 officers, I must needs command 600 in France in order to give proof of powers of command. Since my return, apart from my personal friends, not one hand has been held out to me; if any advice has been proffered to me, it has been only to advise me to disappear into a hole, to sham dead, as if I had to atone for something, to make penance for the eight years with neither rest nor truce that I have given to the service of the country. When my name does happen to be mentioned in connection with colonial developments, it is almost as a grievance against me, as if with some accomplice in a crime, or some officer compromised in the Affair. And I am not to be bitter and disheartened! Heavens above! I never felt more full of sap and life and strength; I never felt better armed to serve my country with words, or pen, or action, and all they can say to me is—"Hide yourself, disappear! Don't stir a finger! Keep mum!" as they would say to some one who had a great deal that ought to be forgotten. . . . And you don't want me to choke and foam at the mouth! But, my dear fellow, I can't stand it any more!

Here I have made myself a mask which I push on to my face when I wake up, smiling, satisfied, the complete hussar. I doff it only when I return home. They can't ask any more of me, and what I write to you is certainly not for the public, to whom I convey the impression that I really was born for nothing more than carrying out inspections of harness, examinations of non-commissioned officers for promotion and horse-training; this I conscientiously do from six in the morning to six at night. But I can't go on! Excuse this outburst. All my efforts are being strained to keep myself going until October 24th, 1930, the date on which I am entitled to retire, and then to resume my independence, which with my modest pension will then mean poverty, but will at least allow me to fix myself in a fifth-floor room in Paris and fling myself into the battle for the ideas in which I believe and for things I know about, unless between this and then I have found abroad what I am looking for, an enterprise or industrial company which will consent to employ me on any job at all to bring me my daily bread, but at least planting my lines far from a country where nobody wants to make use of me and where I cannot resign myself to being merely a wasted force.

Well, my friend, there's a fine outburst! It relieves my feelings, for I had long had it on my mind and it didn't suffice any longer to confide it to my four walls between ten o'clock and midnight. I am very fond of you; cherish your friendship for the corpse that I am becoming, and above all remember that nobody here is to divine this frame of mind; I insist formally on its not being hawked around; it would delight far too many people to whom I don't want to give such a pleasure, and who will never see me anything but smiling. Most sincerely, I ask nothing and wish for nothing. I may be stupefying myself here, but at least I have found in my regiment devoted souls who are pleased to have me, and that is my compensation in my disgrace. I have just told you my *real* frame of mind, but nothing *visible* betrays it. And I ask you specially to say not a word of this to our friends, and to show only my philosophy. It will be time enough to perceive it when I have disappeared in one fashion—or another.

* * * * *

During the summer of 1903 Lyautey, on his way through Paris, had been invited to dine by one of his close friends, M. Jules Charles-Roux, formerly a deputy for Marseilles, and there met M. Jonnart, the Governor-General of Algeria. M. Jonnart spoke of the anxiety which he then felt from the increasing anarchy and insecurity of the districts along the frontier between Algeria and Morocco. He himself, a few weeks before, had gone out with a perfectly easy mind to survey the neighbourhood of the Figig palm groves, and in the Zenaga Pass had met with an unexpected attack. He had been placed in a very dangerous position from which he had been released only by an intervention of French troops, who suffered several casualties, both killed and wounded. This incident, referred to by the press as "the Figig Ambush," had impressed the Government in Paris.

The problem of the Algerian-Moroccan frontier was becoming serious. All travellers and geographers knew that the logical frontier of Algeria had been the river Muluya, which Marshal Bugeaud had reached by the battle of Isly in 1844. But at that time England had protested, and France had accepted an ill-defined boundary running further to the east, with the result that numerous nomadic and robber tribes had their grazing territory and their palm groves in Algeria, while their defensive bases lay in Morocco. True, the treaty of 1845 granted France a right of pursuit, which allowed the French, in the event of attack, to pursue the offenders into Moorish territory. But twofold authority nearly always means no authority, and the event had shown this clearly enough. In point of fact, chaos had been the rule in the Saharan region of these Algerian-Moroccan borderlands. French convoys and outposts were kept in a state of anxiety by "desert corsairs." And, as a German traveller wrote, it was plain that Algeria would not be complete so long as its frontier, with the Muluya valley, was not defined.

About 1880, after the revolt of Bou-Amama, the French had occupied Aïn-Sefra, a small mountain township, and had made it a regional military centre. Bou-Amama had taken refuge in Morocco, whence he had continued to spread incitements to the Holy War in the direction of Algeria. In order to withstand this a line of fortified posts had been built, but they were not strong enough and were shown to be powerless. It was then thought that one means of holding back the nomads would be the occupation of the oases from which they drew their food supplies. Agreements were reached with Morocco. The two Governments, "by reason of their adjacent territories," were to lend each other supports for the establishment of peace within these regions. But it was rather ridiculous, this talk of two Governments, when one of them was a Sultan with no authority, who certainly could never have visited, save at his own peril, the region in which he was claiming to help France through his prestige.

M. Jonnart, appointed Governor-General of Algeria in 1903, had hardly arrived when a French legionary was murdered, a convoy of foodstuffs carried off, and twenty-five of its escort killed. This was the time when the Governor-General himself, having gone into the southern Oran, had been caught in the skirmish at the Zenaga Pass and had almost been carried off.

M. Jonnart was delighted to meet with an officer experienced in this kind of warfare, and asked Colonel Lyautey about the methods used by Galliéni against the Chinese pirates on the Tonking frontier. At first Lyautey hedged, answering that it seemed to him extremely rash to seek a generalization of methods from purely local conditions, that he had no knowledge of the Algerian-Moroccan frontier, and that in the sphere of action there are no rules, but only situations. Nevertheless, when M. Jonnart insisted and M. Charles-Roux encouraged him, Lyautey explained Galliéni's theory, his methods of pacification and penetration, and above all, his ideas regarding collaboration with the native population. While he spoke M. Jonnart expressed his approval. "I am convinced," he said, "that similar methods will be essential in southern

Oran, and not the heavy and rigid ones which they obstinately stick to there." After which the three guests of that luncheon party separated, and Lyautey rejoined his regiment.

A few weeks later a fresh affair of some gravity startled Algeria and France. On August 17th, 1903, a *harka* of four thousand warriors invested the French post at Taghit. Furthermore, on September 2nd, a supply column had been attacked at El-Mungar, losing thirty-six men killed and forty-seven wounded. It was, in fact, a state of war against an intangible enemy.

Were the Moors accomplices? The attacking bands came from Tafilelt, the governor of which was an uncle of the Sultan. From Aïn-Sefra, the regional headquarters, the Governor-General received the gloomiest news. They were afraid that when they woke up next morning they would find the railway and telegraphs cut. Panic was spreading amongst the people of the little Saharan town, and in France excitement was highly keyed up.

Chance had it that M. Jonnart was at that moment, along with General André, Minister of War, at the camp of Avord, where he had gone to see trials of the new machine-guns intended for the southern Oran. They anxiously exchanged their apprehensions and Jonnart concluded: "What I need over there is a competent and energetic leader. I know one. It is Colonel Lyautey. Let me have him."

General André was not ignorant of Lyautey's name. "A former adjutant of Galliéni? Madagascar? Tonking? . . . That would inspire public opinion with a certain confidence. . . . It would look well in to-morrow's newspapers. . . ." And immediately he gave the order for a telegram to be sent to Lyautey telling him that he was appointed to the command of the Aïn-Sefra division and should report at the Ministry.

Lyautey, Colonel of the 14th Hussars, was then with his regiment on the Fourth Corps manœuvres in the Sarthe. Returning from a field-day to his billet, just as he sat down for luncheon with his officers, he found an official yellow telegram on his napkin. He opened it: "Colonel Lyautey will report to the Minister's office in the course of to-morrow morning." No explanation. Lyautey said nothing, finished his luncheon, giving his orders for the next day meanwhile, and then, as he left the table, summoned his lieutenant-colonel and showed him the telegram. The army in those days was right in the middle of the period of denunciations and *"fiches."* The two officers had a feeling that there was trouble ahead.

The Colonel drove in a gig to the billet of the general commanding the division, General Herson, who had formerly served in Africa and only the evening before had been talking with Lyautey about the happenings at Taghit and El-Mungar, which were filling the papers. He had said to him: "I am sorry for the divisional commander of Oran and the brigadier at Aïn-Sefra. . . . There seems no way out of it." Thence Lyautey went over to General Lallemand, who commanded the Army Corps. "My poor Colonel!" he said. "Summoned to the Minister's office! Can you remember having done anything wrong?" Lyautey said he had searched his memory in vain and could think of nothing. But he had a few days before been present in uniform in the cathedral of Alençon, at the head of some of his officers, at a service on the occasion of the death of Pope Leo XIII. General Lallemand said to him: "We need not look further than that. We shan't see you again." He expressed his regrets. Lyautey caught the train, spent a painful night in it, and arrived at the Gare Montparnasse about six or seven in the morning.

It was too early to report at the Ministry. The Colonel ordered his coffee at the station buffet and asked for a newspaper. He thought that within a few hours he was going to be suspended from duty, perhaps even sent to Mont-Valérien. He unfolded the newspaper. On the front page he saw a large headline: "Colonel Lyautey Appointed to Aïn-Sefra Command." He got other papers. All comments, obviously emanating from the Ministry, were couched in terms of the highest praise, approving the happy choice of General André in picking Galliéni's pupil to put in charge of this southern Oran frontier where the situation was causing such anxiety to public opinion.

At nine o'clock Lyautey reported to General Percin, André's *chef de cabinet*. He was now quite reassured, but he did not disguise the conflicting emotions which had been besetting him. General Percin thought the whole business very amusing. "But I don't understand it," he said. "The telegram we sent to Alençon read, 'appointed to Aïn-Sefra command.'" And it was not until later that Lyautey found out what had happened. The telegram was in code. The junior officer in charge of the cipher at Alençon had not yet received the code-word for Aïn-Sefra (a new command), and being unable to read the end of the telegram had forwarded simply the order to report.

* * * * *

LYAUTEY

M. Jonnart wrote to Lyautey:

My DEAR COLONEL,—I am sure that you will carry out the important mission entrusted to you to the best advantage of your country. I have no hesitation in asking for your nomination, for what is needed at Aïn-Sefra is not only a courageous soldier, but an organizer and an intelligent policy. . . . I need hardly tell you that in the accomplishment of your mission you will have the best support I can give you.

When Lyautey had this assurance of support, he felt the difficulties become a pleasure. At last he would again find definite activity, a country to build up, a native political situation to disentangle, lieutenants whose affection and admiration he could secure, and an absolute authority. When he embarked at Marseilles he was a very happy man.

But with arrival at Oran came a slight disappointment. The divisional general received him correctly but coldly, having himself put forward a candidate for the post. Another general whom Lyautey encountered, formerly in command at Aïn-Sefra, said to him: "My poor fellow! Do you know what you're in for? Aïn-Sefra! It's hell! You know what has just been happening. . . . Dangerous and bloody attacks, and we can do nothing against them because we cannot set foot

in the so-called Moroccan territory, although the
frontier is absolutely vague. . . . It will all start
again. . . . It can't be otherwise, because the
Quai d'Orsay will always refuse to let the cause
be abolished. . . . You won't be able to do anything, and you'll be held responsible. . . . I'm
sorry for you. . . ."

Lyautey was rather pensive next morning when
he took the little train running southward. After
a long and tedious journey (he had to change at
Perregaux—nobody met him—he remembered his
arrival at Madagascar when Galliéni had given him
a ceremonial reception), he at last reached the town
which was to be his residence. Aïn-Sefra, "the
capital of desert Oran, lay alone in its valley of
sand between the vast monotony of the high
plateau land and the furnace of the Southern Territory, a very Saharan, very somnolent little town,
with its tawny *ksar* at the foot of the gold-coloured
sandhill, with its holy *koubas* and its dim blue gardens. . . . Beyond the last poplars the sandy track
ended abruptly at the foot of the sandhills which
showed up against the stern, blue background of
the mountains." After that, the desert.

He found the regional sub-division lodged in a
building of conventional military Engineers' type.
A captain laid a "report" before him to be signed

—a punishment of four days' confinement to the guard-room, an authorization to open a canteen, a transport order. . . . It was becoming comical, but tragic too. The captain was not yet acquainted with Lyautey's bursts of passion. But he soon was. "How many papers like that have you got?" —"Sixty, sir."—"Sixty? Well, there are fifty of them you can very well sign yourself without ever letting me see them. . . . I don't want to waste my time with nonsense like this. . . . If you want to work with me you'll have to understand that. . . . Now what about our organization? What artillery have we got here?"—"The artillery is not under your control, sir. It comes under the division direct."—"Oh! Not in my control? Very well. . . . And the convoys? That's the essential thing in a country like this. . . ."—"Not in your control either, sir."—"I suppose that comes under the division too, does it?"—"Yes, sir."—"Capital! So I have to pacify all this country, but I can't move one camel or one gun without referring it back to Oran."—"Exactly, sir," said the Staff captain of the Aïn-Sefra division.

Next day came word of Colonel Lyautey's promotion to the rank of General of Brigade. A pleasant surprise, for he did not expect it so soon. He set off towards the oases to inspect his kingdom.

LYAUTEY

In a letter to Vogüé he wrote:

After four days of Aïn-Sefra, devoted to turning around and seeing the papers, I took the road the day before yesterday for the south. Yesterday I went round Figig, passing along the walls at dawn; everything was glittering, the rose-coloured mountains, the white domes of the *koubas,* the morning mist on the palm trees; a group of foraging spahis stood out brightly on the horizon; a native contingent with their red burnouses, white burnouses, blue burnouses, escorted me in the joy of the extended gallop. The Figig inhabitants watched us from the terraces. . . . This morning, a ride in the dawn . . . to come and see the wounded brought here from El-Mungar. . . . They were there, at the entrance to the outpost— Quartermaster-sergeant Tisserand and Corporal Betz and all the rest, and I shook them by the hand, one by one, and then assembled the forty survivors and told them what we all feel. At the end I asked the question: "Well, lads, have any of you served with me before?" Five or six stepped forward: "I have, sir. I was with you at Nuiken. . . . I was with you at Ke-Tuong . . . at Fort-Dauphin. . . . It was I who escorted you on such-and-such a day. . . . It was I who brought you such-and-such information. . . ." And the same thing at each outpost I visit: I find my old legionaries at each. And you can't imagine how good it feels— tears come to my eyes every time—to read in the eyes of these fine fellows that they have long ago put their trust in me; they seem to be saying to me: "Now then! Things are going to be all right!"

One thing is certain, that in all my subordinates I find an unbounded trust and support—and after all that's the essential thing. For the moment my position is a stupid one; nothing is arranged; I have no power; my hands are tied.

In the course of this journey he reviewed what the division called the "light column" of Beni-Oussif, that is to say, a supposedly mobile contingent intended for the pursuit of raiders. He studied the composition of this unit with an expert eye, and then said to its commanding officer: "Look here, I'd like to ask you a simple question. You've just shown me a column with the men wearing high lacing boots like infantrymen in Orleans, haversacks laden as if for a campaign of six months, vast convoys (for men who feed on a handful of dates)—and you tell me this is a light column. . . . Good. . . . Well, I ask you—what do you call a heavy column?"—"But, sir . . . those are the regulations."

He took the trains to Algiers, went to see M. Jonnart, and explained the position to him. "Either get the War Office to give me a completely free hand, or else send me back to Paris."—"What exactly do you want?" asked Jonnart.—"I want what I had in Madagascar, what Galliéni enforced for himself in Tonking," answered Lyautey. "I

want to have my territory as a whole. I want
to have under my orders not only all the military
services, but also all the political services, the intelligence officers, everything. . . . And then, in
case of urgency, I want to be able to have direct
telegraphic communication with the Minister of
War, without having to do so by way of the Oran
division, who would transmit it to Algiers, who
would refer it to Paris, the result being that any
urgent matter will take a month to settle. . . . I
warn you it's a large-scale affair, what I'm asking.
. . . I know what the military are like. The Paris
variety will jump out of their skins. . . . But if
you desire the pacification of southern Oran, this
is essential."

Within a month Jonnart, who had crossed to
France, was writing to him from Paris:

I saw General André last Monday. On the following day he got the cabinet to agree to a reorganization of your sub-division. In a few days, I
have every reason to hope, this will be put through.
. . . So you have no reason to feel disheartened. I
am behind you and with you, and very soon—believe me—we shall attain all our objectives.

VII

THE problems which General Lyautey had now to solve cannot be understood without at least a brief survey of the situation in Morocco in 1903.

In that western corner of North Africa, Morocco still remained a feudal and barbarian enclave in the heart of modern life. The existence of this anachronistic empire, a few hours from Gibraltar and Algeciras, a few days from Oran, was in itself paradoxical. It is not easy to induce two civilizations to live as neighbours in space, when in time they are separated by several centuries. A natural law in such cases makes the pressure of the stronger crush and destroy the weaker. Order and security may not be rights of man, but they have become necessities of man. A country which, like Morocco, cannot meet these necessities when surrounded by more exacting nations will vanish.

Further, if this Empire had been a homogeneous state, its solidity might possibly have accounted for the tolerance of Europe. But Morocco was hardly a state in the European sense of the word. Its population was composed of Arab or Berber

115

tribes, nomadic or sedentary, who obeyed their marabouts or their councils of elders more than they obeyed the Sultan's kaids. The Sultan himself had several capitals—Marrakesh, Fez, Meknes —wherein he resided; he had an administration, the Maghzen, and certain tribes devoted to his sway, the Maghzen tribes. But the strong tribes, and especially those of the borderlands, did not acknowledge the Maghzen and did not obey it. There was something naïve in the official admission that the country was divided into the Bled-es-Maghzen, the territory recognizing the Sultan's authority, and the Bled-es-Saba, the territory living in dissent. During the tax-paying season the Sultan roamed his kingdom, followed by several Maghzen tribes, to secure the payment of his dues, but he took good care not to enter hostile and powerful districts.

Between the years 1875 and 1894 an energetic Sultan, Mulai-Hassan, had been able to command a certain respect. But since his death a child, Abdul-Aziz, had reigned. Until 1900 the child Sultan had been dominated by the Grand Vizier, Ba-Ahmed. During the Maghzen councils the Sultan would sit looking at picture-books or playing with mechanical toys, while Ba-Ahmed, squatting on the ground before him, would work with the secretaries. Since the death of Ba-Ahmed the favourite had been an extraordinary person, a Scotsman who styled himself Kaid Maclean. Formerly a subaltern in the British Army, he had left Gibraltar in consequence of some private difficulties and then entered the service of Morocco. "He was small and round, with a clean little white beard, and the gayest eyes that ever shone above a bagpipe. Arrayed in a turban and a white burnous he would stride along the garden paths blowing with his bagpipes. *The Banks of Loch Lomond* would squeal out into the African sunshine." [1]

Through Maclean the Court came to be filled with British adventurers, who were received at the palace with a favour that emphasized the hostility which was there manifested towards the French, redoubtable neighbours and possible invaders. In the Sultan's palace nothing could now be seen but bicycles and steam-launches, gramophones and cameras. The Sultan's wives were rigged up in silk gowns, wigs and feather hats, and the Sultan used to have himself photographed in the most comical poses.

This frivolity on the part of a sovereign who ought properly to have been also the supreme re-

---

[1] *Lord Carnock*, by Harold Nicolson.

ligious authority was distasteful to his Moslem
subjects. It was not long before the people of
the tribes began to regard Abdul-Aziz as corrupted
by European civilization, and to rally round agitators. About 1902 one of the latter, Bou-Hamara
by name and styled the Rogui, was proclaimed
Sultan by the revolting tribes. He was a villager
who practised conjuring tricks and gained much
prestige by his miracles. Against him the Sultan
despatched several expeditions, which came to
naught. Throughout the Oujda region (one
which interested Lyautey as being right on the
Algerian border), the Rogui and the aged Algerian chief Bou-Amama were much more powerful
than the Maghzen. And in that country of wide
spaces, where pursuit was so difficult, a small handful of rebels could easily trouble the state of peace.

*   *   *   *   *

How had Morocco survived in face of this
anarchy? The rivalries of European powers exer-
cised conflicting influences on the different forces
which might possibly have acted in the country.
Certain French statesmen would gladly have occupied Morocco, in order to rid Algeria of a dangerous neighbour, and more especially to avoid
the danger of another European power installing

itself there and so creating a new military frontier by making the Muluya into a new Rhine. But French ministers were made prudent by the lesson of Ferry's disgrace,[1] by the distaste of the French electorate for colonial ventures, and by the fear of international complications.

Spain also was a neighbour to Morocco, separated therefrom only by a narrow strip of sea. She had always maintained, at great expense, some colonies in the Mediterranean ports, and believed that she had certain rights over that Empire which were supported by other European nations. In Bismarck's time Germany had favoured the colonial expansion of France, believing it to be favourable to European security; but faced by the development of French power in North Africa she was beginning to regret her possibly ill-conceived generosity. On several occasions she had proclaimed her disinterestedness in regard to Morocco, but a very different story was told by the behaviour of her agents and of German colonists. England was not yet France's friend: it was an axiom of her traditional policy to allow no nation to place itself opposite Gibraltar and so bar the

---

[1] [Jules Ferry (1832-1893) was the statesman largely responsible for the colonial expansion of France in the East and in Africa. His prestige, however, was gravely damaged by certain reverses in Tonking in 1885.]

route to India. She had long hoped to make
Morocco into another Egypt, and without openly
supporting Maclean she had not disavowed him.
Thus the Sultan Mulai Hassan had throughout
his reign been able to play the easy game of setting off one European nation against another.
About 1900 the British representative at Tangier,
Sir Arthur Nicolson, a man of steady and sure
judgment, set out the position in these terms: "The
more I have seen of the members of the Government, the more hopeless seems any prospect of
reform or progress. The main policy of the Government is to set the tribes by the ears, to support
one side, then wring money out of the beaten one,
and then later to extort money out of the victors
for assistance rendered. They wish to ruin the
tribes, leaving them but the barest necessities, so
that they may be harmless. The idea is that if a
tribe becomes quiet and orderly it becomes rich
(relatively) and that they will purchase arms and
munitions and shake off subjection to the Government. No wonder that with this system the country is going backward and backward. . . . From
what I hear the Moors would welcome any European invader. They are tired to death of this
grinding system of government. . . ."[1]

---

[1] *Lord Carnock*, by Harold Nicolson.

But French policy had been much confused by a conflict regarding the Moroccan question between two of the great administrations of the Republic. The Quai d'Orsay,[1] then ruled by Delcassé and represented at Tangier and Fez by M. Saint-René-Taillandier, who was seeking in this disintegrating country a definite authority on which it could exert the influence of its activity. "With whom, if not with the Sultan, do you wish us to negotiate in Morocco?" asked Delcassé. "One cannot negotiate with nothingness." The objective of the French Minister in Tangier was to induce the Maghzen voluntarily to entrust France with the task of carrying out the necessary reforms in the country, training its army and setting up a police force, and later to undertake the building of railways and harbours. In fact, the Quai d'Orsay sincerely desired collaboration with the Maghzen, and the Quai d'Orsay official could not but be startled by any act arousing the Sultan's distrust of France or any act arousing the attention of jealous Powers.

The Algerian Government, no less naturally, regarded such a policy as a fool's paradise. In the provinces bordering on the hypothetical Algerian-

[1] French Foreign Office.

Moroccan frontier, French troops could see for themselves, and at the cost of their lives, that the authority of the Sultan was non-existent, that it was useless to obtain promises from a Government incapable of fulfilling them, to negotiate, in fact, "with nothingness." Geography and common sense alike made it clear that, up to the Muluya, the country was Algerian: "Need it be indefinitely closed to our authority, even to our police expeditions, by the vain phantom of a shadowy Sultan, when certain tribes were only too anxious to come over to us and to be taken into our control, when all that we needed to have peace within our borders at last would be to advance a few kilometres further, to go beyond a certain fold in the land that concealed our views, to set up an outpost at certain wells, to organize a patrol system in a certain group of hills?" [1] To which, no doubt, Paris would have answered that a pact with a Sultan, even a phantom one, put us in a strong position with regard to the rest of Europe. No understanding seemed possible between these two groups of Frenchmen, both perfectly sincere, but one of which was seeking to establish a quite abstract harmony between European myths, and the other to transform the all-too-real images of white bur-

---

[1] *Quinze Ans de Politique Marocaine*, by Saint-René-Taillandier.

nouses, of horsemen armed with rifles, of ambushes in the palm groves.

* * * * *

General Lyautey, then, on the other side of the ideal and sandy frontier he was deputed to guard, had the following prospect before him. At the gates of the "Saharan and somnolent" Aïn-Sefra began the endless sandhills, broken only by the green strip of the oases, "that street of palm trees leading without a break from the Atlas to the heart of the Sahara." Here there lived about two hundred thousand men, in a strange living amalgam of nomads and peasants. The natives of the oases, the tillers of the gardens within the palm groves, were native negro agricultural workers, slave farmers; the owners of the land were Berber or Arab nomads, always busy with warfare, hunting and trafficking, who came to the oases between two expeditions to seek at once fresh provisions and repose.

Nothing could be more strange than these Saharan towns. "They are *ksars,* that is to say, fortified townships. . . . The houses have several stories, with staircase wells; the streets have covered passage-ways, and both the outward appearance and the social life are urban in character; there

123

are markets, shops, strolling-places, cafés, pleasure
resorts. This is all indispensable to the nomad,
who requires of the oasis what the sailor demands
of the port—easy means of revictualling, and gross
compensations for long abstinence. However tiny
a *ksar* may be, it is never a village; it is a town
in baked mud. Herodotus's Babylon was on this
model." [1]

The French occupation placed the nomads in
an ambiguous position, as it frequently happened
that one and the same tribe owned palm groves
and grazings in Algeria and others in Tafilelt, in
the heart of Morocco. Their strength and head-
long bravery made them dangerous. "These continual desert expeditions, imposing as they do an
extreme degree of physical effort on the bodily
frame, together with extreme sobriety, produce
magnificent physique, slender and muscular bodies.
. . . The physical side is matched by the moral.
One must picture to oneself these Saharan tracks,
where a moment's heedlessness, a brief weakness,
or a failure to keep one's head, will bring death
from thirst. Nor is thirst the only danger: there
is also man. An unknown track crossing the path
is perhaps the warning of an ambush. Men do
not linger at the wells, which are too conspicuous;

---

[1] E. G. Gautier, *Le Sahara.*

the leather bottles are quickly filled, and they pass
on, to stop farther ahead, generally after making
a loop calculated to put possible pursuers, always
a possibility, off the track. One is in the *'bled-el-
khouf,'* the land of fear, or the *'bled-el-sif,'* the
land of the sword. Such a life endows the eye
and certain sides of the intelligence with a sharp-
ness that is the admiration of Europeans. A
totally uneducated nomad, questioned by an ex-
plorer, will draw an intelligible map on the sand
with his finger. He has the topographical sense,
because direction is to him a matter of life and
death. He recognizes So-and-so, of such-and-such
a tribe, by the print of his naked foot, as surely
as a European detective identifies a criminal by
his thumb-print. It is needless to say how far his
character is tempered by the ever-present shadow
of violent death. Such is the individual, and we
should consider the bonds which unite him with
the other members of his tribe. This is an exact
equivalent to those imposed by military discipline
between our soldiers. A nomadic tribe is by birth
a regiment."

These poor and hardy lords of the land, within
their old sphere of activity, saw a prosperous agriculture and richer villages developing under the
French protection. Naturally they were tempted

by the new wealth spread out before them, and began to make continual raids into French territory. The conventions of 1845 and 1902 certainly authorized the French to pursue raiders right into Moroccan territory, but as these conventions also forbade the French to have permanent outposts there, these punitive expeditions were useless, and the palm groves of Tafilelt offered a safe asylum to the armed bands.

This mass of hostile tribes, this "bubbling cauldron" as Lyautey called it, was kept boiling at one time by Bou-Amama, that old enemy of the French, who had remained very powerful in the Figig region, at another by the Rogui and his partisans. But a restoration of order did not seem beyond the bounds of possibility. Tafilelt, the most dangerous point of the country, was populous and comparatively speaking rich, containing, therefore, a conservatively minded majority who were anxious for peace and for commercial relations with Algeria. But, as often happens, the agriculturists and traders were dominated by the intransigent and warlike minority.

Fortified by his experience of Tonking and Madagascar, Lyautey wanted to apply here the methods he had tested elsewhere: namely, to investigate the internal politics of the country, to handle

each tribe according to its own temper, to depend
upon the most intelligent of the chieftains, to win
over territory from the tribes succesively without
fighting—the "spreading stain of oil"—to acquaint
the oppressed sedentary peoples with the blessings
of peace, and step by step to consolidate the acquired results by setting up outposts which would
radiate patrols with wide range, crossing their
beams like those of lighthouses.

It was an intelligent and humane policy, but
from the outset it clashed with the policy of Paris.
"The frontier must not be crossed by so much as
an inch"—such had been the existing instructions
formerly issued by General Gallifet. But how
could one not cross a frontier which was quite theoretic? How could one halt cavalry sent out in
pursuit of marauders in these sands, before an
imaginary line of which one's enemy was in total
ignorance? From these first weeks Lyautey was
both in love with his work and baffled by the difficulties.

During the years of his colonial apprenticeship
he had learned the handling of natives from
Galliéni. He had now to learn the secrets of central administrations. Jonnart showed him that
even within the rigid Napoleonic organization of
modern France an energetic man can act with

something approaching freedom if he masters the rules of the game. He taught Lyautey to put up as little resistance as possible, to have things accepted as provisional which would never be considered if put forward as definite, but which would become so later by the provisional being left as a permanency. In the Tonking days Galliéni had said to him: "In your communications with Ministries, make everything look smaller than it is." Jonnart showed him how one ministry can be played off against another, how realities count for nothing with an administration, how in their zeal for preciseness they have an overwhelming passion for making a report coincide with a regulation, but that if they are given some means, even artificial, of contriving such an agreement, these monsters of verification will be duly appeased. Later he taught him the art of handling ministers, vain though often intelligent men, rivals of each other even within the same cabinet, jealous of their prerogatives and standing in terror of Parliament. This apprenticeship was necessary for Lyautey if he was to become one of the proconsuls of the Third Republic. Hitherto, in Tonking or Madagascar, a Lanessan or a Galliéni had been interposed between him and this mysterious mechanism. The fortunes of his career had now placed him at Aïn-

Sefra, a point which, although lost on the very
edge of the desert, turned out to be one of the
nerve-centres of a sickly and sensitive Europe. He
must learn for himself the art of placating the
jealous gods of Paris and making them propitious.

From Jonnart he had a letter dated July 20th,
1904.

My dear General [it began],—Like all men
of action you are bound to find that things move
very slowly, that certain trifling gentle resistances
are parried with absurd arguments, and that central
administrations are far too ready to obstruct
initiative and set up opposing arguments. Believe
me when I say that, in my care for my duties
and responsibilities, I chafe, as you do, against
certain delays and certain obstacles. But the world
is like that. We shan't reform it. The important
thing is always to move forward, however little the
distance, and to achieve one forward step in one's
task every day. When the exact goal is clearly
defined, I am convinced that a strong will enables
one to dominate both men and things in the long
run. I make the experiment daily myself, and
every one, both here and in France, who is capable
of judging our Oran problems, is united in admiration
of the splendid results you have achieved
in so short a time. You have justified, even more
than justified, our hopes, and the trust we placed
in you; you have given evidence of qualities of organization
and of political capacity; these are plain
to every one, even in the Ministry of War, where

certain very human jealousies have failed to overcome the keen feeling of sympathy felt for you by
all your colleagues and all your superior officers.

The main difficulty was the setting up of the
sentinel outposts, the keystone of the work of pacification. They could be placed only beside wells,
which were very scarce in that country. When
these points happened to be on Moorish territory,
there was some risk of injuring the susceptibilities,
not only of the Sultan, but also of Europe and
the Quai d'Orsay. On the other hand, to abandon
these projected outposts for the protection of the
pacified regions only meant condemning oneself
to be for ever starting the same task again. In
November, 1903, a dispute arose regarding a post
set up at the entrance of the Bechar oasis, commanding the passes of the Bechar mountain region, which harboured innumerable marauders.
Hitherto no general had ventured to occupy that
point, which without any doubt lay in Moroccan
territory. Lyautey gave the post the name of
Colomb, in memory of a French officer who had
been killed there. "What! You have occupied
Bechar?" said the minister to M. Jonnart. "You
must evacuate it—you're in Moroccan territory!"
—"But we're not at Bechar," replied M. Jonnart.
"We're at Colomb."—"Oh, that's a different mat-

ter." And the post was maintained. Later on it was called Colomb-Bechar; it covered the Figig region.

But in the following year a more serious incident nearly put an end to Lyautey's career; and it must be recounted in some detail, because the episode shows more clearly than any other the character of the man, one who was always ready, following Goethe's maxim, to stake everything on one card.

* * * * *

In June, 1904, Bou-Amama, "the instigator of all the surprise attacks on Algeria, abandoned the southern regions, which had become too well organized for him, and came up to the north, right into Morocco. With him came a thousand well-armed followers. He was thus in close proximity to the frontier, and consequently in a very good position for continuing his attacks, being at the same time well protected from French attack because of his being within the Moroccan zone." General Lyautey despatched a reconnoitring party to cover the friendly tribes, placing it under the command of his Chief-of-Staff, Colonel Henrys, in whom he had the most complete and close confidence. Henrys proceeded to Ras-el-Aïn, Berguent, the only water-point of the region, and the only place which met the military and political conditions necessary to remain there and cover the south. The local representative of the Sultan declared his happiness at being defended by French troops against Bou-Amama and the Rogui. Indeed, he could hardly have felt otherwise; but the inhabitants of Berguent showed manifest sincerity in their sense of reassurance by the presence of the French, whom they welcomed with enthusiasm. So all was going well:

I had been there twice myself [wrote Lyautey]. I had given the people a solemn promise of our protection, and had begun there on the large scale my usual policy of the "stain of oil" and my methods of attraction, which had already gathered six hundred tents around me. The occupation of this important point, with the adherence of the Maghzen, accomplished without one rifle-shot, was a fine result.

This had lasted for six weeks when a press campaign began, originating in Tlemcen, where Lyautey's policy had certain opponents. At the same time the Maghzen protested to the French representatives in Fez: "What was all this? French troops penetrating Moorish territory, setting up barracks, giving every appearance of staying there! So what was happening to the idea of winning

132

over the Sultan simply by persuasive means, and bringing him to carry out gradual reforms within his dominions?" The Tangier legation informed the Minister of Foreign Affairs.

On July 28th the latter arrived at the Cabinet meeting in high dudgeon; he declared that the difficulties met by the French minister accredited to the Sultan were attributable to the conduct of the military authorities in Algeria, who had crossed the frontier and were thus giving the Maghzen the impression that conquest was beginning. He forthwith asked the cabinet to decide on formal instructions being sent to Algeria that the General in command at Aïn-Sefra should be requested to resume the proper limitations of his territory. M. Combes, the Prime Minister, started when he heard this account of events. He told General André, the Minister of War, that such initiatives on the part of the military authorities were not admissible, and had a telegram sent to the Governor General ordering the evacuation of Berguent. M. Jonnart was at that moment away, and the telegram was transmitted through Algiers and Oran to General Lyautey.

He, in his turn, reacted violently. He had always been impatient of obstacles in the way of his desires, and in this particular case he was convinced of being in the right and indignant that he had not been asked for any explanation before the order was issued. He regarded this evacuation as an infamy. It would destroy all French authority in this region and expose the friendly populations to the terrible reprisals of Bou-Amama and the Rogui. He was then at Oran. He asked permission of General Herson, who had handed him the order for withdrawal, to leave him for a moment, summoned one of his officers, Captain Georges Renouard, and dictated to him the following telegram:

Sefra Subdivision to Ministry of War: . . . Existence alone of Ras-el-Aïn observation post can hold back tribes which formerly made common cause with Bou-Amama. . . . Sections having completely joined up with us urgently request us maintain their protection and not abandon them to Bou-Amama reprisals. I have given formal promise of this, not believing this desertion possible. In virtue of strong points occupied by Bou-Amama and his thousand rifles, in Moroccan territory but against our frontier, Ras-el-Aïn is sole point where we can now maintain observation post, in view of absence of any adequate water-supply in neighbourhood. Withdrawal now can be interpreted by population as flight in face of pretender and Bou-Amama. Whatever point column may be withdrawn to, this step will entail real disaster, repercussion on all our front to Figig and Aïn-Chair, and will cause defection of all wavering tribes, brought in with great pains during past six months. Provisional maintenance at Ras-el-Aïn therefore absolutely easy to justify: (*a*) by strict necessity protection Algerian frontier in consequence of Bou-Amama's new strong points and his reinforcement by pretender; (*b*) by necessity covering our Hamyan tribes at present reinstated in Chott-el-Gharbi; (*c*) by special situation at this point, where agreements have foreshadowed market and mixed police; (*d*) by support given to Maghzen by our presence.

This withdrawal, contrary to all pledges given to inhabitants, who will suffer instant reprisals, will deal mortal blow to our influence and loyalty, and will cause loss of all gains in situation won during past ten months. It is with the deepest conviction and the most solemn sense of my responsibility for security of southern Oran entrusted to me by Government that I beg you to present Government with these observations, which might be overlooked by those not on the spot, and I ask at least for delay of execution of order pending detailed report and until local situation created by union of pretender with Bou-Amama is clarified, so that we do not appear to be taking flight in face of them and leaving inhabitants to their vengeance. Moreover, having personally pledged myself to populations in the name of France that we should not abandon them and would protect them, and having thus brought them to rally to us and recover security and trade unknown for seven years past, I could not honourably proceed myself to this step; and if it is maintained, I respectfully request to be immediately relieved from my command in such a way that I may appear solely responsible with regard to the inhabitants, and so that they may realize that it is I alone who have improperly pledged the word of the French Government, and, seeing me disowned, can suspect only myself and not the honour of the Government of the Republic.

I declare upon honour, in conclusion, that position attained during past six months, without use of force and without one drop of French blood being spilt, will be instantly compromised, and I respectfully express desire to be summoned to Paris if possible to demonstrate this, and that, in the name of French interests and honour, there should until then be delay in execution of this order, the local bearings of which have certainly been overlooked.

Oran. July 31*st,* 1904.

The captain wrote with startled feverishness. Lyautey completed his dictation, and added:

"Have you followed it? Put it into cipher for me. . . ."

The captain rose.

"Yes, sir," he said, "I'll do so. But I have something to ask you first. Allow me to embrace you— at last I have found a leader!"

"Come along," said Lyautey. "Go and get it into cipher quickly."

He returned to the office where General Herson was waiting.

"Do you still hold to those orders, General?" he said.

"Certainly."

"Then here is a telegram which I am going to send immediately to the Minister of War."

Herson read it, and handed it back to Lyautey with the words:

"I shall never forward that."

"You won't have to, General. It's already gone."

"What! You have taken it upon yourself to communicate with the Minister without passing it through me?"

Lyautey reminded him of the permission he had obtained a year earlier, entitling him to send such communications. He had it in his pocket. He handed it to his superior, who returned it, remarking coldly:

"I admit you have the right."

The result was a brief delay in execution of the order of evacuation; but three days later came the confirming order, the only modification in which was that the withdrawal should be carried out in progressive stages. But this, in Lyautey's view, was not any better, because any backward movement sacrificed friendship and in the eyes of the tribes signified the flight of the French when confronted by Bou-Amama and the pretender. Lyautey appeared to bow to the decision, sent proposals regarding the steps to be taken, but also forwarded his request to be relieved of his post:

As I have already had the honour of informing you, my personal word is totally pledged to the inhabitants who have rallied round us and to whom I believed I could guarantee French protection. That I did so improperly is proved all too well by facts, but the responsibility must be mine to bear. If as a soldier I must make provision for the execution and transmission of the first orders, I myself should not be able honourably, or without gravely compromising the word and prestige of French authority, to proceed to the total evacuation of Ras-el-Aïn; this would be tantamount to abandoning populations to whom I have solemnly guaranteed the protection of the French Republic. Accordingly, I have the honour of forwarding to you, attached, for transmission to the Minister of War, my request to be relieved of my command. I have too much confidence in the equity and sense of honour of my superior officers, and of the Government, to doubt their approval of my action.

But he was too much of a realist to refrain from one last effort for victory and survival after this bold and sincere step. In Indo-China he had seen Galliéni make profitable use of threatened resignation in order to obtain certain reforms. It was a dangerous weapon, but properly handled it could be efficacious. Simultaneously with this telegram to the Minister of War, he despatched another to M. Jonnart, informing him of the situation and suggesting what he regarded as a possible and honourable means of saving the situation: namely, that an understanding should be reached with the Sultan, and that some Moroccan troops should be attached to the troops in occupation of Ras-el-Aïn, a solution which would perhaps placate the self-respect of the Shereefian Government and also secure the safety of the inhabitants.

But Jonnart had to be found. The Governor-General, being in need of complete rest, was travelling in Belgium and had refrained from leaving an address, not having foreseen any serious developments during the period of general holidays. At last the telegram reached him. He acted instantly, with adroitness and despatch. M. Combes, the Prime Minister, was at Pons; M. Delcassé in the Ariège. Jonnart wired a long despatch to M. Combes, telling him, firstly, that neither in the particular instance nor in general could he accept a decision reached without his being consulted as Governor-General of Algeria; secondly, that the occupation of Berguent had been carried out with his approval (which was not strictly true, for Lyautey had not had time to refer to him, but M. Jonnart was covering his subordinate); and thirdly, that if this decision were maintained, he himself would go and join General Lyautey at his post at Berguent. He added that the Ras-el-Aïn movement had been necessitated by the need for maintaining security, that it would be paying too dearly for a few concessions wrung from the Sultan, to acquire these at the cost of weakness which might well be "measured in terms of human lives," and asked M. Combes to name a rendezvous with him, no matter where.

M. Combes, of course, was anxious to retain Jonnart, and this message made him decide to return to Paris. Just then the death of Waldeck-Rousseau obliged Jonnart to do likewise. He saw the Prime Minister.

I firmly declared [wrote Jonnart to Lyautey] that I declined to cover the timidities of our Moroccan policy. Further, M. Combes, who goes straight to the point and (I am bound to admit) places the highest confidence in me, had a spirited exchange of views with the Foreign Minister this morning. I wrote you from Algiers three weeks ago: "You are at Berguent: stay there, whatever is said." It has required an extraordinary combination of circumstances, and furthermore my absence from Algeria, for such an incident to arise. But all's well that ends well. Stand firm at Berguent and come and see me soon.

LYAUTEY

A few months later, in Delcassé's room, the Berguent affair was settled in the presence of M. Saint-René-Taillandier and General Pendezec, Chief-of-Staff, on the lines already suggested by Lyautey: namely, the maintenance of the occupation, but the reinforcement of the French troops by a Shereefian detachment. The incident was closed. It had gained great prestige for Lyautey; amongst his officers he had earned the reputation of a man who did not go back on an accomplished fact, and amongst the native inhabitants that of a man whose word was to be trusted. And certainly he himself was relieved that the matter had been settled without his leaving the army, or even Aïn-Sefra. In a letter of September, 1904, he wrote: "This discreet penetration of Morocco, which I began surreptitiously and which is hardly under way, is so intensely interesting that to leave would really be cruelly heartbreaking." The Minister of Foreign Affairs was not entirely wrong in his fear that in this soldier there was a diplomatist with far-reaching views.

*   *   *   *   *

There are certain species which can live only in circumstances where all others would perish. Lyautey was now happy in the Saharan desert, as he had been in the forests of Tonking, because he was alone and because he was master. With Jonnart as his only superior, living far away and in any case giving him a perfectly free hand, he felt himself the almost absolute sovereign of this kingdom of the oases, and his insatiable appetite for action was almost satisfied. Rounds of inspection, establishment of outposts, the transformation of unattached groups, tribal politics—he was gulping down life in mouthfuls. These Arabs, with their passion for birthright and the sanctity of their forefathers, "proud as Artabanus, quick to take offence, difficult to hold," were even better suited to understand him than Annamites or Tonkinese. They liked his fine horses, his saddles covered with tiger-skin, his embroidered burnouses. "You are the son of chieftains," they told him. "We asked an officer about the sword you carry beside your saddle; it is not like other swords; and he told us it was the sword of your grandfather, who was a general and waged war with Napoleon. That is the kind of man we like to command us!"

His letters describing this life took on the keen, singing radiance of a sketch by Delacroix:

It is ten o'clock at night. My lamp is lit on my camp table, in the great tent of the Bach-Agha Si-Eddin, of the Oulad Sidi Cheikhs. He has sent it

from Géryville, with three other tents for those who
are with me. It is as large as an apartment, lined
with cloth and silk, and the thickness of the moss-
like carpets covers the ground. The door is wide
open; my ensign is flapping; a great red spahi is
mounting guard; my officers are finishing their
pipes round a red fire; a horse whinnies and tugs
at its halter, the servants are taking away the remains of the meal under the eye of the kaid of a
neighbouring tribe in his purple burnous, and the
moonlight quickens the night, so cool after the heat
of the day. . . .

Day in, day out, it is all the purest Fromentin,
Decamps, Guillaumet; Arab feudalism has here retained its splendour and integrity, and I did not
think that it could still exist with such life and
colour. . . . I am here amongst the greatest chiefs
of all Algeria, perhaps of all Africa, the Ouled Sidi
Cheikhs, and I try to be as great a chief as themselves, which is certainly the best method of dominating and holding them—as too many of our
people here, even amongst the military, fail to
understand.

Then a night picture:

The splendid moon and the silvered palm trees,
the violet shadow of the ruddy earthen houses, the
milky *kouba,* the fires where the sheep are roasting
in the centre of a circle of long beards chatting to
each other, two white Arabs at their prayers, our
purple spahis passing, far away the muted sound
of flutes and tambourines, and the great screen of

the mountains with their deep, soft shadows—it is a vast fairyland.

Back at his own quarters in Aïn-Sefra he made a point of still living like a great lord of the desert. Open table, silver, flowers, and German singers from the Legion singing sentimental *lieder* during the meals—it was the atmosphere of a miniature Court whose monarch had a taste for artists. Visitors from Paris were enchanted, if a little surprised. They hardly expected on the edge of the desert to find a well-run house or to hear a Bach chorale.

In this populous solitude Lyautey found, or refound, his essential self. He had changed but little. As at Nancy and Saint-Cyr, he required for the living of his life an atmosphere of ardent trust, the need, as he said, "to be swallowed whole"! He had remained youthful, almost, indeed, a spoilt child, and he found his favourite collaborators amongst the young. The colonels who were placed under his command were sometimes far from happy. One of them, on seeing the light native troops equipped by Lyautey according to his own notions, natives in rope sandals and freed from their burdensome packs, said almost in tears: "I can't be in command of a ragamuffin regiment!" The General's complex and difficult character could

be understood better by lieutenants and captains
than by older men of set character, slaves of their
own respectability. His spirit was divided against
itself, for ever torn between the fondly loved past
and the insistent present, and he solaced himself
with freaks of fancy which might seem brutal and
unjust in the eyes of those who did not know them
for symptoms of a deep inward unrest. As soon as
one worked in contact with him, one found that he
emerged from these vehement outbursts lucid, cool,
and ready to take the most reasonable and well-
calculated courses of action.

The General used to think aloud before the
young officers by whom he liked to be surrounded.
Like them he was fond of a smart uniform and a
flowing burnous, lively horses and ornamental saddles, gallops without bridles and caracoling at the
gates of the *ksours,* unexpectedness, the outbursts
of gaiety that ease the tension of the mind. He
knew how to judge and test these young officers,
and how to employ them in the right place; he
bound them to himself by the confidence of his ideas
and schemes, and by his disappointments no less.
He regarded them as collaborators and associates
rather than as subordinates. Following the tradition of Lamoricière he addressed them familiarly

and treated them like grown-up sons. Towards them he himself offered no mystery or concealment; he lived his life with open doors, right under their eyes. Each one of them in turn found a place laid for him in his welcoming house. After the swiftly served meal he found an occupation for each of their several tastes; to the musician he handed a score, to the artist a box of colours, to the reader the latest reviews; and then, at the exact hour for duty, he pushed them cordially out. In this way there grew up the *zaouia,* his chapel of the faithful.[1]

His relations with M. Jonnart and the Algerian administration remained friendly. The letters written to him at this time are full of two interwoven themes—praise for the astonishing work accomplished, and counsels of serenity. On December 16th, 1904, Jonnart was writing:

MY DEAR GENERAL,—I should greatly like to have news of your health. I hope you are quite yourself again and that you will take care of yourself. It is essential that you should do so. I know from experience that it is not always easy, but it is possible, provided one bears in mind that logic and sound ideas do not triumph immediately in this world and that one must be very patient. What I can tell you is this, that you will always be colliding with critics, because you are a man of action and because only men who do nothing have their minds

---

[1] Britsch.

at rest. But there is only one opinion about you—
that you are doing an excellent piece of work, and
that you are one of our greatest hopes. No doubt
you will rouse jealousies, but that will be just because you are what you are! We are in partnership
and acting for the best, in our country's interest.
What need we care for the curs barking at our
heels? There are still plenty of sound men in
France who understand and approve what we are
doing. Nothing is easy.

And again, on September 6th, 1905:

MY DEAR GENERAL,—I have read with interest
the despatch informing me that the *djicheurs* had
this time paid for their rash enterprise with their
lives. Thanks to the new organization the Moorish
bands will certainly soon lose heart. . . . That is
why I congratulate myself heartily, and all who
have any idea of our southern Oran congratulate
themselves, on your efforts; and we rejoice to be
able to say that, notwithstanding the serious gaps
persistently and wilfully left unfilled by the inertia
or hostility of the ministerial departments, you have
within two years restored our prestige on the
Algerian-Moroccan frontier, and assured our defensive system along rational and logical lines, and
by means that are new to Algeria. The results are
very fine. But your ideal would ask much more;
I know it, I approve, and often I feel sorry for
you; but I beg you not to feel disheartened.

I have just spent a few days in Paris. It was
impossible to catch the Minister of War. He is un-
veiling street fountains, and occasionally following

the manœuvres at a slow trot. He finds much
amusement in this. He was in Paris last Saturday,
but he double-locked his door. I imagined he must
be actively concerned with the question of munitions, stores and mobilization; the circumstances
would appear to impose such duties and such grave
responsibilities upon him! But no: he was preparing a speech for heaven knows what inauguration ceremony at Maubeuge, and his civilian *chef
de cabinet* pointed out to me how ticklish it was to
speak in a town where the municipal council is cut
asunder, where the deputy is a Socialist and coun-
cillors belong to the Left Centre. I had to agree
that nothing could be more difficult, and that it was
criminal on my part to disturb the meditations of a
Minister absorbed in such lofty preoccupations. I
had at first left this gentleman profoundly stupefied by a modest suggestion that perhaps (I said
perhaps) the Minister could have contrived not to
accept the invitation to the inauguration at Maubeuge. I am informed that between now and
October 15th this extraordinary man must attend
nine further inaugurations. Evidently he possesses
the dominant quality of the military leader—endurance. But to myself, who had merely to discuss
service matters with him, he was invisible.

I visited the finance branch. Virtue is making
serious ravages there. . . . You are about to receive a letter in two parts: the first throwing blame
on the irregular book-keeping of the "camel section"; the second recognizing that you have made
able and opportune use of the credits. But if any
indiscreet question is asked in the Chamber, only

the first part will be read. I admired this little
arrangement. The Minister thought of it; his virtue revolts at the thought of a credit assigned to his
department having been "irregularly used"; but to
make up for that, his common sense rejoices at a
utilization of credits thanks to which the troops are
no longer decimated by dysentery and typhoid
fever. Facing the enemy, Berteaux would show
dash and courage; facing the Chamber, he is capable of any cowardice. I have told the heads of
the department distinctly that the matter was no
concern of mine, but that I wished to make it known
by an official letter addressed to the Minister that
I had congratulated his officers on their practical
foresight. . . . I shall ask M. Berteaux to read my
letter to the Budget Committee or in the tribune of
the Chamber in the doubtful event of explanations
being asked about the "camel section." This is all
a shabby business. Sign of the times.

The frontier organization had been transformed.
A whole line of outposts now shielded Algeria.
South of Colomb-Bechar the Figig region was covered by Talzaza, and in the centre Fortassa kept a
bellicose tribe well in hand. The system of small
posts strung out in a line had been replaced by the
Galliéni-Lyautey system of larger forts capable of
sending out strong scouting parties. Quietly and
prudently Lyautey was rounding out the zone of
security. In his view this policy of peaceful penetration remained the only practical one. He did

not believe in diplomatic pressure on a powerless Sultan, and still less in a military conquest of Morocco:

I am afraid of foolishness, whether it be a resumption of "stoical pacifism" consequent on the first suspicion of visible satisfaction, or, what would be still worse, the ill-timed use of force. I can hardly be surprised that our rulers have not read my essay on the rôle of the colonies, nor the conclusions of my book on the Madagascar campaigns, but nevertheless it is infuriating to have expressed a complete new doctrine of subdual by the "oil" method, of penetration by organization ("an organization on the march," as I wrote), and to observe that nobody has read it or understood it, or even questioned it, and that the problem should still be debated in the twofold terms of pacifism or a full-blown military expedition. All or nothing. Yet Madagascar is there as an object-lesson in the flaws of *both* of these systems; for one (the palavering of Le Myre de Villers) and the other (the '95 campaign) have both given proof of their worth. In the interests of final success, of national prestige, and of the health of our finances, I should like this year to be not the "hammer" as you say, but the gimlet, piercing slowly but irresistibly. I would answer with my eyes shut and with all my conscience for the result and the economy.

All the politicians who visited the southern Oran left the country amazed and won over. A year before, this country had been dangerous; but here was peace restored again, with its harvests, the flourishing townships in the palm groves, the bustle of Arab festival. Deputies like Etienne and Thomson saw this French general holding a court of justice amid the respectful Berbers, and returned to Paris filled with wonder. The faith of Lyautey's childhood had served him in good stead in inspiring him with a respect for all faith. Nothing had done more to heighten his authority than his respect, constantly made public, for the Moslem religion.

I conclude with a pilgrimage to the sacred tomb.[1] . . . The keepers were awaiting me; I was admitted not only to the sanctuary, dimly lit by three or four candles held by the Abids, but further through the sacred door hiding the coffin covered with a burnous of green stuff broidered with gold. It is most venerable, most worthy of respect, and from the place there emanates a strong force which it would be folly not to reckon with.

This evening we are dining on the terrace of the Arab office. The grandeur and melancholy are incomparable . . . what a night! The twelve *koubas* are glittering like a constellation, a few fires gleam on the dark walls of the *ksours,* the desert is asleep; at our feet lies the cheerful, glowing encampment where the dark burnouses make Chinese shadow-plays. Here one is in the very heart of Islam, without one jarring note, a thousand miles from every-

---

[1] At El-Abiod-Sidi-Cheikh.

thing, touching a degree of isolation in time and space which I have never before attained.[1]

This isolation delighted him. From France came the distant and discordant rumour of these internecine quarrels of Frenchmen which he held in such horror. The law separating Church and State, passed in 1905, ordered the taking of inventories of church furnishings and religious objects. The fiscal officials were ordered to carry out this order in the churches. The bishops protested, and the valuers were threatened by the faithful. In several towns churches were barricaded, and soldiers were called upon to force admittance. In Flanders a demonstrator was killed by a rifle shot. Lyautey wrote to his friend M. Etienne, then Minister of War:

You speak with pain of the obligation you are under to punish the officers who have refused to obey the law. I have been deeply moved by the way you tell me of this. I have felt grievously sorry for you, as by the terms of the regulations and the letter defining your duties you could perhaps do only what you have done. But poor fellows! You know yourself, from the confidences I have given you, how free-thinking I am, and that this freedom of thought has forced me to painful breaches with things and people who were very dear to me. But I cannot detach myself from my

[1] To E. M. de Vogüé.

Catholic matrix, and I am only too well aware of the dreadful struggle that must be going on in souls who have kept intact their faith in divine law and the supernatural. And what courage they need to sacrifice everything! To sacrifice comfort, the security of the home, a career, in turning their backs on the human law with its immediate sanction, rather than violate that other law, the sanction of which is hypothetical and without material effects! Of course, I know the argument—the men, whom to-morrow they must order to march against the strikers! But why place the army in this horrible position? Yes, make haste to establish the mobile gendarmerie of which you feel the urgent need, and still it will be hard to recruit. Over here, when the *kouba* of El-Abiod-Sidi-Cheikh was blown up, they did not dare to use Moslem troops; only French were used, and to-day too nobody would dare to make use of Moslem soldiers to break into a mosque. Well? A very moderate officer writes to me from Lunéville: "Colonel du Manoir is about to retire from the service in despair: he was forced to use his Chasseurs to break in the doors of a church. *Some of the soldiers wept.*" Melancholy words—*some of the soldiers wept!*—poor lads, obeying without understanding, terrified to have to touch things which they have been brought up to hold sacred. Here *every single* officer was agonized by the news. Most of them are indifferent, and many are unbelievers; nevertheless they are anxiously asking themselves what they would do in like circumstances, so little can they admit that, having assumed the uniform for the noble art of

153

war, they should be condemned to this job of bur-
gling and chasing women and children. I give vent
to my feelings with you, forgetting that you are a
Minister and remembering only the friend with
whom I have always been so open-hearted; besides,
I know and feel that you realize all these things,
because you are suffering more than anyone from
having found the execution of this trumpery piece
of law-making to be part of your ministerial
heritage. . . .

Forgive me: I must be very fond of you and hold
you in very high esteem to dare to write thus to
you. . . . Before closing this letter, I owe it to you
to tell you in all sincerity that I have fixed on a
firm point for myself. In one region of France
there are certain churches which hold the most
sacred memories for me. . . . On the day I learn
that men wearing my uniform have been forced to
violate them, I am resolved to ask leave to resign
from the army. It may be to-morrow, for I should
feel that were I to pass their threshold in uniform
my forbears would rise from their tombs before me.

Such action will certainly not be disobedience;
it will be the laying aside, with a broken heart, of a
uniform which I could no longer wear without dishonour. And you could not fail to understand it,
you who have fought from the days of the Empire
for the respect of your convictions, and have lauded
those who then shattered their careers to avoid dishonour. Really, unless you want the army to lose
all its best elements, outraged in all that they feel
most intimate and sacred, work—and work quickly!
—that the army shall be reserved for the sole tasks
we are destined for—and let this nightmare end!

It is difficult to know whether it was Lyautey's letter that made M. Etienne resolve to abandon the use of troops for these operations; but in any case they were suspended. Soon afterwards M. Clemenceau, the new Minister of the Interior, decided to suspend the whole inventory-taking. "I shall not risk one human life," he said, "for the sake of counting church candlesticks."

Considering Lyautey's desire to be the man of a unified France, he was fortunate in being so far away during 1905 and 1906 from a France that was then so disunited. He was aware of this fortune, but aware also that it rested on frail foundations.

My thoughts now are only of the present hour, and I cling on here so long as I'm forgotten. I produce a suggestion in myself to delude myself and those about me concerning the practical effect of our activities. And I more or less succeed.

For twelve days past (and there are six more before me) I have been parading a few hundred rifles and swords along the slope separating me from the Muluya, which diplomacy forbids us to go beyond (one of my detachments has even pushed right up to the edge of this river); and my officers have come back with the feelings of the Israelites before the Promised Land. In this way we have explored and overcome all the country of the Beni Guils (*terra incognita*). What is the good of that? you may ask. Well, there is good in it! It is some-

thing to be still carrying somewhere a respect for
our name, amongst these fine warrior races; they
are amazed by our justice and moderation, our ab-
stention from all violence, no less than by the turn-
out of our troops; and faced by this warlike instrument of which we need only press the trigger, they
hasten to us to settle old disputes according to our
wishes. I have thus completely wound up my
year's accounts without a single rifle-shot, though I
was ready to fire, as they very well knew. And I
feel that I have the country in hand as it has never
been. And it was in this fashion that I used to
dream, in the days when dreams were allowed, of
penetrating Morocco step by step, sure of my instrument and my method. But the dream has vanished. Here at least we forget the gloominess of
things around you at home. We live. We are all
"men of the *bled*" over here. You know that the
bled ("country" in Arabic) is here the generic
name of the steppe, whatever it be—high green pla-
teaux or yellow Sahara. . . . It is the "forest" of
the Tonkinese.

To-night for the first time we have landed on an
islet of vegetation. My tent looks out upon the
bank of a *wadi* filled with pink laurel. Opposite,
on the other bank, are fine bushy trees beneath
which the camp of my *agha* has been pitched—the
very picture of warrior Turkey that you've seen
rendered over and over again, but of which one
doesn't grow tired when it is "really and truly."

Yesterday the bivouac was wonderful (the site
was simply made for it); there was a great gathering of tribes coming to make submission to me, and

bringing as offering the equivalent of the marauding they have done for a year past; and the spreading out of these camels and sheep and coins (counted out one by one on the carpets) at our feet, before my tent, before my horse, was all like something in the Bible. My troops had put in sixty kilometres, the distance between two wells; two companies of the Legion, my extraordinary sharpshooters, an invention of my own brand who travel light and can now cover any distance you like; my spahis, my native scouts, and all keen, cheerful and sober, with not one complaint against the terrible heat of the end of the march or the improvised shelter, and led by a band of young officers whose like I have never seen. I could embrace them! 'Splendid fellows! And how powerless one feels to reward them! All I can do is to "interest them," and I succeed in that; I muster them at each stage of the march, and explain the day's policy on the map, the result obtained, the reason for each movement—an unusual practice, and all the more appreciated.

Since the 19th I have been getting up every morning at three o'clock to break camp at half-past four, march for seven or eight hours, roast in the tent and lie down fully clothed on my camp-bed (most of my officers simply roll themselves in their burnouses). I am truly content with the persisting resistance.

He had reason to be content. "In action," Alain has said, "men seek outlet for a captive genius within themselves which is stirring. In so far as they rule their actions, they find pleasure in them; and there is no pain like the sense of slavery and impotence." Lyautey, out amidst these unvanquished lands and these lords of the desert, was succeeding by virtue of the very traits which would have made him a failure in Paris. By birth, and in virtue of his childhood and education, he was an aristocrat, and so a pessimist. In times and places of disorder a people has need of leaders who believe at once in their mission, their duty and their natural authority. The thirteenth-century villages respected a lord who defended them. The French of 1900, strong in a seeming security, had no desire to be commanded. Lyautey had been reared on a noble but proud ideology, and could not find in an old and optimist country an employment worthy of his genius. In a wild and unhappy country he was the man of providence.

These two civilizations were out of gear in relation to each other, and the fact gives some explanation of the radical cleavage in the endless and indecisive struggle carried on between Lyautey and the officials in Paris. An administration is an organism slowly formed by the evolution of a people whose individual members have become sufficiently alike for general laws to be capable of application throughout their body. "Regulations" are not a piece of abstract folly when they are applied to beings who can understand the abstract. They become absurd if an attempt be made to transport them into a world a thousand years younger. One of Lyautey's sources of strength amongst these barbarian folk lay in the fact that for him every problem was fresh and individual, and that he governed for this kaid or for that tribe, and never for a citizen or a commune. Even his weaknesses helped him. The most intelligent of his officers had not been slow to note his restless desire to please, his coquetry, his humours, his outbursts of anger followed by gentleness, his mixture of suppleness and obstinacy. And they only loved him the more for these things. A disciple is almost always grateful to a great man for being but human. One night when he came back to his tent in camp he found an envelope containing an unsigned composition on his table. Opening it he was surprised to read:

Extracts from the Survey of France, 1906.

Lieuvin de Hautevue, Marshal of the Camps and Armies of the King, and Governor for his Most Christian Majesty of the Marches of Barbary, studied his art under the Marshal de Gallibray whom he followed in the Isles, where he aided him puissantly and gained both honours and reputation by well deserving them, which is rare in these days.

He was, albeit negligently, a colonel of cavalry. Dry and quick to spark like a flint, lively and bubbling like the wine of his Moselle hillsides, he wishes to be lovable and is so by nature, wishes to be liked, and is so with deplorable facility, for he is as indifferent as he is caressing. He is able in the extreme, and has perceived that in the old age of our King the favour of the nobodies, of the common herd in fact, is not to be despised, and he makes sure of it very deftly, without ruffling his lace, like a man who is sure of cleaning up the hands he touches without blackening his own finger-nails. To this perilous game he brings a smiling good-nature, with just such a trace of mockery as to make it invincible, something rare and worthy of admiration.

Loved by his officers, by the soldiers, by courtiers, scribes and functionaries, he himself loves women, pretty faces, flattery, workers because they serve him, fribbles because they amuse him, action because it is a necessity to him, and lofty aspirations because he feels himself worthy of them.

A trifle deaf in one ear, of tall and youthful mien, he listens to one speaking without seeming to, looks at things and at men with a keen clear eye, and judges them quickly and often justly. He has no time to be modest.

Marshal mintage: and may our King never strike a coin less good.

It was a severe portrait, but a good enough likeness, he thought. He had a hunt for the author, and when he found him—a certain Captain Jaegle —he made a friend of him.

VIII

DURING these two years events had been happening far from Aïn-Sefra which had altered the Moorish problem. The pattern of European friendships had shifted as abruptly as the shapes in a child's kaleidoscope. England's anxiety had been aroused by the new German naval policy, and she had discovered the virtues of France. King Edward VII and President Loubet, at the Elysée and then at Buckingham Palace, had exchanged smiles pregnant with promises. M. Paul Cambon and Lord Lansdowne had discussed Morocco. M. Cambon had said that France realized that the Moroccan question could not be solved by her alone. And this sybilline and reassuring phrase had pleased Lord Lansdowne. For some time now the Foreign Office had been growing weary of the Sultan and Kaid Maclean. "My dear Nicolo," Sir Thomas Sanderson, Permanent Under-Secretary of the Foreign Office, wrote to Sir Arthur Nicolson, "Kaid Maclean is rapidly developing into a perfectly phenomenal bore."

London had let Paris know that Great Britain was prepared to leave France a free hand in Fez, if France, on her side, renounced any claims in Egypt, if Tangier, the Gibraltar of Africa, remained neutral, and if Spain were a consenting party. In 1904 France and England had signed an agreement, England recognizing that it was the rôle of France, as a neighbour of Morocco, "to assist the Sultan in the necessary reforms." The Chancelleries have a taste for these chaste and virtuous formulas. Both Governments admitted the Spanish rights on the Mediterranean coast. Italy had already been placated with the promise of Tripoli, and Germany had always declared that her sole interest in Morocco concerned her traders there. As the Quai d'Orsay's intention was to leave an open door, it looked as if France would now have her hands free.

The first difficulties came from Spain. "Spanish opinion," said M. Cambon, "was excited, and ran very high on anything concerning Morocco. Fortunately there were cooler heads to bring more objectivity into their judgments." In the end France and Spain signed two agreements; one was public, guaranteeing the integrity of the Empire of Morocco; the other was secret, defining the limit of the zones of influence which the two Governments recognized for each other. The secret agreement, like all secret agreements, became public. The

162

Germans, who were connected with the opposition of the Spanish cabinet, got to know of the clauses of the treaty and communicated them to the Sultan.

France had been mistaken in supposing that Germany would ask no more than equal trading rights in Morocco. It was quite true that the Wilhelmstrasse had little interest in Morocco itself, but Germany here saw a means of asserting her power and breaking this new intimacy, which was forming so dangerously for her dreams, between England and France. Advised by Germany, the Sultan refused the French "proposals of assistance," and suggested a conference at which all the European powers, as formerly at the Congress of Berlin, would discuss the status of Morocco. M. Delcassé opposed this, replying that "he could not have an intermediate power between the French and Moorish Governments, there being no intermediate country between Algeria and Morocco." Von Bülow caught glimpses of a chance to shatter the Anglo-French entente. He insisted that the Emperor William II, who was then cruising in the Mediterranean, should land at Tangier to affirm the interests of Germany in Morocco and the independence of the Sultan. That clumsy ride of the Kaiser along the ill-paved streets of an African town echoed on every boulevard in Europe.

The request for a conference, formulated by the Sultan, upheld by Germany, rejected by Delcassé, brought about the downfall of the last-named. He was replaced by M. Rouvier, who wanted "peace at any price." The conference sat in the Spanish town of Algeciras from January to April, 1906. Its opening stages were marked, as is customary, by attempts at intimidation, threats of breaking off negotiations, and general discouragement. The French Government, of course, fell from power at the critical moment, and at the climax France was left unrepresented for a fortnight. Then, as is also customary, just when every one was desperate "formulas" were found. The Anglo-French entente triumphed. Germany, placed in a minority and all but isolated, agreed to leave the reorganization of the police force and a large part of the capital of the State Bank to France and Spain. It was a rebuff for Germany, from which she was to harbour a dangerous sense of grievance. And France was left in the position of having her plan of reorganization adopted, though under an international control. The situation remained confused.

General Lyautey had followed these negotiations with the passionate interest of one whose work might be consolidated or destroyed by the outcome of the conference. After Algeciras he was ap-

pointed Divisional General, and entrusted with the
surveillance, at Oran, of the whole of that frontier
of which he had so far ruled only the southern part.

It is only since you have been at Aïn-Sefra [Jon-
nart wrote to him] that we have had an Algerian-
Moroccan policy. I regard it both as an honour
and a great piece of good fortune to have had at
my disposal a general officer who is at once a gallant
soldier, an administrator, and an able diplomat.
From the time of your arrival you have conceived
this programme which provides us with a military
organization of particular ingenuity and suppleness, and assures us the success of a policy of
victualling the Moorish tribesmen which leaves a
universal impression of strength, justice, and humanity. At the present moment the plan you have
prepared is going easily forward, clearly illumi-
nated and defined. Where we were losing ourselves
in useless demonstrations, you have indicated the
clear path. . . .

My dear friend, to myself it is both a consolation
and an encouragement to see you working, achieving, and succeeding, whilst the Parisian colonial
officials are saying and doing so much foolishness. . . .

* * * * *

As Brigadier-General at Aïn-Sefra, Lyautey
had insisted on being made independent of the
Divisional General of Oran; and now, with a characteristic stroke, on becoming in his turn the Di-

visional General, he secured the restoration of his authority over Aïn-Sefra. If it seemed a contradiction, what matter? He might well have exclaimed with Whitman: "Do I contradict myself? Very well then, I contradict myself." Was not the situation different? The Oran region was now to have a chief who had made his own Algerian-Moorish policy. The important point now was the application of that policy to the whole of the borderlands.

Lyautey's objective at Oran would be quite simple. The Algeciras Conference had deprived him of any certainty that France would occupy Morocco. As the Sultan's Empire, then, was not likely to be long-lived, perhaps some other European nation would one of these days be planting itself at Fez. It therefore seemed both urgent and necessary to improve a frontier which, in its 1906 form, was impossible to defend. It was necessary, by means of the "gimlet" policy, to bore a way through as far as the Muluya without causing an outcry in Europe. That was henceforward to be Lyautey's direction.

In Morocco, Abdul Aziz, the modernizing and anglomaniac Sultan, was now fallen into complete disrepute. Many of his Moslem subjects were deserting him for his brother, Mulai Hafid, a traditionalist and an enemy of the Infidels. The country lived in a state of anarchy. Assaults on foreigners became more frequent and more violent. In 1907 a Frenchman, Doctor Mauchamp, a man of charm and erudition, was murdered at Marrakesh; and as a reprisal General Lyautey was authorized to occupy Oujda, the small capital of eastern Morocco. But Paris forbade him to advance further, to go beyond the confines of the town, or to carry out his usual "stain of oil" policy. Under such conditions the occupation of Oujda was dangerous, being a source of irritation to the Moors and at the same time giving them an impression of weakness. Around him Lyautey could see the restlessness of tribes, and in particular that of the strong and warrior tribe of the Beni-Snassen. He sent in warning reports, but in vain; no attention was paid to them.

About July 1907 the state of western Morocco became more and more disquieting. Some Frenchmen employed on works at the harbour of Casablanca were massacred by the inhabitants, and sailors sent to free the French consulate were attacked. Casablanca was easily occupied by a body of troops disembarked under General Drude, but his orders were to go no farther. The tribes who had just been "making the powder talk" round

the town, regarded this immobility as weakness,
and became more and more restive. Lyautey was
following these happenings from Oujda; they sad-
dened him:—

Not that I have for one moment regretted my
not being at Casablanca. . . . But I am deeply
sorry that such a bad start should have been made.
. . . Whether one likes it or not, Morocco is a
fireship on the flanks of Algeria, and short of evacuating the latter, a forcible intervention in Morocco is essential, for the anarchy of that country
has close repercussions on our interests and authority in Algeria. . . . But the whole problem
lies in the fact that our military and civilian authorities can only conceive this intervention in the
form of an "expedition," and that is rightly regarded as alarming. Yet what makes me furi-
ously angry, what makes my blood boil, is the
realization that after these four years, after all I
have written and done elsewhere and here, no one
understands anything of my method. . . . Let me
be given, with the first incident or massacre, a free
hand, the choice of means and men, and my own
choice of time, and I undertake to bring pressure
upon Fez in a definitive manner, painlessly, and
at small expense. And I shall do this by making
use of military and political means, of my intelligence services amongst the tribes, disintegrating
them, making a friendly party ahead of me, making a snowball—in a word, putting into practice
my formula of the "organization on the march."
I should do a fine and original piece of work for

you! What a pity. . . . I give you my word that it is as a Frenchman that I am suffering, far more than just as a man.

In September he thought he could see a gleam of light. M. Regnault, the French Minister at Tangier, was despatched to Rabat to negotiate with the Sultan Abdul Aziz, and Lyautey accompanied him thither as his region was involved. They had of course to proceed by sea, for the country was in a state of complete anarchy and one could not travel from Tangier to Rabat, nor even from Casablanca to Rabat. The Sultan was blockaded in his own capital. And there Lyautey saw for the first time the white and peaceful city which was to play so great a part in his life. M. Regnault and he obtained important results; a convention was signed dealing with the organisation of a police force on the Algerian-Moroccan boundaries. But on his return to Oran he found the position increasingly grave. The storm was gathering; all the native informers foretold the imminent rising of the Beni-Snassen, and the War Ministry, far from preparing for resistance, was depriving Lyautey of his troops in order to add men to the landing force at Casablanca, the position of which was causing the Government anxiety.

Lyautey sent in severe and outspoken reports

to M. Jonnart regarding the strategy of the Paris
offices. The Governor was prudent enough in general to forward to Paris only adaptations of these,
carefully toned down. But in M. Jonnart's absence a secretary "accidentally forwarded, quite
raw, one of these reports from the Divisional General of Oran. M. Clemenceau was furious. 'I'll
send this General to Perpignan!' he said.—M.
Jonnart, who was in Paris at the time, defended
Lyautey.—'What can you expect?' he said. 'He's
a thoroughbred, and sometimes he kicks against the
traces. . . .'—'I daresay,' said Clemenceau, 'but I
shan't allow his droppings to be sent to the Government.' "[1]

Before long a letter from the Ministry reached
Algeria saying that the reports were coloured by a
preconceived pessimism, and that the General at
Oran was conjuring up dangers in order to be
given the stick to knock them down with. General
Lyautey was accordingly deprived of his title of
Commissioner at Oujda, and was instructed to
transmit his powers to the Consul, M. Destailleurs,
as civil Commissioner, and to the officer commanding the column of occupation at Oujda, and then
to return to Oran. Immediately Lyautey left for
Algiers and saw General Servières, commanding

[1] Britsch, 107.

the troops in Algeria. "General," he said, "there is nothing for me to do but leave."

He had not been twenty-four hours in Algiers before news came of a serious rising of the Beni-Snassen. They had broken through the Algerian frontier *en masse,* burnt the Kiss factories, and were drawing near to Nemours, where the terrified inhabitants were calling for help. Next day the newspapers were full of this tragic story and demanding the proper defence of Algeria. The Minister wired to the Governor: "If letter No. — has not yet reached you, do not transmit it to General Lyautey and regard it as not despatched."

Once again Lyautey had become the indispensable man; he was entrusted with the task of repulsing the Beni-Snassen; and there was a desire that he should attack instantly. It was now Lyautey who had to soothe the officials at home. He forcibly said that he would not attack before completing the preparations for the expedition in every detail, and this he did with such precision and mastery that it was successful almost without dealing one blow. Within a fortnight this great tribe, surrounded in its hilly fastness, had surrendered, and on January 1st, 1908, General Lyautey celebrated the new year amidst his victorious troops.

LYAUTEY

That evening he wrote to Vogüé:

Yesterday, the 30th and 31st, they carried out for me the finest *raking* manœuvre you can imagine. Four columns coming up from the south drove their way simultaneously into these hitherto inviolate gorges and cliffs, whilst my Branlière column, to the north, held all the exits. This was carried out at night, a surprise move, under conditions calling for incredible boldness; the weapons fell from the hands of the most unconquerable groups; one party surprised at night one of the most active of the chieftains hidden beneath a rug, and brought him captive to me; the ringleader of the whole movement, a *marabout,* found himself hunted down in the hills with every way out blocked, and came in to give himself up at nine o'clock. . . . The caches of weapons were traced down, and herds, guns and trophies were brought back . . . and at four o'clock yesterday I was at the mouth of the mountain pass, greeting the heads of the columns driving all their captures before them. That was the end. The men felt it; a company of the Legion were passing, *"Bonjour, mes légionnaires!"* I called to them. *"Bonjour, mon Général, tout va bien!"* came the answer from two hundred throats with one single voice, and everything thrilled around me! Unforgettable hours! And the joy is to feel the mutual trust reaching its climax, that confidence which superior officers cry out to me, of which young officers come and tell me individually, at all hours, and which comes to me also from the eyes of the rank and file as

I go round the bivouacs. With that instrument
in my hands I would go everywhere, lead them
anywhere. . . . And then I rode round the bivouacs, wishing them a happy new year. The
trumpets rang out clear and full—it was the
France of the old days, the good France! Yes,
indeed, how I wish you could have been there,
to enjoy it like the good Frenchman of old, and
the good friend too, that you are! I don't give a
damn for the morrow—the present is enough for
me. . . . The weather is splendid. From my tent
I can see, across the defensive parapet, the camps,
the Kiss, the Beni-Snassen hill-country—all iri-
descent, living, stirring, singing—it is sublime!"

In the Casablanca region the situation was still
difficult. General d'Amade had succeeded General Drude. Abdul Aziz, driven from Fez and
Marrakesh, was unfortunately becoming "the
Frenchmen's Sultan" to his peoples, and had lost
his religious prestige. His brother, the pretender
Mulai Hafid, was supported by the German consuls and colonists, and had installed himself south
of the town along the bank of the Oumer-Rabia,
between Marrakesh and Settat, and was a nucleus
round which hostile tribes gathered. M. Clemenceau felt anxious about this Moroccan question,
which might at any moment become very serious
indeed, and wished to consult this General Lyautey whose success on the Algerian frontier had

given him great prestige. He summoned him to
Paris. Lyautey came over in February, 1908, and
was immediately taken to the Place Beauvau,
where he found in Clemenceau's room Pichon,
Thomson and General Picquart.

"General," said Clemenceau, "let me tell you
why we have summoned you. . . . You have lately
carried out an excellent job in Algeria, and done
so at small cost. Well, we know nothing about
what is happening in Chaouia; we can see no positive results. We have decided to send you to
Casablanca. We shall double the effectives and
you shall take command. . . ."

"Excuse me, sir," answered Lyautey. "I know
General d'Amade very well, and he is an officer
of great merit. Before replacing him I think one
must be certain that somebody else can do better.
That is not proved."

"But, General," said Clemenceau, "d'Amade
could very well remain there under your orders.
There could be nothing humiliating in that, for
you are a divisional general whilst he is a brigadier. Another brigade would be sent out, and
as you have just shown your strength you would
take command of the whole force. What could
be more natural?"

"At present, sir," said Lyautey, "d'Amade is

holding the chief command. This would mean a moral diminution, and probably unfair. . . . Now this is what I should suggest. First of all I shall try to grasp the situation on paper, at the War Ministry, and then, as nothing can take the place of a study on the spot, I shall go out there. . . . Three eventualities have to be kept in mind: first, that d'Amade is doing all that can be done, and it is over here that his difficulties are not being appreciated. I have enough experience of these things to make me regard this as the most likely hypothesis. Second, that d'Amade is doing very well, but that my experience enables me to give him some advice: I shall give it gladly and then return. Third, that d'Amade is not the man I take him for; he has changed or is deceiving himself. Then I shall replace him."

"Very nice," said Clemenceau.

"One last point, sir," said Lyautey. "I shall ask you to let M. Regnault accompany me. He is a man I know well and value highly, and the presence of a diplomat will give the mission a distinctive character and deprive it of any element which could wound d'Amade's feelings."

"Agreed, General," said Clemenceau.

For a week the name of Lyautey was always

on his lips. "I've found a real man," he told all the deputies who called on him. He discussed poets and historians with him, and said to him: "I swallow you whole!" The General did not seem to hear the words. "Well?" said Clemenceau. "The Prime Minister tells you that he swallows you whole, and you pay no attention! What's in your mind?"—"If only it lasts, sir. . . !" said Lyautey. M. Clemenceau recounted the conversation at the Elysée that night, with much laughter.[1]

Lyautey left for Casablanca in March, 1908, carrying in his pocket a letter empowering his command, but being resolved not to take it out. When he landed at Casablanca, General d'Amade showed at first a somewhat reserved demeanour towards him, which Lyautey understood and approved. It was a delicate situation. He knew that, if the rôles had been reversed, he would have suffered from such a control. Further, he saw, as he had anticipated, that d'Amade was perfectly qualified to exercise this command. By a show of warm friendliness and by evoking common memories of Saint-Cyr, he quickly restored his trust. He accompanied d'Amade to his columns in Chaouia, and then to the occupying force in Settat. This was the first point on the southern

---

[1] Britsch, 106.

route from which it was possible to survey the enemy's lines of approach from the direction of Marrakesh. But Settat, this important strategic point, was beyond the ridges bordering the Chaouia, and beyond these the Government did not intend operations to be carried on. As Lyautey was about to leave, a telegram arrived ordering the evacuation of Settat. Lyautey was beginning to grow used to these orders incapable of execution. "Don't do anything about it," he said to General d'Amade. "I'm going back to France. I shall be in Paris in four days' time. I'll get this order cancelled." Whereupon he set off, having left General d'Amade all the time in ignorance of the letter in his pocket empowering him to take over the command.

On reaching Paris he found the same group in the office at the Place Beauvau. Clemenceau gave him a warm welcome.

"Well, General," he said, "we've been awaiting you impatiently. Tell us the news. . . ."

"One preliminary question first, sir," said Lyautey. "You sent an order to evacuate Settat?"

"Yes. I think it has been done."

"No, sir."

"Why?" exclaimed Clemenceau.

"Because I ordered General d'Amade not to

evacuate it. . . . The evacuation is impossible and
I ask you to recall the order."

"We'll discuss that later," said Clemenceau.
"Tell us about your mission."

"No, sir, I shall say nothing. . . . I must first of
all explain why General d'Amade's position is impossible unless he occupies Settat."

Immediately opposite the Minister's large desk
in the room were two doors. Suddenly Lyautey
crouched behind the desk.

"Do you see those two doors, sir?" he said to
Clemenceau. "Those are the approaches from the
south. . . . This desk is the plateau which is called
the 'balcony' of Chaouia. . . . My position here,
kneeling behind the desk, is the one you are assign-
ing to General d'Amade. I can't see the doors; he
can't see the routes. What must I do to be able
to watch the exits leading from the south?"— He
raised his head above the desk.—"Look over the
'balcony,' that is to say—occupy Settat."

"Is it really like that?" said Clemenceau.

"It's just like that," said Lyautey.

"Well, that's better than all their reports," said
Clemenceau.

And he instructed General Toutée to send the
telegram. On April 18th General d'Amade re-
178

ceived the authorization from Paris to maintain a detachment at Settat.[1]

Lyautey's report written after his journey is interesting as being his first dealing with a Morocco policy proper. Already he was adumbrating "an occupation as light as possible, showing no signs of any direct administration, or of a substitution of French machinery for local machinery, but on the contrary, the reconstruction and education of the latter." He was realistic in his judgment of the problem of the two Sultans: Abdul Aziz, infinitely preferable but greatly enfeebled, who must be shielded from being further compromised by too obvious measures of support; Mulai Hafid, "Champion of fanaticism," a man certainly to be fought, "but without any preconceived rejection of grounds for an understanding."

In the realm of facts, this question of the two Sultans was settled by the fortunes of war before the year was out. On June 20th Mulai Hafid entered Fez. In July Abdul Aziz decided on an attempt to recapture Marrakesh and left Rabat with a Mehalla of five thousand persons. He showed a desire to confer with General d'Amade, but the latter referred the point to Paris, where they decided, wisely this time, not to intervene. Attacked on its

---

[1] General d'Amade's report, p. 127.

southward march by partisans of Mulai Hafid, the imperial Mehalla was routed. Abdul Aziz mounted the few women in his train on horses, tried bravely to put up a fight, and then, swept away by fugitives, took refuge in the French lines, where he at once took childish delight in using the telephone.

By November Mulai Hafid was recognized as Sultan, even in Casablanca. He was a man of intelligence, who saw quite clearly the danger to his prestige arising from the presence of the French at Casablanca. He asked Ben Ghabrit, the interpreter of the French legation: "Why are the French on the coast of Morocco?"—"To maintain order," answered Ben Ghabrit. "I could understand that," said Mulai Hafid, "in my brother's time; for he was a monarch without power, but for my part I am quite able to maintain order within my own territories."—"The French will observe that," said Ben Ghabrit. "The occupation is only provisional."—Mulai Hafid looked at him for some moments, and gave a toss of his head. "When Allah created the world he said it was only a provisional creation," remarked the Sultan.

*   *   *   *   *

Lyautey profited by the credit he gained with the Government from his missions in Morocco, to secure a new organization of the frontier better suited to his own temperament. If a French general could not, without the risk of Moorish and European complications, rule the eastern districts of Morocco, where in actual fact the French were in occupation, why not set up a High Commission of the Algerian-Moroccan borderlands, this territory being subject jointly to French and Moorish High Commissioners? It was a wonderful arrangement. As head of the Oran Division, General Lyautey would be under the Ministry of War; as High Commissioner of Morocco he would be under the Ministry of Foreign Affairs. In this way, no doubt, he would be under nobody but himself—which was just what he had always desired.

He obtained these powers by wonderful feats of skill, dexterity and determination, and made good use of them for the native populations and for France. By the end of 1908 he was able to send to Paris a general report regarding the organization of the frontier zones, which was a model of clarity, of ethnographical and geographical accuracy, of economic, financial and military organization. To north and south, at Oujda and Bou-Denib respectively, two strong centres, solidly composed, were set up against the two hotbeds of trouble, the two "bubbling cauldrons" of Tafilelt and the lower Muluya. Between these two strong-holds, a light police force was sufficient.

The principle on which this police force was based was *"that protection depends on movement."* The string of small and weak posts was abolished. According to Lyautey's view it formed a sort of Great Wall of China, and would no more have saved Algeria than the Wall had saved China. Posts, he felt, like police reconnoitring-parties too, ought always to be strong. "It is a grave mistake to believe that small reconnaissances mean modera-tion and prudence, while large ones imply military operations. It is just the opposite. Six hundred men always pass where one hundred get held up. In dealing with the policing of native populations, one should always bear in mind the formula that *force should be displayed in order to avoid using it."* Finally, and this was the cardinal point, every post should be a centre of political activity, and every commander should have unity of control in his hands—the old principle of Galliéni.

The results of this method had been remarkable. "A real buffer-state now covered our Algerian frontier, and thrust back the zone of insecurity by several hundreds of kilometres. The populations were already acquiring a taste for ordered life, less costly than anarchy, the kaids for regular administration, more fruitful than the pettifogging of former times, the Maghzen for the well-gathered revenues of a country which had never recognized its authority. . . . The policing of the wide territories had cost France but little: 4000 men had been enough in the Oujda area, 1600 on the Haut-Guir. Further, the Shereefian troops and budget were gradually to replace the soldiers and money of France. Rarely had a soldier conquered with so little expense. . . ."[1]

Lyautey's success had even been recognized by Bou-Amama, that old foe of the French in Algeria. As he lay dying the aged chief had said: "Lyautey is a great master. . . . I cannot submit to him myself, but my son Si Taieb will submit." Si Taieb became a loyal friend. Arabs and Berbers were fascinated, as the French officers were, by a man who in high places remained human.

---

[1] Britsch.

IX

AT the end of 1910 General Lyautey was appointed to the command of the Army Corps at Rennes. Before leaving Algeria he had married Mme. Fortoul, widow of Colonel Fortoul, and daughter of Baron de Bourgoing. He believed that his return to France was final, and that his colonial career was over. He accepted the change of front. Henceforward, he thought, a military man's hopes of service would lie in France; for it was the universal impression in the army at that time that official Germany desired war, and that this would break out within the next few years.

But although he came back determined to work with all his heart and soul, Lyautey did not return without anxieties. Always concerned about what might be said or thought about himself, Lyautey believed that on account of his colonial career he was regarded by the officers of the French army as an interloper. At the Ministry, he knew, they liked to style the regular colonial officers "the bashi-bazouks," and considered them as men ignorant of real war "because they had never done written exercises on tactical questions." On his

184

return from Madagascar, General Pendezec, then Chief-of-Staff, had said to him: "Well, Lyautey, so you've decided to come back to the Army?" He had started; but the remark had thrown a light upon deep misapprehensions. Notwithstanding the higher rank, this return from Oran resembled his return from Madagascar. Lyautey's objective would now be to teach himself, to bring his colleagues to appreciate his worth, and to gain their affection.

A palace revolution had lately broken out in the higher command. General Joffre had replaced General Michel as Commander-in-Chief. Joffre was a friend of Lyautey's, who had known him in Madagascar. He had just set up a centre of advanced staff studies, and Lyautey asked General Brun, Minister of War, for permission to follow its courses before taking over the command at Rennes. General Brun sceptically shrugged his shoulders: "What's all this about?" he asked. "It isn't a course for generals; it's a course for colonels and lieutenant-colonels. What would happen to us if all the Army Corps commanders made the same request as you?"—"But they won't," said Lyautey, "and they'll be quite right. . . . They know their lessons. But think of all the years since I have held a command in France. . . . I don't want to risk having a Chief-of-Staff at Rennes who turns up from this centre and will teach me my own job. . . ." He followed the course.

Once at Rennes, Lyautey began work whole-heartedly. Map exercises, formation exercises, garrison manœuvres. . . . Two months after his arrival General Pau came to inspect him. Never had a General-Inspector stayed so long with one Army Corps. He behaved with Lyautey as the perfect superior and colleague, examining every-thing, giving a series of lectures on all subjects, which appeared to be meant for the officers, but in reality went over their heads to the new com-mander. After a few days he took Lyautey aside: "Don't be vexed, Lyautey," he said, "at seeing me so very particular. I'm doing it for your own sake. I know just what you are. I also know what you may lack. You haven't served in France for twenty years. And I wouldn't at any price give you les-sons in front of your officers. But I give you them indirectly."—"I realized that, General," said Ly-autey, "and I am deeply grateful to you."

A little later General Joffre, directing important manœuvres in eastern France, with General de Castelnau as Chief of General Staff, brought in General Lyautey, entrusting him with one of his sides. When Lyautey, living with him, thanked him, and expressed some astonishment at being thus chosen from among so many for this display of confidence, General Joffre replied that he would enter the Super or War Council before two years, that there should always be one member of it coming from the cavalry, and that he, Joffre, had Lyautey in mind to appoint as adjutant to the Commander-in-Chief in case of war. And so Lyautey now gladly saw the highest military posts opening to him.

* * * * *

A French officer at that time had to work all the harder because Europe was going from bad to worse. In July, 1911, the German gunboat *Panther* had anchored off Agadir. M. Caillaux negotiated. The whole summer was spent in long conversations between M. Cambon and the Ministry of Foreign Affairs. "They concluded," said M. Cambon, "in the definite recognition by Germany of our political primacy and our liberty of action in Morocco. On the other hand, they cost us the abandonment to Germany of a strip of territory which enabled her to join the Cameroons to the Belgian Congo. This arrangement was badly received in France, where the enormous gain accuring to us was not appreciated, and in Germany

was regarded as a serious setback. The Crown
Prince himself was seen giving expression to his
discontent in the Reichstag tribune, and the Minister for the Colonies, Lindequist, resigned with a
flourish. However that may be, the threats of war
were for the moment averted, and the Moorish
problem was at last settled to our advantage."

Early in 1912 M. Regnault, French Minister at
Tangier—an excellent representative who had long
played an important rôle in Morocco and was destined to be the first Resident-General—had left for
Fez to submit for the Sultan's signature a treaty
for a protectorate.

Mulai Hafid protested, threatened to abdicate,
and then, during the morning of March 30th, 1911,
signed. "He accepted the protectorate for the
whole of his Empire, provided that France, on her
side, pledged herself to lend him constant support
against any danger threatening his person or trou-
bling the peace of his territories. A Resident-
General was to exercise the powers of the Republic
in Morocco." [1]

On April 15th M. Regnault gave a great ban-
quet. The Maghzen and the Residency exchanged
toasts which seemed cordial enough. During the
night of the 17th-18th a riot broke out in the town.

---

[1] Poincaré.

Some *tabors* (Moorish troops officered by French) massacred their officers, chased the colonial officials and threatened the Sultan with death. These outbreaks were attributed to a plot, or to fanaticism; the Sultan was accused of having fomented them. This was not accurate. They were the work of one of Lyautey's great foes—"the regulations." There had been an attempt to submit the *tabor* troops to the French system of *"l'ordinaire"*: that is, instead of letting the men receive their whole pay (as they were accustomed to do) and feed themselves at their own expense, they had tried to hold back their subsistence money and cook the food purchased therewith for the whole company. It had overlooked the fact that most of these Moorish soldiers were married. "What!" they said. "One franc for the mess! That only leaves twopence for our wives and children!" Whence the mutiny.

After murdering their instructors, the armed soldiers scattered through the town and over the countryside. The citizens of Fez were well-to-do and peaceable men, fond of talking politics but taking little action. But in every large town there exists a rabble who are always ready for a surprise stroke; and the Fez rabble, seeing a chance of looting, joined hands with the unleashed soldiery. They

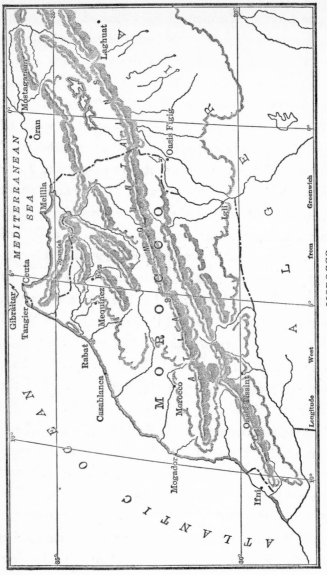

MOROCCO

rushed to the Mellah, they sacked the shops and the houses of the Jews. The latter fled; ten thousand of them took refuge in the Sultan's palace, and they were found even in the menagerie, in empty cages alongside those of the lions. The Sultan in his excitement did not know what to do. "Don't move," Ben Ghabrit told him. "There are ten thousand men in Meknes whom the French can bring quickly to Fez."—"I shan't move," said the Sultan. "But what am I to do with all these Jews?" The disorder was great. Certain military men wanted to bombard Fez, but M. Regnault rightly opposed them. This duality of powers in a revolting country could not last. The Government did not wish to sacrifice M. Regnault, "a very gallant man," who had long been working his hardest. But the outlook seemed grave. If unity of command was to be made a reality, it was essential that, willy-nilly, a soldier should be sent out as Resident-General.

M. Millerand, Minister of War, and M. Poincaré, Prime Minister, hesitated for some time between General d'Amade and General Lyautey. "On Saturday, April 27th, a cabinet meeting was held at Rambouillet, interrupted, as was customary, by luncheon in the great dining-room with its Gobelin tapestries, overlooking the ponds where the water-fowls, ducks and swans disported themselves. M. Fallières would have preferred a civilian Resident-General, invoking the Republican traditions, to which we would all gladly have been able to conform immediately. 'No one is better aware than myself,' answered M. Léon Bourgeois, 'of the force of the President's argument, but the course of events at Fez has convinced me that it would be premature to appoint a civilian to the head of affairs in Morocco. We shall doubtless have fresh alarms there, and at certain times the need for military authority can make itself felt instantly.' To these reasonings President Fallières yielded. General Lyautey was selected." [1]

Summoned from Rennes by telegram, Lyautey lunched next day at Millerand's house in Versailles with Poincaré. He already had a programme for Morocco, and laid it before them. It was learned from Fez that the Sultan had taken the news of General Lyautey's appointment very badly, and was once again talking of abdication unless he were allowed to go and live at Rabat. It was a matter of urgency that the new Resident-General should proceed to his post. M. Poincaré had justly observed for himself that General Lyautey's qualities were of the kind that could

[1] Poincaré.

flourish only in an atmosphere of confidence, and
before Lyautey's departure, in agreement with him,
he reorganized the African arrangements at the
Quai d'Orsay. As he had to take with him a civilian
adjutant, he asked for M. de Sainte-Aulaire, then
attached to the Embassy in Vienna, whom he had
known in Tangier and whose firmness, intelligence
and independent character he appreciated.

X

LYAUTEY embarked at Marseilles on the cruiser *Jules Ferry,* and landed first in Algeria in order to have a consultation with the men who had succeeded him in charge of the Algerian-Moorish borders. He was now going to be working in liaison with them, as one part of his kingdom, eastern Morocco, separated from Fez by the unconquered region of Taza, could only be reached through Algerian territory. His instructions were cautious:

I have made it clear in the most definite way that any idea of activity directed towards Taza ought to be set aside until further orders. . . . I have asked General Alix to convey this intention to all his subordinates, a step which I regard as indispensable in order to put an end to the state of excitement and nervousness produced in every one by this expectation, which was indeed becoming rather an obsession, to the detriment of more urgent and more useful concerns.

Then, veering round very much as he had done when he transferred from Aïn-Sefra to Oran, he defended against Algeria the integrity of the Moroccan territory which had now become his own:

194

LYAUTEY

I was informed yesterday of a fresh incident, namely, the despatch of a detachment of Senegalese to Aïn-Chair by the commandant of the Aïn-Sefra territory, without the knowledge of the borderland authorities. This is a step as imprudent as it is inopportune. I telegraphed in that sense to the Governor of Algeria, and have no doubt that the order for the withdrawal of this detachment will be given.

It was the Ras-el-Aïn incident seen from the other side of the hierarchy.

He landed at Casablanca, spending a couple of days there. And there he found a young colonel, already famed for his capture of Samory—Colonel Gouraud. Lyautey had formerly met him as Captain Gouraud. "What are you doing here?" he said.—"Nothing, General," said Gouraud. "I arrived here with a colonial regiment. It was replaced by sharpshooters, with Mangin, and I'm waiting." —"Well, that's capital," said Lyautey, "I'll take you on. You shall be in charge of my escort. You shall make all detailed arrangements for my march on Fez. I don't want to have to occupy myself with them." They set off on horseback for Rabat. The *kasbah* of the Oudaias, a hill of white cubes, shone peacefully in the sunlight near the Arab cemetery. The Engineers had already started building barracks of the conventional type.

Lyautey burst into one of his fierce rages. Was this beautiful native town to be ruined by these hideous official constructions? In this fresh new country he was going to find the zinc washing-places, the black strip along the bottom of the flaking whitewashed walls, the smell of coal-tar. "Heavens above!" he cried. "Can't you pull that down and wait for my plans?" No, the Engineers could not pull it down. They had already spent 150,000 francs. Lyautey gave orders for the work of construction to be held up, taking it upon himself to seek another solution, and proceeded on his way towards Fez. He was getting the feel of the country, sketching out roads and railways in his mind.

At the gates of Rabat he met two Frenchmen and talked with them. They had come from Fez, and described the plight of the town as dangerous. From all sides the tribes were coming down from the mountains, stirred up by rumours of disorder and promise of looting. A siege seemed all too likely. The new sovereign would have to conquer his kingdom. In his talk with the two travellers he discovered that one of them was an artist, an architectural expert, and he told him the story of the barracks at Rabat. "No doubt, General," said this man, "they can't be demolished; but they can be clothed or transformed." And sitting beside Lyautey on the grass beside the road he drew a sketch. "What is your name?" said the General abruptly.—"Tranchant de Lunel, General."—"Will you stay on with me? You shall be my Director of Fine Arts." He accepted the offer, turned on his tracks, and went back towards Fez with the escort.

In two days' time the little caravan of the Resident reached Meknes. A few officers came out to the General, with apologies for not having fired salute guns. "It would have been enough to loose an attack, General. The populace are very excited. A general rising in the country is expected."

The journey from Meknes to Fez was made in two stages. A couple of hours from Fez an intelligence officer, known to and valued by Lyautey for a long time back, Commandant de Lamothe, came to meet the Resident.

"How are things going?" said Lyautey.

"As badly as they could, General. By to-morrow you would not have been able to enter the town. All the tribes are coming down. We are going to be surrounded. The officers in command here are swimming in optimism. But for my part, I fear the worst."

An hour later, a cloud of dust. It was General Moinier.

"Good-day, Moinier," said Lyautey. "So things aren't going very well, I hear?"

"Not well?. Who said so? It's all over. . . . I'm delighted to see you arrive, but from the military point of view everything is settled."

And soon they came into view of the wonderful background of ramparts and cemeteries. M. Regnault welcomed his successor at the entrance to the town with smiling courtesy, and placed himself with good grace at the General's disposition.

Lyautey was led to the palace which he was to occupy, the Dar Menehbi, and put on full dress to call upon the Sultan. Whilst he was pinning on his ribands and medals, General Brulard, an old officer of his, set forth the situation: "It is too late, General. . . . If you had been here a week ago, you could still have tried your method, you could still have plunged into the native politics and managed things with honour. . . . But it is too late." And he repeated: "Too late, too late. . . ." There were tears in his eyes. And while Lyautey, in his French General's uniform, white breeches, high boots, white plumes, was on his way to the Sultan, shots were heard ringing out in the town. Gouraud, who was now unoccupied, heard them.

"Hullo! What's that?" he said. "Oh, nothing," said his host. "Looters stealing apricots."

That night the French colony gave a ball in honour of the Resident. There were about twenty colonial officials present. About midnight, when the dancing was in progress, there were shots in the garden. "Apricot thieves again?" asked Gouraud. Then came a regular volley. The attack was beginning. And next day the tribesmen, who had been slowly gathering since the riots, had invested the town.

A few officers, Poeymirau, Benedic, Guillaume and Drouin, shared the Resident's mess. Action had to be taken. It was not easy. There they were, in the middle of a large town of 90,000 inhabitants, with a tortuous tangle of streets for the most part so narrow that two men could not pass abreast. The true military conception of defence would have been to carry the defensive action outside the town, into strongly entrenched positions from which both Fez and the attacking forces could be kept under fire at the same time. Such an evacuation was not possible. Within Fez were a hospital with sick and wounded, and a whole French and foreign colony, scattered over various points in the town. The defence had to be made on the spot.

But how? Not only were they defending a town beset on every side by warrior tribes, but the town itself was in a state of fiery unrest. Its middle-class inhabitants perhaps wanted peace, but the populace had found both pleasure and profit in pillaging the Mellah. They had to keep an eye on a prison, on barracks crammed with old Shereefian troops, dangerous men. The Sultan, whom the noise of battle had made very nervous, could talk of nothing but abdication or escape. If he had left the town he would have placed himself at the head of the rebels to save his own life. It was a heart-breaking situation. There was no native support. Inside the town 4000 Frenchmen were drowning in a flood of 90,000 Fasis. Outside the town were fanatical assailants in unknown numbers.

Lyautey was reluctant to despair of his "method." Under fire he summoned a meeting of the Ulemas and Shorfas, who might be able to rally the better elements of the town. It was a sound calculation. The rich merchants of Fez had no fancy to see their town entered by the poor and pillaging tribesmen of the hills. The massacre of Frenchmen might well be succeeded by a massacre of Fasis. But, just like the officer the day before, they could only repeat: "Too late, too late. . . ." The revolt was unleashed. From the terrace which

served as his observation post, the Resident, in an
agony, saw the Legion companies surrounded,
forming square, and retreating from the position
on the Merenides which commanded the town. All
seemed to be lost.[1]

About four in the afternoon General Lyautey
decided that the last reduit of the defence would
be the hospital, and he had drums of paraffin placed
alongside his baggage so that it could be set alight
as soon as the Dar Menehbi had to be evacuated in
order to reach the reduit. A little later, dinner was served. Bullets were whistling. Threatening sounds drifted over from the town lying there
in its sombre beauty. Orders were given. There
was nothing more to be done. Lyautey remembered Galliéni reading John Stuart Mill on the eve
of an engagement. Amongst his officers was a
poet, Drouin.

"Come along, Drouin, give us some verses.
Have you written any to-day?"

"I have written a sonnet, General."

"Good, let's have it. . . . And then give us
something of Vigny."

---

[1] As a matter of fact this withdrawal saved the town. Until then
the artillery had not been able to fire on a mass wherein French and
rebels were mixed. From that moment it could rake the tribesmen.
But from the terrace of the Dar Menehbi it was impossible to follow
what was happening, and the danger seemed to be increasing from
one moment to the next.

While Drouin was reciting a poem of Vigny's, M. Regnault came in.

"Good evening, gentlemen," he said, with the same smiling courtesy, very calm and self-controlled. But a sign showed the General that he wished to speak to him alone. Lyautey took him into his room, and when the door was closed M. Regnault asked him:

"The situation is very serious, isn't it?"

"I fear so," said Lyautey.

And he informed him of the steps already taken, and of those which he had provided for the last extremity. When the door opened again, the diplomat resumed his smile. If Lyautey thought him rather optimistic the evening before, he now thought him perfect. Night was falling. The battle still went on. No message was getting through to the commander's position. For two days Lyautey had not slept.

"I must rest for an hour," he said.

He gave instructions that he was to be roused if any news came or anything happened, and flung himself down on a camp bed.

On waking he was amazed to see sunlight. He looked at his watch. He had slept for ten hours. No more firing. Everything was quiet. He summoned his officers. They explained the miracle. The retreat of the Legionaries, which had seemed to be the beginning of defeat, had actually enabled the artillery to bombard the tribesmen and save the town. Colonel Mazilier, an experienced colonial officer, who lay to the north of Fez with some battalions at the camp of Dar Debibagh, had got round, taken the tribes on the flank, and set them to flight.

The situation was still far from favourable. When it was possible to go round the town in the morning, a lieutenant and forty sharpshooters were found killed at their posts. A combination of military and political action was now urgently called for. The military side was entrusted to General Gouraud, who, with five battalions, freed the immediate environs of Fez on the morning of the 29th. On the 31st reinforcements arrived from Meknes, and on June 1st Gouraud moved eastward with five or six battalions, two or three squadrons, and a battery. The 75's put the hostile tribes to flight. Gouraud marched right round the hill region, through country that was a veritable garden, and his action gave Fez a breathing-space, and time to receive mails and foodstuffs from the neighbourhood.

Lyautey wrote to Captain de Mun:

The town itself feels the tension gone. It was suffering for two reasons. On the one hand, considerations which I cannot well account for have prevented the terrible repression which ought by rights to have followed the outbreak instantly—which is a great pity—but on the other hand, in consequence of this failure in repressive measures, rightly a source of annoyance to the military authority, the latter have made up for it by a series of mean, ill-timed and prolonged inflictions of forced labour. They have let themselves be mastered by far too summary and simple a conception, and have lumped the whole population together in a common measure of blame. They have not discerned that, side by side with the mob who lent their hands to the military mutiny, there was also a middle class of industrious and peaceful-minded tradespeople, whose sole part in these events was to suffer from them, whose only wish was to be sheltered behind constituted authority, and that, above them again, there was a whole class of enlightened people, holding a traditional influence of their own, large classes of Ulemas wielding effective religious authority and divided into two distinct groups, and lastly, the Shorfas, the highest class in Fez, whose origins go back to the beginnings of Islam, and without whom nothing efficacious can be done here. The military authorities saw nothing of all that; everybody has been treated on the same footing, jostled, ignored, humiliated, left with running sores; several well-known families have started an exodus to Tangier in order to find shelter from the vexations here. The information of the War Council handling the repressive measure has, at the behest of any tale-bearer, lumped together as accomplices in the rising many honourable people who have had nothing whatever to do with it. It is here that I have had to draw distinctions, disentangled, destroy, by intensive action on my own part, hour by hour—and it is still going on—with the sole help of my own colleagues, those whom I brought here with me, and the civilians: Monsieur Gaillard, who is perfection itself; the Consulate staff; Frenchmen long established at Fez, and also the British Consulate, who have given us such loyal aid; a personnel of which the military authority was systematically ignorant, and which is the best source of information here, and the best instrument of action. Every day I see the native notables, individually or in batches; I restore their confidence and lend an ear to their plaints, and more often than not give them their due (for most of them are justified): in fact, it is through them that I have begun to find a few bonds of union with the tribes, and thanks to them that Gouraud actually has a few native personages with him now who are accompanying his column and lending their co-operation.

All of which is to the good, you may be sure, but it is very localized, and there is all the rest of Morocco, where my personal action cannot yet be felt, and where it would be chimerical to seek to make myself understood simply by correspondence.

Well, the south, the Haouz and Marrakesh, are causing me the liveliest anxiety. I have no one I can send there. If I had a couple of months to go back in, I should go down there to see the great feudal chiefs, the Glaoui, Si Aissa Ben Omar, Anflous and Mtougui, and take it upon myself to act on them, to bring them in, make them sit down, set them opposite each other. But for the moment I must first of all complete and cement my Fez construction, which is the key to everything, and that is a matter of several weeks—and between this and then, very serious accidents may occur in the south.

Just imagine, it takes me a week to get from here to Casablanca; that slowness complicates everything.

So the general situation remains very bad.

* * * * *

The first difficulty, and perhaps the prime one in importance, was the character of the man with whom Lyautey would have liked to collaborate— the Sultan Mulai Hafid. Lyautey's doctrine was based on the possibility of using the Sultan's prestige for the maintenance of order amongst a religious people. "The continued maintenance of a protection without a protected sovereign would have been a dangerous paradox."

But Mulai Hafid wished to depart. He was an intelligent but nervous man, and was placed in a completely false position. In days gone by he had reached power as the symbol of resistance to Europeans. It was hard for him to admit that he could possibly be the Sultan of the Protectorate. For several months he had been alarmed by the successive outbreaks, and he was greatly afraid of General Moinier. "He makes inquiries about my past," he used to say. "You'll see that he will kill me." He knew, moreover, that the French Republic had more than once allowed dethroned monarchs to live at its expense in very pleasant conditions. He was no longer a sovereign defending his political rights, but a private individual seeking to liquidate his affairs on advantageous terms. In vain did Lyautey seek to restore his confidence, to "restore the façade" of the crumbling Maghzen. "To restore to Mulai Hafid the taste for power, the practice of authority, and confidence in the future, while for months past all his thoughts had turned to the comfortable, care-free, material life of a retired sovereign in a pleasant country retreat, with a nice income and nicely provided for, was an insoluble problem."

In order to obtain the Sultan's signature to the treaty of protectorate it had been necessary to promise him an authorization to leave Fez for Rabat. This had become an obsession with him, and consent was obligatory. Lyautey began to wonder whether the Protectorate would be practicable with a sovereign in whom the most trifling act produced crises of extreme neurasthenia. His attitude of sulky indifference was interpreted by the natives as evidence of his moral captivity. "The Sultan is the prisoner of the French; he approves us"—such was the password spread amongst the hostile tribes.

Mulai Hafid was all the more difficult to hold as he was well aware of the international and domestic difficulties of France. He had a competent press service, and had *Le Matin* and *Le Temps* translated for him every day. When he left Fez, Lyautey said to him: "I shall keep you in touch with what is going on in the country by telegram." The Sultan's reply was given by the interpreter: "His Majesty offers you his best thanks, but prefers to receive the regular and integral communications of the Havas Agency." It was picturesque, but dangerous.

The Quai d'Orsay dreaded his abdication, as the Protectorate had not yet been recognized by all the European Powers. Lyautey was exasperated by Mulai Hafid, and was coming to desire his abdication. As a matter of fact, the problem was solved by the Sultan himself. For on reaching Rabat he announced that he would not remain in Morocco after August 31st. He wished to leave for France, for the sake of tranquillity and to escape his responsibilities.

Who was to replace him? Mulai Hafid wished one of his sons to do so, but that would have presented serious drawbacks. The reign of a minor would have meant, as in the days of Abdul Aziz, the supremacy of a Grand Vizier, several ministers, and later, of unknown favourites. There remained the Sultan's brothers. The eldest, Abdul Aziz, who had shown in childhood too strong a tendency to be influenced by court intrigue, was at Tangier. The other, Mulai Yussef, for some time back Khalif of Fez, was a man of good will, respected by the better-to-do classes of Islam; he was correct in behaviour, calm and kindly. The Fasis said of him: "He has a fine way with him." All that was to be feared was his shyness and his lack of prestige amongst the tribes. On him the choice fell, and later history was to show that the choice was an excellent one.

Once this decision had been made it was important that Mulai Hafid should leave as soon as possible. But now that his abdication had been accepted, this weathercock man was anxious to remain, to make a pilgrimage to Mecca, and to return thence to Rabat. There were endless discussions.

Si Kaddour Ben Ghabrit had to get control of his sovereign with dexterity and firmness. It was essential that the Sultan should hand over his powers with good grace, if the position of his successor was to be secure in the eyes of his people and the European powers. On August 10th he accepted General Lyautey's invitation to dinner, where he was treated with every consideration to put him in good humour. That evening he had a long and strange conversation with the General, during which he said that France had been wrong in demanding a treaty of protectorate, that the English in Egypt had never so much as spoken the word and yet had all the advantage of the situation. He spoke with plenty of intelligence and coolness, and paid Lyautey various compliments.

Next day he was again in a state of extreme nervous collapse. Ben Ghabrit was afraid that he might go down to the harbour, excite the negro guard, appeal to the population, refuse his letter of abdication. His baggage and his women were already at the harbour; the Sultan persisted in declaring that the harbour bar could not be crossed, that it was dangerous to start. For Lyautey that was a day of real anguish. The whole population of Rabat was present at the embarkation. The launches were blocked with women, negresses and secretaries. Mulai Hafid declared that he would not go so long as one of his followers remained on the beach. Suddenly, a few minutes after five, before the bar ceased to be passable, he took the tug and crossed it. He had not yet handed over his letter of abdication. At last, on board the tug, he made up his mind to transfer the famous letter from his wallet to that of the Grand Vizier. General Lyautey's relief can be imagined when he heard the twenty-one guns booming out to announce the sovereign's arrival on board the cruiser *Du Chayla*.

Mulai Hafid to El Mokri: Praise be to Allah alone!

May Allah bestow his grace upon Mohamed and upon his family!

To our well-beloved servant, the Grand Vizier and best counsellor, El Hadj Mohamed El Mokri: may Allah be propitious to him!

We address to you Our greeting accompanied by the benediction of Allah!

As followeth:

You are not unaware of what fatigues and cares We have experienced of late, in such measure that Our health has been shattered and We find Ourselves prevented from adequately fulfilling Our duties towards the people. For which reason, We have chosen to repose Ourselves, and have decided to leave the throne of sovereignty for reasons connected with Our bodily health.

Consequently, it will not be unsuitable should you choose, for the purpose of taking into his charge the interests of the Moslems, one of Our brothers who may be agreeable to you and regarding whose person the people may be in agreement.

May Allah choose for the Moslems some one who may be of service to them!

Greetings!

Mulai Hafid to Lyautey: Praise be to Allah alone!

There is nought enduring save His empire!

We cease not to ask for news of you and are eager that you may be continuing in good health.

As followeth:

We desire to make it known to Your friendly Excellency that Our Shereefian Majesty is satisfied in heart and contented in mind, and that Our Majesty is pleased to recognize that Your Excellency is entitled to high praises for the perfect courtesy, the attentions and delicate kindnesses which We have received at your hands of late, and which oblige Us to address to you Our most exalted compliments now and hereafter.

You have acted with us following the course of friendship and sincerity in all circumstances, and mutual liking has been born therefrom between us. But Allah has decreed our separation, since Our decision was taken to leave power for reasons of health touching Our personal expediency.

We trust that you will fully appreciate the truth of this.

However that may be, We shall not forget you and shall retain the happiest memories of you.

LYAUTEY

If the people are agreed on the choice of Our brother Mulai Youssef to take the direction of affairs into his hands, there is no objection thereto.

May Allah choose some one who has within him the well-being of the elect and the common people!

XI

RABAT. August, 1912.
A native city of mystery. The Sultan, the
sole official link between the French and Morocco,
had just embarked. Lyautey was now to have beside him, as the exile's successor, a sovereign as new
as himself, a man of good will, but timid, inex-
perienced, and recognized by only a portion of the
country. Around Rabat stretched a vast territory
unvisited by the Resident, and in a state of semi-
anarchy. In the south a pretender, El Hiba, had
raised powerful tribes against the French, tribes
beyond the latter's reach. Certain Arab notables,
like those of Fez, still retained some respect for
the religious person of the sovereign, but the mountain Berbers, wavering believers, hardy Moslems,
ignored this Mulai Yussef, the Frenchmen's Sultan. Lyautey was in the plight of "a naval officer
appointed to the command of a doomed vessel."

The crew was as small as the vessel flimsy. The
Resident was surrounded by only a few men. No
director of public works. No director of finances.
Everything had to be faced with a few officers and
the former French personnel of Morocco. The

first headquarters was symbolic of this poverty. Lyautey occupied a small house which had been the German Consul's. Access could be had to it only through ravines bristling with aloes. When the General wished to entertain a few guests the dining-room was too small. A tent was pitched on the day when the first president of the court of appeal came for the first time, a storm flattened the canvas, and the depressed guests had to go home on mules down the sodden ravines. Never have conquerors settled more precariously in a conquered land.

Yet one's impression is not of a miracle, but rather of one of the most deliberate and successful of human adventures, when one reflects that two years later, out of his chaos of centuries, a modern country had arisen, and so securely had French roots penetrated that in 1914, on the declaration of war, Lyautey would be able to send the greater part of his troops to Europe, not only without losing Morocco, but without arresting the country's progress. It is interesting to ask how such a change came about, and to analyse the form of character that made it possible.

* * * * *

All his life long, even in those childhood days when his comrades had styled him "Emperor,"

Lyautey's dream had been the exercise of an absolute and beneficent power. In the days of almost universal democracy, such a desire may well have seemed chimerical to the man who secretly cherished it. Morocco was to be the answer to his prayer. Having once conquered his kingdom, Lyautey was to be the most absolute of sovereigns, under cover of a Sultan of his own creation. He would still, doubtless, negotiate with the French administrations and the officials of the Quai d'Orsay; but he would do so in the name of a Maghzen whose prestige would buttress his will, and he would deal with ministers who dreaded Moorish anarchy and would long stand in need of him. In Morocco itself he would have to keep an eye on public opinion, but there he was to be more free than any constitutional sovereign, and the fiction of the Protectorate was long to save him from any representation of interests. From 1913 to 1925 Lyautey was to be as omnipotent in his African empire as any human being can be. We must explain how this "enlightened despotism" which, placed in other hands might have become so dangerous, in this particular instance bore infinite fruits.

Let us look back here at the traits which united to make Lyautey a focus of energy. The first was

his craving for action, an incessant, tyrannical craving which killed even sleep. Remember those
notebooks of his youth, that "eternal ennui," that
Lucretian disgust, that *"Act, act, act . . ."* which
he inwardly cried with the violence of despair. The
man has remained akin to the adolescent. No
activity will ever tire or sate that tragic appetite
for action. His power of work is terrifying. He
"knocks out" all his helpers. In Tonking and
Madagascar and Morocco he finds the fuel to feed
this insistent inner fire for twenty years, but there
are times when even the creation of a country no
longer suffices to tear him out of himself. One of
his orderly-officers tells of a terrible day in Morocco
during which Lyautey presided over councils of
war and councils of notables, traversed hundreds of
kilometres, harangued tribesmen, preached, argued,
and dictated dispatches until two in the morning.
At last, towards the middle of this short night, the
officer was summoned to the General. His look
was one of gloom. "What is the matter, General?"
he asked. "What's the matter?" said Lyautey.
"Can't you see that I'm *bored?*" For he is a romantic of action, as other men have been romantics
of sentiment.

"But when you speak of me," he orders, "never
say *or,* say *and.*" Is he, then, romantic or reason-

able? Do not say *or,* say *and.* He is ardent *and* reasonable. He is romantic *and* classic. From the Lyauteys he had inherited the ancestral passion for devotion to the state. He gives himself up to his work of sovereignty with a disinterestedness that even his enemies have never failed to admire. From thirteen years of absolute rule in a country where vast business concerns were growing up, he emerged a poorer man than on the day of his arrival. More imaginative than his paternal forbears, he inherited from them the austere rectitude of a great administrator. From his Christian training he had kept intact the profound and beautiful conception of the importance of every man, not only as a subject and citizen, but as a brother individual. That feeling, which led him in earlier days to work with Captain de Mun and to set up clubs for his troopers, led him in Morocco to an understanding of the natives. And there his aristocratic mould joined up with his Christian mould. It was his manifest duty, as a leader, to be the protector of this race. He was constantly to be seen in the streets of Fez or Rabat like some sultan of the Arabian Nights, walking unescorted, accompanied only by an interpreter, questioning merchants and passers-by regarding their needs and wishes. Never would he give the impression that he was in a conquered country. "He is a man who likes us," they say. He respects their religion, their institutions, their kaids, their pashas, their religious properties. In no circumstances was he puzzled to catch the right note. "How should one talk to these people?" asked a newly arrived officer of Gaillard, the consul, a man well acquainted with Morocco. "For my own part," said Gaillard, "when I talk to a Moorish peasant I talk to him as if to a French peasant; when I talk to a Moorish bourgeois, I talk as if to a French bourgeois; when I talk to a Moor of high rank, I talk as if to a Frenchman of high rank." That is what Lyautey instinctively did, and his naturalness delighted them. "What do you think of Lyautey?" a traveller asked some Rabat townspeople in 1913. And they answered: "You know the words of the Prophet: 'The soul is drawn towards the man who heaps benefits upon it.'"

A man of the Borders scion of Lorraine and the Franche-Comté, he had always regarded local institutions with respect. He had not that taste for "centralization," for the standard code of regulations, which is the mark of so many great officials. He was anxious, whilst introducing French civilization to this country, to let Morocco retain as much of its own character as possible. The first rule he imposed on his Director of Public Works is to respect the native towns. By his orders the European town was everywhere built alongside the native one. As soon as he realized that Morocco, regarded by Europe as a homogeneous kingdom, is in reality formed of two peoples foreign to each other, Arabs and Berbers, obeying different institutions, he insisted on the customs of each race being protected, and obtained a decree from the Sultan to exempt from Moslem justice the Berber tribes who were accustomed to the justice of their councils of elders. He wished to be as much the representative of Morocco in France as he is that of France in Morocco. He believed that a colony should be governed for its own benefit, not for that of the home capital, and that it will become a source of strength to the latter only in virtue of its own prosperity. Whence his maxim: "The two fundamental institutions of a colony are—free trade and no gendarmes."

And so it came about that his inborn characteristics, certain of which would have baulked him in France, made him in Morocco the very man who was needed. In a country where prestige matters, his taste for splendour served him good stead. An excellent horseman, he was admired by the Arabs when he galloped to visit the Sultan, enveloped in a great black burnous braided with gold. His love of a fine background and a well-appointed house had grown to the scale of a great potentate's, and had become a love of well-planned towns and unspoilt landscapes. For it was one of Lyautey's truly original qualities that *his spirit admits no degree of greatness.* He gave himself with equal passion to whatever interested him. "It is just as important," he said, "to set a picture correctly on a wall as to set a town correctly in a country." He always lived completely in the present moment, and from his colleagues demanded that same darting concentration of the searchlight of attention which, in himself, illumined one single object at a time in the field of the mind, that exact coincidence with the instant of time which he called by an outlandish, but perhaps useful, word—"immediacy" (*l'immédiatité*).

Another trait: *an acute sense of relativity of things.* He had no absolute doctrine regarding anything. He arrived in Morocco with a few general principles, inherited from Galliéni or formed for himself in the southern Oran. But he was ready to throw them overboard if the facts seemed to contradict them. In the realm of action there is no theoretic method true for all times and all

places. You have to be supple. Model yourself
on the past event so as to create the next one.
"Man rules nature only by obeying her." And
politics is a natural science, experimental and
poetic. In Morocco Lyautey was everywhere doing what Galliéni taught him—making the "regulations" give way before common sense.

Constantly absorbed by a single idea, nothing
could restrain him where his work is concerned.
In France this man had had, and again in old age
would have, very strong prejudices of caste and
education; yet he found himself freed from them
by the toil of creation. Just as a great artist will
forget everything for the realization of the picture
or the novel which is necessary to make life endur-
able for him, so Lyautey sought even amongst his
enemies the elements for his success. Whence his
confident collaboration with the most advanced Republican statesmen, whenever one of them understood and supported him. His freedom of mind
found play likewise in the choice of his own collaborators. Whatever their official priority, whatever their political views, it was the men most apt
for usefulness that he needed for the building up
of his team.

"I remember one fine outburst of General
Lyautey's," writes M. Guillaume de Tarde. "He

had just been visiting a small outpost in Morocco, and the young official who had been his guide during the visit had impressed him by his intelligence and energy and practical gifts. Stepping into his carriage, the General said to his *chef de cabinet:* 'That's a remarkable young man. We must make him a comptroller.'—'Out of the question, General. He hasn't been long in the service, and the regulations. . . .'—'Then have I to leave a living force mouldering in these minor posts? Have I to condemn this man to mediocre jobs on the pretext that he isn't old enough? What damned nonsense! As if we had too many men! And where does this regulation come from? From Paris, of course! But what may be all right for Paris and dozing ministries is detestable out here where we have everything to create. . . . Come along, hunt round and find a means. That lad has got to be made a comptroller immediately. . . .' He was beside himself, curt, quivering like dry wood, and the phrases sprang straight from his fury. At bottom he was quite self-controlled, but he was not annoyed at being heard a long way off."

When once he had thus placed his confidence in a man and given him a place in his team, he slackened the reins. He did not believe that a leader's rôle is to take the place of each of his assistants. "I have my technical men," he said, when asked about subjects that do not interest him.—"And what do you do yourself?" he was asked.—"My technical job," he said, "is general ideas." But from time to time he would come and note practical results. Any slowness or indecisiveness threw him into terrible rages, in which, as with Napoleon, there was a certain element of "effect." In such cases he has been seen to throw his cap on the ground and trample it. The man who is used to power often has caprices like a child's. In Lyautey this trick was not unconscious. "Deliberate spontaneity," he says himself in moments of unbending. There are times when he seemed to need flatterers, because, like every creator, he could work only in an atmosphere of sympathy. "I need to be swallowed whole," he says; and if he feels a single hostile being in a listening crowd he will be put out. "B—— is there," he says. "He doesn't like me. He isn't answering to the reins." But if he had a horror of the half-hearted supporter, he respected the rebel. His best friends, those whom he has kept longest by his side, were the open-minded who dared to tell him the truth.

One nearly always finds, in studying the lives of artists, that their genius springs from some deficiency. The rule seems no less true when touching

the poets of action. Lyautey's success was born
of his restlessness and his youthful pride. The
normal man does not transform the world; he submits to it. The man of genius imposes the form
of his spirit upon materials whose resistances he
controls. All those who know Lyautey and travel
through Morocco are surprised to see how much a
country can become the image of a man. They
find there his method and his flights of fancy, his
imagination and his caution. They observe there
the extraordinary potency of his radiation. From
1913 he had been for every one, officers and officials, *le patron,* the Chief. And they can imagine
none other. Sometimes he irritated them, tired
them, exhausted them; but in the darkest days they
knew that it was from him that they drew their
strength, that they would be backed up by him,
that he would be faithful to all *his* people. The
announcement of a visit from him worked miracles,
for (a sovereign who would have enchanted Stendhal) he united the prestige of his intelligence,
and the strength of his passion, with the potent
charm of caprice.

XII

INTO every human success there enters an ill-defined element of good fortune. In the dangerous situation of the French in Morocco in 1912 the first piece of luck was the choice of the new Sultan. Lyautey had taken him because there was no one better; he did not dare to hope for any wonders from him, and he only judged him to be a lesser evil than his brother. He soon discovered that this heavy bearded man, swathed in white muslin, had the soul of a sage within him. Mulai-Yussef was lettered, kindly and shy, but not devoid of guile. He was not in the least European; he was by nature devout, and as Lyautey encouraged him in remaining strictly faithful to Moslem traditions he was not long in winning the esteem of his Arab subjects. He himself had taken a strong liking for the General, who was grateful for a respect which he had scarcely expected, and he soon became in a short time a support and a useful force on the French side.

At Fez, Lyautey could count on Gouraud. In June the latter had set off eastward again at the head of a column, to round off the subjection of the rebels. It was a strange campaign. The troops traversed quiet villages which accepted the coming of the French with resignation. The column halted near a farm, and the friendly peasant came out with his little girl to see the horses and the rifles. "Your little girl's got pretty eyes," said the officers. Suddenly shots were heard, and the old man said something to the child. She came back with a gun. "What! Do you want to fight us now? What's happened?" asked the surprised Frenchmen. *"Baroud!"* said the man. The tradition of powder. . . .

Lyautey's instruction to Gouraud had been on the expected lines: "Show your strength to avoid using it. Never enter a village without reflecting that a market should be opened in it next day. In so far as you are not forced to impose your will in order to avoid disorder, leave the Moors in peace." To apply this policy, Gouraud had with him two intelligence officers with an admirable knowledge of the country, Captain Mélier and Captain Sciard. He himself, so manifestly a chivalrous and generous man, quickly inspired confidence in the Fasis.

The great mosque of Mulai-Idriss was surrounded by a zone forbidden to the Infidels, and Gouraud had given strict orders that nobody was to set foot on it. A few months after the occupation, on a great day of festival, the Ulemas refused to illuminate the mosque, insinuating that the French had taken the religious funds. The inhabitants of the district came to Captain Mélier and complained. "Your Ulemas are treacherous liars," said Mélier, "and I will prove it. Ask them to examine with yourselves all the accounts of the religious foundation, and I defy you to show that the French had taken the smallest sum." The Fez townsmen made the examination, and were so convinced of French good faith that, after forcing their priests to light up the mosque, they invited the French officers (an unprecedented action) to attend the festivities. In the Fez region, of which Gouraud became the Kléber, all was quiet and the moral conquest making good progress.

In the rest of the country, however, grave causes for anxiety remained.

(a) Firstly, in the south, where the pretender, El Hiba, was making dangerous progress. Marrakesh ought to have been occupied, but that would have been an immense undertaking. In such countries it is easy enough to advance and even to be victorious; but then one has to maintain oneself and protect lines of communication, without which an army has neither stores nor munitions. In a country having neither roads nor railways, the number of men who can be kept alive in such conditions is very limited. Lyautey had already had great difficulty in never letting his 7,000 men in Fez lack for nothing.

(*b*) Eastern Morocco '(neighbouring Algeria, the Morocco on the confines of which Lyautey had formerly held sway and where General Alexis was now in command) was still separated from Morocco proper by a group of hostile tribes with Taza as their capital. It would one day be essential to link up these two Moroccos, but there also Lyautey was anxious that roads and railways should accompany any forward movement, failing which an advance would be precarious and might easily end in disaster.

(*c*) Lastly, a strong and dangerous group of dissidents lived in the mountains of the Zaïan bloc, round Khenifra.

Three expeditions, then, were necessary to assure peace in Morocco. But these three expeditions the General was anxious to postpone at all costs, for there were working lines to guard, flanks to be covered, and many men be kept alive. At no price would he expose his troops to useless risks until he had consolidated his foothold.

As regards Marrakesh, his hand was forced.

The pretender El Hiba, proclaimed Sultan by all the Sous tribes, had entered that town and captured eight Frenchmen there. As a march on Marrakesh did not appear practicable, intelligence officers tried to obtain the handing-over of the captives. But in the course of these negotiations, which in accordance with the instructions of the Resident were to be political and not military, it was discovered that the pretender's marauding had roused the wrath of the great Kaids, who were all-powerful in this region. Several of their number, notably the Glaouas, made very definite advances to the French, whose officers were told by their emissaries that if the French came nearer the scene they would themselves attack El Hiba and prevent him from massacring the prisoners. Whereupon Colonel Mangin was sent towards Marrakesh, which he entered on September 7th, after crushing El Hiba.

Very soon the Resident-General followed him into his southern capital. And a splendid entrance it was:

I have been living for the past ten days in a real fairyland; none of the Orientalist painters can have touched the splendour of my arrival at Marrakesh on a dazzling morning. The Arab throng, the great unfolded standards, the successive processions, the glad fanfares of our troops, the odour of

victory and joyousness, the scenic background of
the great snow-covered Atlas. Then the encampment of the victorious column in the great gardens
of the Sultan, the reception of the officers in a
palace washed by waves of greenery. It evoked
pictures of Napoleon's armies in Egypt. My own
quarters, in a little pleasure-pavilion surrounded
by orange-trees, grenadines, olives and cypresses;
my reception hall, thirty feet high, with its mosaic
facings; the encampment of my staff, swarming in
gardens of Scheherazade. . . . Here, as I write,
I have beside me the panoply we are keeping for
General Niox: a cannon, two flags, Hiba's ceremonial umbrella, and his headdress, flung on the
ground in rage when he took to flight. Moreover,
for a week past, as well as the heavy tasks of reports and telegrams and political palaverings, there
have been state receptions, at my quarters as well
as at those of the great Kaids, feudal lords of the
fourteenth century. They have all come to see me,
down from the hills and up from the coast, with
trains of hundreds of horsemen. They all have
their town residences at Marrakesh, and seek to
outstrip each other in magnificence. The Glaouis
live in real palaces, wherein European furniture
and superb silver and tables served à la française
are displayed against a Babylonian background.

And now, to consolidate this result and to impress the imagination of the southern peoples,
Lyautey was anxious to bring them his Sultan.
Mulai-Yussef was growing in importance. Even
after the first successes there were many who con-

tinued to think that "he would be merely a puppet, the shadow of a shade, the creature of the Roumis, incapable of assuming any prestige of religious authority." But Lyautey had concentrated with meticulous attention on refashioning royal dignity for him:

I kept him scrupulously aloof from any European promiscuity, from motor-cars and champagne banquets. I surrounded him with old Moslem ritual. His own character, as a good Mussulman and a worthy man, did the rest. He restored the great Friday prayers with the ancient ceremonial. He celebrated the festival of Aïd Seghir with a degree of pomp and veneration for tradition unknown since Mulai-Hassan. At Fez Gouraud has tutored him on these lines with the utmost intelligence, tact and reserve. So now he is suddenly standing forth as a genuine Sultan. His journey from Fez to Rabat is being made at present with old-time pomp, and, in accordance with my instructions, we hardly appear on his line of march. I shall be at Rabat in four days' time to receive him and instal him there, and then, in a month, I shall launch him on Marrakesh. That will be the touchstone. . . . I do not want to count the chickens before they are hatched, for things may go wrong, but it is an interesting game to play and to follow. . . .

In France there were certain ministers eager to send heavy reinforcements and have done with independent Morocco. But Lyautey would have nothing to do with their reinforcements, and it is of surpassing interest to study, in the correspondence of this period, the moderation and prudence of a man who was outwardly so violent.

This country ought not to be handled with force alone. The rational method—the only one, the proper one, and also the one for which I myself was chosen rather than anyone else—is the constant interplay of force with politics. I should be very careful about attacking regions which are "asleep," which are lying still, which are waiting and questioning, which would burst into flames if I entered them, at the cost of many men and much trouble, whereas, once all the neighbouring regions are dealt with, these others will find themselves isolated and will fall into our hands by themselves. Take an example: the great Zaïan bloc, south of the route between Fez and the Tadla. This is a Berber hill-country, populous, warlike, and extremely difficult of access. When I arrived four months ago, military circles inclined to urge me towards the conception of large combined operations with three columns approaching the morsel from the north (Meknes), from the centre (Rabat), from the south (Chaouïa). I formally avoided this, having no wish to put my hand into a wasp's nest, and confining myself to the programme familiar to you. . . .

Another example—Taza. I can see clearly how many people are still surprised that I do not carry out this linking-up immediately—after Marrakesh.

There, too, I should be very cautious. Indeed, I
have harnessed myself to the task of driving my
60 cm. railway tracks to their goal. Everybody is
harnessed to that. I am even hopeful of having,
by April, my eastern terminus at Taouirt or
Mçoun, and my western terminus at Meknes. This
accomplished, the problem of supplies will be
transformed from top to bottom. It will result in
an incomparable economy of forces, effectives,
escorts, fatigue, and expense. I shall then be relieved of the terrible burden of these interminable
lines of communication and their subjection. Am
I to neglect an advantage like that in order to do
the job badly and slowly and at a high price three
or four months sooner? It would be absurd. And
the more so because, during this delay, time is
working on our behalf: in the east, Alix is still
scratching away, grilling the Beni Ouaraïn; in the
west, Gouraud is scratching and grilling the
Tsouls and the Branes. The wall is wearing thin
and growing frail, and a push of the shoulder will
bring it down. If impatient views (and oh, the
impatience of the colonial officials and the national-
ists above all!) prefer premature spectacular action to this slower but certain method, they had
only to refrain from sending me here; but nothing
will make me relax my grip from this method,
which is, for myself, one of conscience.

*　　*　　*　　*　　*

The whole of the year 1913, then, is one of military unobtrusiveness and economic and moral

penetration. Road and narrow-gauge railways make the occupation less precarious. Political action is carried on by collaboration with the native structures. Every effort is made to give them, not a superficial semblance of power, but as large a share as possible in affairs. A new life has been given not only to the Sultan, but to the great Kaids and the Berbers' councils of elders. Pacification is making good progress. Already Mulai-Yussef can proceed from Fez to Rabat, from Rabat to Marrakesh, and even to Mogador. Never have the most powerful of his ancestors been lords of so vast and so peaceful a country.

By 1914 the narrow-gauge railway had been pushed forward far enough, and Lyautey decided to effect the union of the two Moroccos. He made minute preparations. He took Gouraud, who was to command the troops coming from Fez, to General Baumgarten, who was in charge of the attack from the Algerian side. At Baumgarten's headquarters he sketched the whole programme on the map, provoking and accepting criticisms. And at last, on May 10th, the Gouraud column set off. It was hard enough going. One great tribe, the Tsouls, occupied the ridges and were like a nest of wasps on the column's flanks. On the 12th Gouraud turned off after them, perpendicularly to his line of march. A point-blank engagement took place; it was a sharp one, but the last. Before long the two French armies met at a spot which General Baumgarten named the Crête du Baiser. And on the slopes of Taza, Lyautey, who had joined them, reviewed his united forces.

In June General Henrys subdued the Zaïan bloc and occupied Khenifra. There remained a few tribes of hillsmen in what was known as the "stain" of Taza. On July 26th, 1914, Gouraud decided to force his way into the hill-country with three columns, and telegraphed next day to Lyautey that all was going well. He received in reply a telegram which he did not understand: "Good. But in view general situation take defensive attitude." Gouraud had been in the field for two months, and had not followed the European situation. He imagined that some question of financial prudence was in question, and replied "Bad economy." A fresh telegram came from Lyautey: "If situation allows, come at once to Rabat." What was going on? A European war? Gouraud could not believe it: "After all, one doesn't make war because an Austrian archduke has been murdered by a Serbian student. . . ." Two days later he arrived at Rabat with General Henrys. And there he learned that war was declared.

XIII

JULY, 1914. A Bosnian student, with a Serbian revolver, had murdered the Archduke Ferdinand, heir-apparent of Austria. The Emperor William was cruising in Norwegian waters. M. Poincaré was on his way to Russia. Telegrams passed between the Quai d'Orsay, the Wilhelmstrasse, Downing Street, and the Ballplatz. Out in Morocco these events read in the news columns of *Le Temps* seemed unreal or futile. "The Balkans!" said Lyautey. "The old story! I can remember it all so often for twenty years past! Let's get on with our work. . . ."

He had spent part of that July at Casablanca, which had become his economic capital. It was the most active and least agreeable of the towns of his empire. "A vast modern region of suburbs, a flowering of stone shooting haphazard from the stones of the soil like the vigorous plants on the walls, improvised warehouses, waves of houses breaking all along the bay and right up the hillsides, overflowing native villages," [1] amongst the dwarf palms and thistles. In the primitive har-

[1] Alfred de Tarde.

237

bour merchandise and passengers were disembarked in flat-bottomed boats, and when the harbour bar was troublesome, vessels had to sail again without discharging their cargo. Along a few yards of docks bales and packing-cases stood heaped under corrugated iron shelters. Here and there rose new factories, their chimneys smoking above the minarets. Lyautey's eye was upon this seething chaos, and mentally he was sketching out the future town.

It was a difficult situation. The French population had increased tenfold within three years. Morocco had been painted as a sort of Eldorado, and immigrants were now pouring in at the rate of three thousand a month.

In the whole coastal region of Morocco [said Lyautey later] it was a real invasion, at a time when nothing was ready to receive it, and the very restricted administrative staff I then had at my disposal was positively submerged. Excuse a familiar comparison: you are building a house where you propose to receive your friends and acquaintances with open doors; but look! here are all the guests arriving when nothing is finished. The staircase has not yet got all its steps, the rooms are not yet furnished, nothing is arranged. In vain do you ask the few days' respite that are indispensable for the completion of your installation. But nothing is of any avail; the crowd rushes on,

eager to come in. You may want them at least
to be lined up, and take their turn of entry, but it
is no good insisting—everybody wants to come in
and to be looked after all at once. You raise your
hands heavenward, your inadequate staff struggle
under the pressure, sweating blood to satisfy the
visitors notwithstanding, but they don't succeed
and everybody is discontented. That is exactly the
position in which my administration was placed in
Morocco for three years.

For the occupation and transport of these new
colonists, roads and railways would have been
essential, but notwithstanding all Lyautey's horror
of slowness, speedy work in the Morocco of 1913
was an impossibility. France was bound by the
Treaty of Algeciras. She had promised to submit all purchases of material for the Moorish government to international adjudication at Tangier.
Morocco could not buy a roller for crushing stones
on a local roadway without setting six or seven
great European administrations into motion. Germany had caused the introduction of a clause into
the treaties forbidding France to have any ordinary
railway-track before that from Tangier to Fez.
And the Tangier-Fez line encountered endless
difficulties in the Spanish Cortes. There were, of
course, the military 60 cm.-gauge railways, but
another clause forbade their use for commercial

purposes. The German representatives, active
and well-drilled consuls, kept a strict and meticulous watch over the application of the treaties.
Lyautey chafed and fumed, but had to mark time
before these closed barriers. The tide of immigration kept rising, and with it the number of
malcontents. At Casablanca the disappointed colonists had shown signs of a rebellious movement
and set up an independent municipal commission.
Lyautey decided to take the opportunity of the
festivities of July 14th to address the population
and tell them the truth.

That speech of July 14th was like an "examination of conscience," loyal, clear-cut, "looking
straight in the eyes. . . ." ("The greatest proof
of esteem one can give to people whom one has the
honour of controlling," said the Resident, "is not
to wheedle them, but to talk seriously to them,
showing them things as they are.") It was also a
definite programme of what must needs be accomplished to provide Morocco with its economic tools.
Few phrases—facts—figures—dates—the plan of
a road system which, pending the railways, would
make lorry transport possible—a whole plan for
expanding the town—a reform of land-tenure—
and, infusing everything, that indefinable liveliness

of free action which was the essence and peculiar
virtue of Lyautey.

July 14th.—It was stiflingly hot at Casablanca,
and Lyautey was preparing agricultural exhibi-
tions. On the 27th, when he was presiding over a
meeting of officials and farmers, two of his officers
on duty, the naval Captain Fortoul and Captain
Noguès, received by telephone a message from the
Minister of Foreign Affairs, deciphered at Rabat,
the sense of which was as follows: "The most prob-
able outcome of the present diplomatic conflict is
war. . . ." General instructions followed. General Lyautey was instructed "to maintain in Morocco only the minimum of indispensable forces,
as the fact of Morocco would have to be settled
in Lorraine, to reduce the occupation of Morocco
to an occupation of the chief coastal ports, and
if possible of the Khenifra—Meknes—Fez—
Oujda line of communication; all advance-posts
should be abandoned for the present, and the Resident-General's first care should be to bring back
to the coastal ports the foreigners and Frenchmen
in the interior." The two officers stared at each
other, dismayed. This meant the abandonment of
Morocco and the ruin of the work begun. One of
them entered the room where the agricultural dis-

cussion was proceeding and handed the telegram to the General. He read it, folded it without a word, put it in the pocket of his tunic, and continued his discussion with the notables of Casablanca. Shortly afterwards arrived a telegram from the Ministry of War, confirming the first, and adding: "I consider it indispensable and possible for you to envisage the despatch to the main French armies of the whole body of your battalion of Chasseurs, Zouaves, Colonial infantry, Algerian and Tunisian sharpshooters, and field batteries. . . ."

At last the meeting ended, and joining his colleagues again, Lyautey could speak. "But they're mad!" he cried. "They're mad! A war between Europeans is a civil war! This is the greatest piece of stupidity the world has ever contrived!" Then he re-read his instructions. They were only too clear: the goal to be aimed at was to send to France the greatest possible number of troops. To set them free for this, it was necessary to evacuate the whole interior of Morocco and limit himself to holding a few points on the coast.

He gave orders for a meeting at Rabat of his regional commanders, Brulard, Gouraud, Henrys and Peltier. He then returned there himself, and on the way, as was his wont, he did some thinking aloud before his right-hand men. His first impression was that, although the Government were right in asking him for the greater part of his troops, they were wrong in instructing him to evacuate Morocco, because that was impossible. It would result in "such a shock throughout the country, and such boldness in our adversaries, and such disheartenment amongst the Moors who had really submitted, that a general rising would surge up beneath our feet. At every point, caught in an eddy of the tide, our battalions would have the utmost difficulty in forcing a way through to the coast, and would only reach it exhausted and decimated, abandoning their dead, their wounded, and their stores." As for the civilian Europeans, there was reason to fear massacres of the kind that had formerly been known in British India. For Morocco, the declaration of war had arrived "three months too late or three months too soon." Three months too late, because they now had a foothold at Taza and at Khenifra, with enemies whose courage would be completely restored by a French withdrawal; three months too soon, because with the coming of winter this campaign would have been ended. After twenty-four hours' reflection, Lyautey wired to the Government and pointed out these dangers.

On July 30th, Gouraud, Henrys, Brulard and Colonel Peltier arrived at Rabat. He questioned them. They agreed with him that if they conformed with the instructions received from France and fell back along the coastline, everything would break up; and that if, on the contrary, the French stood fast, maintaining, even with the most reduced effectives, an armature, the semblance of a line, the "egg-shell," the "bark of the tree," and if they gave the natives an impression of calm and security, it would then be possible, under cover of this screen, to send France all the men she asked for, and still to hold Morocco.

Lyautey asked General Henrys:

"What do you need to keep Meknes?"

"Hardly anything," said Henrys, "so long as Khenifra is occupied, because I shall be leaning upon subjected populations. If not, all the forces I have—and more as well!"

General Gouraud gave the same reply.

General Brulard said:

"I guarantee to hold Marrakesh with three battalions, and Agadir with three companies. If I evacuate, the whole of the Atlas will turn against us. The Kaids will not be able to resist the movement; it would sweep everything away."

After this council of war Lyautey spent the

whole night in reflection. The responsibilities facing him were terrifying. Eighteen months, no more, had elapsed since the Fez massacres, and he was about to propose carrying on the Moroccan adventure by staking everything on the submission of this people, on his personal prestige, and on the devotion of a few great Kaids. On July 31st, after once more going through certain calculations of effectives with his generals, he wired to the Ministry saying that he would keep Morocco in its entirety, and that he would send back instantly twenty battalions and six batteries; the remainder of the troops demanded would follow as quickly as precarious transports would allow.

All this was taking place in the tropical heat of late July in Africa. The offices at Rabat where the military staff worked were only wooden shacks, almost all covered with flowers. The Resident was still living in the small house belonging to the German Consul, guarded by the "blue blades" of the aloes. The telegraph office was in a shelter a hundred yards off. One morning an officer ran in carrying a telegram: "War declared." Around Lyautey there was a moment of enthusiasm amongst the young men. France had allies; victory was certain; Sedan and Versailles would be effaced. But Lyautey remained grave and anxious. To this master-builder the gigantic destruction which he already foresaw seemed criminal, and what is more, absurd. In the morning he notified the Sultan, convoked the great Kaids and explained the war to them. They declared their loyalty, which later events substantiated.

At Fez Gouraud assembled the notables and reminded them of the disorder prevailing before the coming of the French, and of the anxiety in which they had lived for centuries through the proximity of the tribes and the impotence of the Maghzen. He contrasted that anarchy with the tranquil prosperity enjoyed by the town since the Protectorate. He then expounded to them the causes of the war, and the French alliances, declared that a French victory was a certainty, and that the interest of the Moors lay in fidelity to France. One of the notables rose and said: "What you say, General, is true. But if you want the people of Fez not to stir during this war, do not remove one single battalion. . . . We Fasis love you and are not minded to fight you, but if the tribes see that you are weak, they will attack you. . . . The second condition is that the war does not last too long."

Well, the troops had to be sent back, and Lyautey thought the war would be one of long duration. But the die was cast: *Inch Allah!* An attempt was made to give the impression that the French forces in Morocco were not diminished by replacing the departing troops of the active army with territorial troops hailing from Cette, Béziers and Narbonne. To transform these middle-aged family men into colonial soldiers, they were given Legion uniforms, with broad belts and white helmets. The colonists who were left were given the high round head-dresses of Zouaves, and were armed with rifles. Improvised Zouaves were to be seen in peaceful shops carrying on their trade. Bayonets gleamed on counters. With these territorials and a part of the battalions returning from the interior Lyautey was able at the beginning of the war to review at Rabat 25,000 men before the eyes of many of the Maghzen notables. This made a great impression. By the end of August the battalions asked for by the Government had all been sent home. Lyautey had been loyal to the governing conception—the subordination of everything to the success on the French front. But over and above that, and at the same time, he had taken the initiative—apparently foolhardy but actually prudent—in maintaining the secondary front with the most fragile scaffolding. "I've scooped out the lobster," he said, "but I've preserved the shell."

But to embody these territorials, who were so new to the country, it was absolutely essential to retain officers with colonial experience. But they all wanted to go. They all felt that the real game was being played on the French front, and that to remain in Morocco would mean their being kept out of the war for which they had been fitting themselves throughout their careers. It would be a short war, they thought, and if they did not leave at the earliest possible moment they would see nothing of it. Lyautey persisted in his refusal to believe in a short war. After the Marne he remarked: "I mistrust those steep banks of the Aisne. Blücher hung on to them in 1814." To officers who begged him to let them leave he replied: "You shall go when I tell you. . . . You've been taught that the war would last for six weeks. . . . They gave you good reasons to prove it. . . . Remember that in war, in action, two and two never make four. . . . I tell you this will be a war like Napoleon's wars. . . . You'll all have time— too much time—to take part in it."

But frequently these scenes were painful, and Lyautey, who felt so strong a need for perfect harmony in working with his team, suffered from a feeling that some of his best adjutants "were not answering his touch on the reins."

Another danger was the presence in the country of natives under the protection of European powers which, since July, had become either enemies of France or neutrals. They numbered twenty or thirty thousand, and hitherto they had set French laws at defiance. Incorporated and protected by the consular corps, they retorted to every observation with: "I'm under the German Consul." This had to be cleared up. The officer commanding Casablanca, Colonel Targe, closed the Consulate there. Numerous German protégés were working at the harbour, and anxiety reigned amongst them throughout the day. From time to time they would look at the flag still floating over the roofs. Towards evening the flag fluttered down. Work stopped for a moment, and then the astonished, fatalistic natives resumed their loading of bales.

A final unfavourable factor in the French position was the adhesion to the ranks of the enemy powers of the European Moslem peoples. Turkey's declaration of war, followed later by the evacuation of Gallipoli, the British reverse at Kut-el-Amara, the Italian reverse in Tripoli, were all facts capable of exploitation by hostile emissaries.

Such feelings could be minimized only by the religious autonomy of the Sultan. The Sultan of Morocco, the successor of the Emirs of Andalusia

who formerly held sway over all Northern Africa
to the borders of Egypt, was the crowned Shereef,
the religious as well as the political chief, totally
independent of the Sultan at Constantinople and
the Shereef of Mecca. It was in his name that
prayers were said, and not only in Morocco itself,
but secretly at many places in the Tlemcen region,
in Algeria, and as far as Timbuctoo. In the eyes
of all who acknowledged him, the Turks were
heretics. And consequently Turkey's entry into
the war, cleverly exploited, became a score in
favour of the French, for the Sultan proclaimed a
Holy War, and the word by itself had an incalcula-
ble influence. Moorish battalions set off against
the Infidel, and throughout the war the Sultan
sent them Shereefian Letters, veritable encyclicals,
which the wounded could be seen receiving in hospital and kissing them as they read.

Dissension was fostered on every hand by
foreign emissaries. Several times in 1914 and 1915
the military situation became difficult. General
Henrys, with a self-denial and devotion that
touched Lyautey's heart, had remained faithful to
the man who had been his chief at Aïn-Sefra and
Oran. Lyautey had put him in command of the
north, and from Henrys at least there never came
a word of complaint. But many officers grew more

and more restless. "What are we *doing* here?" they kept asking, and recalled the phrase in Messimy's first despatch: "It is in Lorraine that the fate of Morocco will be decided." During the early stages of the war Lyautey and Henrys no longer found, even amongst the High Command, the enthusiasm which had been so characteristic of Morocco in 1913. This restlessness was the cause of several rash deeds, one of which had serious consequences.

One day when General Lyautey had reached the end of one of his countless journeys across Morocco, exhausted and suffering from liver trouble, his staff received a telegram informing them that Colonel Laverdure, in command of the Khenifra front, had broken all orders and abruptly assumed the initiative of attacking the great Zaïan chieftain, Moha or Hamou. It was a crazy enterprise. The disheartened Zaïans had already been sending their sick for treatment in French outposts. According to General Henrys it was only a question of a few days' patience and of waiting for the snow, which was already capping the mountain-tops, to come down into the valley hollows, driving the herds before it. But Colonel Laverdure, obsessed with the idea of a bold stroke, had attacked and had been caught on his way back, losing his own life, as well

as twenty-three officers, 580 men, and nearly all his
arms. It was a terrible lesson. Fortunately it did
not lead to a more widespread disaster, thanks to
the energy of General Henrys, to whom Lyautey,
faithful to the Galliéni method, left full powers.
In October, 1915, when Albert Sarraut brought the
Médaille Militaire to General Lyautey, it was on
this Khenifra front that he agreed to receive it
from the hands of a non-commissioned officer.

*   *   *   *   *

Military action was but one aspect of the problem. At first Lyautey had feared that he would
have to abandon the economic programme which he
had set forth to the French colony at Casablanca on
July 14th. "Construct roads—build harbours—
dig drains—build schools? In the midst of a war?
Why?" On closer reflection, that *why* did not seem
to lack an answer. Firstly, because the Moors had
to be impressed with the sense that France had no
doubts regarding victory. A peace programme
carried out in war-time would fortify that sense.
Whence, formula number one: "the policy of the
smile." The second argument was the idea which
Lyautey had formed from his first contacts with
Tonking: revolt is born, not from the natural
wickedness of men, but from unhappiness and

poverty. Rebelliousness, no doubt, also contained a natural element of pride, of opposition to a foreign invader, but the great mass of the Moorish people were more or less indifferent to political problems; they ought to be kept in that spirit of indifference, and to that end these wild tribes of the mountains must be fed, kept busy, provided with well-paid work. Formula number two: "a workshop is worth a battalion."

In a report of Lyautey's we read:

Maintenance of the mass of the Moors in that indifference; development of the material interests; conviction on their part that we were, and would remain, the stronger power. It followed:

1. That as little as possible should be said to them about the war, and everything should be done to avoid arousing in them a curiosity, so far nonexistent, regarding this. Such was the absolute rule here, and for that reason I have been observed to offer little support to projects for organizing counter-propaganda within the country in the form of newspapers, proclamations, or *fetvas* obtained from the Ulemas. Wherever I have yielded to urgent demands of this kind I have had reason to regret it.

2. That an air of complete nonchalance should be assumed with regard to the course of the European war, with the object of letting such nonchalance be interpreted by the natives as proof of our wholehearted and serene confidence in success. We have been able to do so only by maintaining here

the whole outward façade of life, even its decorative and spectacular side. Nothing has been more painful, and nothing is more painful, under the burden of mourning and anxieties that oppress each one of us, but at the same time there is nothing that I regard as more essential for our political hold on Morocco.

3. That, on the other hand, to prevent the curiosity of the general mass from being attracted to war matters, it was necessary to be continually diverting it in other directions, and to that end, to ensure that, throughout the war, the people should not only enjoy a security and well-being that would almost entirely preserve them from the results of the war, but further—what may seem paradoxical but was on the whole actually brought about—that they should find in the very fact of the war, in certain points at least, a steady increase of prosperity.

Such was the goal. Was it possible of attainment during the war? A great man of action is cautious of prophecies and takes each wave as it comes. In July, 1914, every argument would have proved the impossibility in war-time of finding the resources necessary for the equipment of a new country. It happened that in Morocco, on the contrary, the war helped Lyautey. There are some men who are paralysed by an excess of freedom as by a dizziness, and can only act if they can feel supported by the rigid and reassuring warders of hierarchies and regulations. Lyautey was truly himself only in an all-powerful position, modified solely by friendship, by the reactions of the team, and by his own natural moderation. And never had he been more free.

The international controls imposed by the Algeciras agreement, which made the simplest and most necessary acts so difficult in this closely watched country, were suddenly abolished by the state of war. Germany and Austria could no longer intervene; Great Britain and Italy, as allies of France, no longer wished to. There was no more trouble about the Fez-Tangier railway or international adjudications. France was henceforward alone in Morocco, and could get to work there.

But it was not only freedom from foreign constraints that Lyautey obtained through this exceptional situation: it was also freedom from the French capital. In peace-time, notwithstanding the protectorate régime, he had had Parliament to placate and the necessary resources to obtain from Parliament. This he had managed by dint of intelligent dexterity and personal charm wielded upon the statesmen who came to Morocco, but he had nevertheless been living in an atmosphere of struggle which enhanced the difficulties of the constructive task. But the Ministry and Parliament now had other cares than Morocco; they were more than content to find a man who would answer for the African provinces, and to make a sovereign of him. In the year 1915 no monarch on the face of this planet wielded a personal power more widespread and untrammelled than General Lyautey.

Even in executive details the new situation made everything easier. As the war had checked the flow of immigration, equipment was able to catch up with population. Money, so harshly bargained for in Morocco during the previous year, had suddenly lost all value. When Lyautey required for his projects an extension of a sixty million franc loan, he could write to Paris: "What are sixty millions? One day's war-costs!" They could hardly refuse him the price of a bombardment for the preservation of an empire. Besides, France had need of Morocco's prosperity: the commissariat authorities were obliged to make purchases there; the agricultural products which the country could supply were useful for feeding the capital. The Regulations—Lyautey's terror—bowed to necessity. One almost incredible fact was that the military administration lent its 60 cm. lines for commercial transport. And even the replacement of active service troops by territorials turned out to be a favourable factor, for amongst these latter Lyautey found workshop foremen, architects, financial experts, engineers—colonists despite themselves—who but for the war would never have set foot in Morocco, and who, like so many Frenchmen torn from too facile an existence, suddenly revealed astonishing adaptive and creative qualities. They formed the combination of civilian and military personnels that he required for the policy which was his individual conception.

From 1915 new roadways were being traced out by tractors. Casablanca and Rabat were now only two hours from each other. "The thing to see," wrote Guillaume de Tarde, "is all those road engineering depots created together and working together: from Ber-Rechid right to the gates of Marrakesh, from Mazagan to the edge of Doukkala, between Kenitra and Salé, along the whole of the Meknes-Fez route. I know nothing more picturesque than those of Mazagan. There every element has set about the work—men, women, children, mules, camels, horses and horse-power. The men dig, clear the ground, raise embankments. The children break road-metal. The women lay stones carefully on the road, like the fragments of a puzzle. Rollers go by, hauled by disdainful camels. From all this ant-like industry there emerges a long strip of road straddling the hills in the distance. And before the end of December there will thus be nearly 270 miles of road in the whole of Morocco."

Not only roads were being built. The harbour of Casablanca was making progress; that of Kenitra, a completely new creation, Lyautey's personal project, seemed to be a success. Everywhere they were opening schools and infirmaries. ("A native infirmary is worth a regiment.") Madame Lyautey organized maternity institutions and infant clinics, and the Berbers of the mountains came to be tended by French doctors.

When the German Consulate at Casablanca was entered, it was found to contain the framework of a remarkable commercial organization—samples of all possible products of the Reich which the Consulate was entrusted to offer to Moorish merchants, and also samples of products desired by Morocco which were despatched to the manufacturers in Germany capable of producing them. "This," said Lyautey, "was an object-lesson to be followed." He himself claimed the title of "chief commercial traveller of the Protectorate." He got into touch with the French Chambers of Commerce, and even (the notion at first seemed paradoxical in wartime) organized an exhibition at Casablanca in 1915, and in 1916 a trade fair at Fez.

The impression made on the natives was surprising. One of the still independent chieftains, who was keeping up a stubborn resistance to General Henrys on the northern front, heard descriptions of the Casablanca exhibition and was seized with irresistible curiosity. He requested a truce, and authorization to go there and then to resume his post of warfare against the French. Strange and impossible as such a request seemed, it was granted. He was cordially welcomed, and after his visit he and his tribe made submission. At Fez hillsmen were to be seen who had been living in rebellion since the massacres. Some of them submitted in order to be able to ride on the roundabouts at the Fez fair. "No doubt," says Alfred de Tarde, "a Berber strolling through the Casablanca exhibition might think, like Socrates visiting the *souks* of Athens: 'what a lot of things I don't need!'" But he enjoyed seeing them, and for the time being forgot the pleasures of gunpowder.

Under the guidance of a great artist in town-planning, M. Prost, plans of extension had been sketched for each town—"projections of the future town." The rule was made that the European town should be separate from the native one, primarily to preserve the charm of the latter, and also because "we must respect not only the appearance of the native cities, but also their customs and ways of life, whether social or religious." A plan of orientation was made compulsory, streets were designed, the speculation of land-jobbers was checkmated. Everywhere the beautiful remains of Moorish art were safeguarded. A central and disinterested authority imposed on private interests respect for the general interest and respect for beauty.

All who participated in this work have retained a powerful and happy impression of it. It was creative action, which is the most constant requirement of human nature. "At all times and in all places the pioneer experiences an austere and legitimate happiness. At every moment of his life that fortunate man is set face to face with a well-defined problem calling for definite action. Accordingly, no rules and no red tape; these things are left to a few bureaucrats; he himself is a creature of perception and action. Now, when these two floodgates are open, a stream of life bears the heart of man along like a feather. . . . What need for desire then, what need for fear? Time is lacking for either: action swallows up regret." [1] The periods when humanity yields to romantic despairs come when the opium of action ceases to veil from men's gaze the strangeness of their destiny. The war

---

[1] Alain.

staff in Morocco had chafed at their exile almost to the point of rebelliousness, but in the midst of battle, in hard toil, they came to know the divine joy of creating.

Alfred de Tarde relates how General Lyautey took him for a tour of inspection at Marrakesh in 1915. They were going across those desert plains where the heat raised mirages over the sand, and on the horizon the mountains, cut off from the ground by a thin white line, seemed to be suspended in the void; inspired by the beauty of the scene, Lyautey spoke of his work and of the joy he experienced in again seeing this town which he would doubtless find transformed and beautiful.

It was a meeting long ago with an Englishman at the mouths of the Danube that gave me a full revelation of myself [he said]. That man was Sir Charles Hartley. . . . Hartley is the man who *made* the Danube. Before his day it was a dead river, spilling its waters into a sand-blocked delta. Hartley spent the whole of his life in re-fashioning that river, in building dykes and channels and dams, and in the end opened it to a great European traffic. . . . The man might die; but he left a work that would never die. . . . From that day, like Hartley, I had a dream of creating, of raising into life countries which had been asleep from the beginning of time, and showing them those riches of their own which they are ignorant of, and breathing the breath of life into them. . . . In Tonking I was the first to penetrate territories into which no European had ever ventured. In Madagascar I made towns grow up. . . . And in Morocco, amongst these ancient lands of lethargy, what a rich joy there has been in giving them desire, in quickening the blood in their veins. . . . There are people who regard colonial enterprises as barbarian. What stupidity! Wherever I have gone, it has been to construct; and whatever I had to destroy I built up again later, more solidly and durably. Our troops left behind them territory restored to peace, scored with roads, and quickening with life; and commercial exchange preceded the exchange of ideas. . . . What a difference from the wars of Europe, which ravage cathedrals and museums and everything irreplaceable, and annihilate in one day the priceless treasures of centuries!

The war, by side-tracking "regulations," had empowered Lyautey to choose his officials and directors from amongst ordinary soldiers, like a sultan of the Arabian Nights choosing his viziers from the ranks of the artisans. M. Laprade, one of the architects of the new Morocco, describes a scene which took place at Fez early in 1916.

There was some question of setting up a hospital. Five different plans lay spread out on a large table. All the authorities, all the Génic officers, all the doctors, captains or colonels, debated the advantages and disadvantages of each side. And, as is only right in any good deliberative body, the question became so confused after an hour or so that nobody could grasp it any longer.

The general had hitherto said not a word. At last he turned impatiently to an intelligent-looking young Zouave who was standing in a modest place at the foot of the table.

"You are an architect," he said. "Which is the best of these?"—"This one, General." Whereupon the Chief picked up a stout red pencil from the table, and wrote right across the plan, in capital letters six inches high: "ADOPTED—*Lyautey*." And the date. "There you are, gentlemen! Be good enough to come back here in a year's time for the inauguration of the hospital."

Another day, when visiting some barracks, Lyautey came across a corporal whose face showed the intellectual. He was carrying out a water-fatigue. The General stopped. "What is your name?"— "Branly, General."—"Branly? You're not a son of the scientist who invented wireless, are you?"— "Yes, General, I'm his son."—"And they put you on water-fatigues! What a waste of energies! What do you do in civilian life?" The young man explained that he was preparing for a post in the Treasury. Two days later he was transferred to an important post in an appropriate branch. A few years later he was Director-General of Finances in the Protectorate.

*   *   *   *   *

Nevertheless, happily as the team worked, the Chief frequently chafed at the bit. He too, like his officers, had suffered in August, 1914, at being tied to Morocco. He had realized his danger, as one who had always dreamed, and still dreamed, of a great rôle in France, in being at such a time so far from the centre of action. On September 6th he had written to Millerand, the Minister of War, when he sent over his troops from Morocco:

I need not tell you what suffering it causes me not to be at the head of what I am sending, the equivalent of more than a whole army corps. The Government is the sole judge of the post which it believes me best fitted for, and there has not been, and will not be, a single word of mine betraying a desire. I consider that the passive acceptance of bounden duty has never been more imperative, and I strain every nerve to set an example of willing sacrifice. . . . But living so far off as this, almost cut off from all news, during such days of anguish, is more than hardship.

"My Lorraine house is in all probability destroyed," he also wrote in that letter. And although he did not know it at that moment, the destruction was already a fact. Crévic had been destroyed, Crévic with its wealth of memories, where he had his letters and manuscripts, his three beloved notebooks of philosophy, his books, the portraits of his friends, and his arms, his African curios, his memories of Lorraine, and the kitchen-garden of his childhood where the plums on the trees were so good. The destruction of Crévic was the symbol of all that was perishing at that moment in France, all that he loved. Yes, this was suffering indeed. He wrote to M. de Mun:

I have a very clear and lofty sense of the service I am giving to my country. That is adequate for my conscience, but does not suffice my heart, because I feel that the country will not understand it, and that here even the officers, except a very small élite, do not understand it. Our race is above all else argumentative, impatient of discipline, and feels command as a hardship. My own command is henceforth devoid of any consolations. For too many years now I have relished the sense of my being loved and understood. I must resign myself here to being so no longer, to being inflexible in the face of the dumb resistances that I encounter, and of the impatience which has to be repressed. I have the close support of an admirable being, Henrys, who for his part has made a complete sacrifice with the utmost calm. I have been less well pleased with certain others, in whom egotism has been far too dominant. My own sacrifice is absolute and I shall hold firm to the end; only, when a man has wielded a command of this kind in such conditions, he is finished, and all he can do is to disappear. . . . The Will of Allah. . . .

In 1915 he had to go to France to obtain a supplementary loan. M. Poincaré notes in his journals the wonderful news brought by Lyautey of the situation in Morocco: "The accomplishment of this marvel has cost only 47 million francs, but the Resident-General is insistent on putting us on our guard against what he calls the moral attrition of his defensive instrument. All who are stationed in Morocco, officers and non-commissioned officers, regard themselves as disqualified or dishonoured, notwithstanding the fact that, although peace reigns in the interior of the country, there is very stiff fighting on the frontiers. The General asks that this should be borne in mind, and that more freedom and authority should be left to himself in the matter of promotions. As is his custom, he speaks with a vigorous and alluring conviction which hardly leaves his listeners time to reflect and sweeps away all objections like straws."

Through M. Poincaré he obtained leave to make a tour of the front, and he travelled from Dunkirk right to the Ballon d'Alsace. On his return to Morocco he wrote to his friend M. Joseph de Reinach, giving his impressions in the course of a long letter:

The instrument as a whole struck me as admirable, and that is the essential matter; for the instrument is not to be improvised, and well-handled from one day to the next it can effect the maximum. But to the minds of reasoning men it is plain that this instrument has limitations in duration and renewal. We are now at the 1879 class, and thereafter there is nothing. Now, more than ever, it is upon us, and us alone, that the whole weight of the war and its issue lies. . . . That instrument, then, must be handled with every care, must be played with the utmost caution, and must not lose one particle through wastefulness. And the unbridled, muddling wastefulness forced on us for long months now, through a lack of united control, method, and a rational play of forces, is one of the things which struck me most strongly and most painfully.

If we pass from the instrument to its motive powers, the scene (alas!) changes. In vain have I sought them, on any level. . . . Let there be no misunderstanding. I am not saying that we shan't get through somehow or other; and I set aside the pessimism of foregone conclusions, because, all things considered, there are two parties to the game, and it is quite possible that on the other side there may be wear-and-tear, cracks, and corroding elements which will prevent them likewise from snatching the prize.

But what I find alarming, and contrary to what has always been the cardinal rule of our commands, is the spectacle of our people "staking on luck." If there is one Napoleonic principle truer than any, it is that in war one must always anticipate the worst. One must arrange the maximum of chances on one's side, and do so in all branches, tirelessly.

When I made my start in Tonking with Galliéni, and as his chief of staff prepared with him my first major military operation, I had spontaneously more or less doubled the forecasts of effectives, in rations and munitions; when I laid these before him, he doubled the figures, to my stupefaction; that is to say, he quadrupled them—and it was he who proved to be right. *No one ever foresees enough of the unforeseen,* of risks, of miscalculations; no one ever reckons broadly or largely enough.

At Chantilly they seem to me to be doing just the opposite; there everything is measured out by the drop; when a decision is reached, instead of throwing the maximum on the scales, they are inspired only by paltry economies; they take the small view; they supply means grudgingly, weighing them on a chemist's balance; and, lastly and most notably of all, they vacillate and always turn up late.

There is no need to expand on the absence of the national motive power. We agree only too well. I was struck even more forcibly than on my arrival by the total absence of a basic organism of national defence, devoted exclusively to what concerns the war in all branches. They will be simply beating the wind so long as there exists no separate and compact grouping of the four or five ministers concerned with that under the control of a *chief,* whether one of themselves or chosen from outside.

What is required is a special and distinct organization, a *war government,* making comprehensive use of all the vital forces of the nation to be utilized for war: effectives, material, factories, crops, preparation of new recruiting classes, finance, organization of social life, spread of propaganda abroad (something grossly neglected, as I here see better than anyone), and taking a forward view.

If desired, this organism should have in juxtaposition to it the normal government, President of the Council and the rest, looking towards the country, doing the talking, forming a screen to assure peace for the active organism, shielding it from disturbance, freeing it from parliamentary wastage of time, leaving it completely to its intensive and continuous production of the forces to be handed over, without a break, to the Generalissimo.

Above all this, the President of the Republic, regulating the two organisms, holding the double reins in his hand.

Finally, the *motive power of the coalition* of Allied powers. Here indeed is not the least of the evils. It is terrifying, faced by the unity of action that confronts us in all its coherence and simplicity, to see this amorphous assemblage of six nations under arms, having numerical superiority, mastery of the seas, superiority of resources, and yet amongst whom nothing definite emerges because nobody is in command, and amongst whom the smallest decision, even a military one, cannot be reached without a long exchange of preliminary negotiations. How is it that this manifest lack of organization and the resultant dangers have not been sufficiently striking to bring about the creation in Paris from the beginning (and it should be created to-day) of a delegation of Chiefs-of-Staff,

269

centring round the leader of France, the undoubted axis of this coalition? Such a delegation should be composed not of military attachés, but of highly placed personalities having powers for instant decision and forming the executive committee of this world-wide war.

To sum up, the instrument exists, the motors are lacking. True, that is better than the opposite state of affairs, for the instrument cannot be improvised, whilst the motors, depending solely on the will of men, could be instantly organized. Only, it is essential that *some one* should will this and dare it—and where is that some one?

My last day in Paris was the most moving of all. I was full of these matters, and for all my awareness that I could do nothing and that my voice had no weight, it was a real agony for me to leave without having given vent to my conscience in the right quarter.

On setting foot aboard ship at Marseilles again, Lyautey had the feeling of a man emerging from a nightmare.

And then there was the return to Morocco:

I am obliged to resist the selfish pleasure I feel on returning to find my command in full activity, in full swing, in the wholehearted confidence of every one. For six days now I have been wholeheartedly savouring the joy of seeing once again achievements brought to pass in the atmosphere of immediate decisions, mutual comprehension, a fully working machine, and being myself surrounded by a team of picked men who believe in me and in our common task, and throw themselves into it with their every fibre. So absorbed am I by a really overwhelming job that it calls for some effort to think of the terrible drama which is proceeding beyond the seas, and on the issue of which depends our life as a nation, and no less the work which I am accomplishing here. Important as it is, I quite realize that this is only secondary, and that it is not here that our destinies are being spun.

"It is not here that our destinies are being spun. . . ." To be the man who would save France. . . . His childhood dream of playing a decisive and beneficent part in his country's history. . . . Was not that suddenly appearing within reach of realization through this general bankruptcy of will? Would it not enable him to apply to the conduct of the war the methods which had been proved so efficacious in Morocco? It was agonizing to feel at once so capable of serving and so far from the places where he could serve.

XIV

DURING the night of December 10th–11th, 1916, the Resident-General received the following telegram:

In the eventuality of your being offered War Ministry under my presidency, could you accept without disadvantage to Morocco? Reply extremely urgent.—BRIAND.

It was one of the darkest moments of the war. The Rumanian front had just collapsed. The Battle of the Somme had been interrupted, perhaps too soon, but after alarming losses and without visible results. In Parliament as in the army a mood of general criticism was abroad. Coteries had formed; round various generals there were groups of officers and politicians, supporters for reasons of conviction or of ambition, all of them pointing to their man as the only one capable of command. Between Paris and the front there was a perpetual coming-and-going of secret emissaries, bearers of advice or of bad news. The whole country was being infected with this anxiety and restlessness. According to their own opinion, friendships, and grudges, some blamed the Briand Ministry, others

the Commander-in-Chief, and others the Allies.
Many politicians in Paris were demanding the sup-
planting of Joffre, who was blamed by some for
doing nothing, for what they called his "stagna-
tion," and by others for his multiplication of par-
tial, useless, and costly attacks. The advocates of
the Salonika expedition complained of the hostility
of General Headquarters, who would only recognize the French front and refused troops for this
other enterprise. Joffre's opponents did not dare
openly to propose the dropping of the General,
whose popularity was still widespread, but they insinuated the idea that in order to give him wider
views and familiarity with all fronts it would be
wise to broaden his powers. He was only in command of the Armies of the North and North-East.
Why not make him a real Generalissimo by substi-
tuting a commander of the French front? This
would give an opportunity for the suppression of
General Headquarters at Chantilly, round which
unpleasant legends had been gathering. Its successor would be pushed nearer to the troops, up
to Compiègne, whilst Joffre, on the other hand,
as military adviser to the Government, would take
up his abode in Paris. But might not Paris shock
him, as being too far off from the armies? Well,

why not install him with a personal Staff near Paris, quite near Paris—say at Neuilly? Thus, under cover of fresh laurels—as often happens— the way was being paved for the dropping of the calm and prudent man who had wielded an almost absolute power from the opening of the war.

For a twofold military and political move of this sort, and to set the battle-worn Cabinet afloat again, it was essential to have a War Minister who could inspire confidence in the country. From the Quai d'Orsay, Philippe Berthelot, who already held in the councils that extensive and durable power attained by those who prefer the realities of power to ephemeral triumphs, had admired the results obtained by Lyautey in Morocco. He suggested Lyautey's name to Briand. Léon Bailby had just published an article in *L'Intransigent* declaring that at least two Frenchmen had proved themselves great organizers—Lyautey in Morocco, and Edouard Herriot as Mayor of Lyons—and that it would be wise to bring them both into closer touch with the conduct of the war. In the universal confusion, public opinion had fastened on to these two names. Whence Briand's telegram.

When Lyautey received it, the military situation in Morocco itself had taken a bad turn. Enemy submarines were reported off the Atlantic coast, and Germans had landed to join El Hiba, the agitator in the south. That very morning the Resident-General had sent in his periodic report to the Ministry of Foreign Affairs. It showed Lyautey in a somewhat gloomy frame of mind. "The situation," he said, "must be regarded as serious."

I. We are faced by two eventualities:

(*a*) Bombardment of the coastal ports, particularly Casablanca and Rabat. This, according to the known plans of the enemy, may occur any day now, and will have moral repercussions in the interior of the country all the more serious because the insufficiency of our defensive material incapacitates us from reply; further, in contradiction of our declarations, it will offer the native population twofold evidence of our no longer having mastery of the sea and of our inability to protect them.

(*b*) German landings in El Hiba's territory. These are dangerous because they can induce a general offensive movement against us from the south, and restore confidence to all the dissident tribes who will lend it their aid.

The general intelligence to hand goes to show that the impression produced by the first arrival of the Germans announced by Hiba, and by their relations with him, is a very deep one. One of the Germans landed is certainly Herr Probster, the former consul at Fez when war broke out, who was exchanged for our consul at Nüremberg. He possesses a perfect knowledge of the language and country, and has numerous connections throughout Morocco. He appears to be taking control of the movement. Hiba has successively sent to him his two chief lieutenants—Najem and Iraa, who have offered him two horses in tribute. They proceeded with him on the 10th towards the Wady Dra, to await with a wireless telegraphy apparatus the new landings announced by him. These appear to be unavoidable, as three submarines were reported three days ago abreast of the Wady Nun, and as the patrolling of the south has been abandoned by the Naval branch on account of insufficiency of anti-submarine armament.

There is therefore no ground for supposing that landings will not be effected, or that others will not follow later. There is every likelihood that before long we shall see Hiba provided with important material, in arms and artillery, with German control and staff.

Local informants, generally cautious, declare the situation very serious and susceptible of sudden aggravation, and advise as prompt an intervention as possible. . . .

II. Morocco is thus confronted by a group of external dangers, the possible nature of which is envisaged on pages 61–63 of my report of November 29th, which you must have received, and to which I drew attention as potentially dominating and compromising the results hitherto attained in the interior.

III. Unfortunately the counter-steps to be taken

to these are very difficult and precarious, on account of the poverty of material means. Each region possesses only the minimum of troops and indispensable equipment for the maintenance of its own front, especially if a general upheaval takes place, and there are neither troops in reserve nor troops available. . . .

IV. To sum up, so far there are only threats, but these threats are very definite and very serious.

After despatching this report, Lyautey had set off on a tour of inspection in the south, so that it was only at night, on returning from Rabat, that he found M. Briand's telegram. What was he to answer? To be tempted would have been natural. To play a great part in France had been the lofty and legitimate ambition of his whole life, and from countless letters he knew that he was regarded by many Frenchmen as the necessary leader. From the inner councils of the War Ministry itself, one officer wrote to him:

The Morocco undertaking is at present unique in achieving the results aimed at. Opinion is noting that quite definitely. The politicians and journalists returning from Fez have been won over by you and by your work, and do not fail to publish it. . . . The days of the existing General Headquarters seem to be numbered; Chantilly will have to give place to a rational organization.

. . . From all sides the leader is called for. I am absolutely convinced that the force of events will cause him to be found where he is.

But if he returned to France at this moment, could he really be the man who would impose one single will upon the coalition? Could he really be the organizer of victory? It was hard to form a fair judgment at a distance, but the situation looked very nearly desperate. The diversion in the East, in which Lyautey had believed in 1915, was by now gravely compromised by the collapse of Rumania and the defeat of Greece. Must he once again take on the command of a disabled ship? Would it be even a command? And besides, did the situation in Morocco admit of his departure? His report of the previous day had provided the Government with the most exact information to come to a decision on that last point. During the night, at 1.30 a.m. on December 11th, he replied in these terms:

Having left to inspect anti-submarine defences, I only found your telegram in the evening, which accounts for delay in reply.

I belong to my country, and I shall sacrifice all personal considerations in order to serve it as a soldier, within the limit of my capacities, wherever the Government may judge me most useful.

It is therefore for the Government to weigh up the situation set forth in Report no. 473, which I sent off yesterday and ask you to read attentively.

I believe that summary to be strictly accurate.

It is beyond question that the present situation is extremely threatening, dangers having suddenly arisen in consequence of the new factor, the German landing in the south, and of the attacks to be expected on the ports. Several days must elapse before it can be seen whether these threats diminish, and whether we are in course of facing them effectively or not.

Consequently, in reply to your definite question, my conscience compels me to say that my departure from Morocco would at the present moment have grave disadvantages, the risk of which would further depend chiefly on the choice of my successor, for there is just now nobody on the spot with rank or authority to assume general control.

Not for one moment is there any question, in present circumstances, of my avoiding a duty. All I can do is loyally to give you the general and comparative elements, and you can judge where my primary duty lies.

Briand's reply arrived during the morning. It asked whether, in the event of General Gouraud being appointed to Morocco, General Lyautey could accept the Ministry.

He answered:

I. General Gouraud is entirely fitted to cope with the situation, and I shall hand over the command to him with every confidence.

II. My personal coefficient, as at present established amongst the natives, and even amongst dissidents, is indisputably our highest trump here; and in order to diminish the element of the unknown involved in my departure and to adjust the transference, it would be highly advantageous to make the appointment of my successor a provisional one, at least to start with, so that in the eyes of the Sultan and the population I should remain the guarantor of the policy hitherto pursued. I mention this point to you because I regard it as essential, and also easy to arrange.

III. From the local point of view it would certainly be preferable that I should await Gouraud's arrival, in order that there should be no break in continuity in the command; but of this too you are the judge in the last resort.

Gouraud was in command of the Fourth Army in Champagne when he was urgently summoned to the Ministry of Foreign Affairs. He arrived surprised, and was received by Philippe Berthelot. "M. Briand has sent for me," he said. "What is the matter?"—"You will be delighted," said Berthelot. "They're going to send you to Morocco as Resident-General."—"Oh, no!" said Gouraud. "Not that, not that!"—"Why?" asked Berthelot. "But don't you like Morocco?"—"Yes,

I liked Morocco before the war, and I shall like
it after the war.   But at the moment I cannot
quit my Army."   Just then Briand summoned
Berthelot, who returned a few minutes later to
fetch Gouraud.—"General," said Briand, "I am
going to ask a very great favour of you."—"I know
already what it is, sir," said Gouraud.   "I implore
you to leave me my Army."

It was a long discussion.   At last Briand concluded: "Listen, General.   I am sorry I cannot
convince you.   Your arguments do you honour; I
must acknowledge that.   Now I should like to ask
your advice. . . . You know that the French are
a difficult people to lead.   I have been thinking
that, in the hesitations we are now going through,
the War Ministry needs a man whose prestige will
reassure this country.   My desire is to summon
General Lyautey to that.   What do you feel about
it?"—"Excellent, sir.   What we need at the Ministry is certainly a great organizer, a leader, and
if there is one such in France, it is Lyautey."—
"I am very pleased to hear that," said Briand.
"But what am I to do about it?   I wired my offer
to General Lyautey, and here are the telegrams
we have exchanged."

Gouraud read them.

Briand watched him with a smile.

"Well?" he said.

Gouraud saw he was beaten, and yielded.

Gouraud's acceptance made Lyautey's possible, and from that moment Briand regarded him as forming part of the Cabinet.

Pending his arrival, Admiral Lacaze, the Minister of Marine, was entrusted with the interim Ministry. But Briand was reluctant to face the Chamber before a new Commander of the Armies of the North and North-East was appointed. He warned Lyautey by wire that this choice would be made before his arrival, that General Joffre would remain as Generalissimo, employed on the conduct of war on all fronts, side by side with the Government and under its authority. Briand asked Lyautey whether he approved these measures. Lyautey replied on December 12th:

Very Urgent: for the Prime Minister.

1. It is not for me to accept arrangements or otherwise, as I have no data for estimating their value. Only when I am on the spot shall I be able to take my share of responsibilities. Until then I must decline to take any, and formally request that there be no possibility of a misunderstanding in this connection before Parliament and the country.

2. Having only remote and incomplete information, I may be mistaken—and I cordially hope so —but it is my duty, at a moment when I shall perhaps be your collaborator, to tell you that since the events in Rumania and Greece, which seem to me to rob the Salonika project of all effective chances, I regard the venture as seriously compromised.

If I have not failed the Government's appeal, it is because every one of us owes complete sacrifice and a maximum effort to his country; I shall give them unreservedly; but whereas in March I saw a possible way out of things, I can no longer discern one to-day, at least from here.

3. But before being on the spot it is impossible for me to gauge whether the projected new arrangements are the best, and whether, to achieve the co-ordinated effect of all the Allies, they ensure that concentration of direction and of really and practically organized action which is indispensable and remains the only guarantee of success.

Meanwhile, in Paris, the new Council of Ministers were anxiously and hesitatingly choosing the successor to General Joffre. He himself was much too acute not to realize that the floral wreaths and proffered titles were destined merely to bedeck a victim. But treated as Generalissimo, and consulted by the Council with the utmost consideration regarding the choice of a General who ought theoretically to be his subordinate, Joffre saw himself constrained to play his part in this tragicomedy. Several names had been put forward: Foch, Castelnau, Pétain, Nivelle. . . . Foch at this time was said by Headquarters to be in too bad a state of health to hold command. General Pétain and Nivelle alone, during this unhappy period, had acquired real prestige by having stemmed, and then pushed back, the German attacks at Verdun. But Pétain, precise, lucid and devoid of illusions, was less congenial to most of the ministers than Nivelle, an optimistic General who promised, if his methods were put into practice, to break this intangible front. Joffre himself was less unfavourable to this choice than to any other. Nivelle was appointed. On the same day too it was decided to set up a War Committee. The new British Government under Lloyd George had just put the formula of the War Cabinet into fashion, and in difficult times public opinion always expects marvels from a formula.

* * * * *

On December 13th, at Rabat, Lyautey was making his preparations for departure when he received, forwarded from Tangier, the official communiqué announcing the formation of the Ministry:

LYAUTEY

Tangier.   December 13th, 1916.
To the Resident-General, Rabat.

General Gouraud appointed Resident-General France
Morocco replacing General Lyautey.

Constitution of Cabinet:

President of Council, Foreign Affairs	BRIAND.
Justice, Public Instruction . .	VIVIANI.
Finance	RIBOT.
Interior	MALVY.
War	General LYAUTEY.
Marine	Admiral LACAZE.
National Economy, Trade, Industry, Agriculture . . .	CLEMENTEL.
Transport, Civil and Military Foodstuffs	HERRIOT.
Colonies	DOUMERGUE.
Munitions, War Manufactures .	ALBERT THOMAS.
Under-Secretary for Health . .	GODARD.
Transport	CLAVEILLE.
War Manufactures	LOUCHEUR.

A Committee of War is established consisting
of the President of the Council, and Ministers of
Finance, War, Marine, Munitions. General Joffre,
General-in-Chief, will be able to attend meetings
of this Committee as technical military adviser to
the Government. The Government will not come
before the Chamber until Thursday afternoon.

Lyautey was profoundly taken aback and dis-
quieted by this communiqué. To start with, he

had asked that Gouraud's appointment to Morocco should be provisional; it appeared to be definitive. As a matter of fact this was only an oversight, and in the *Journal Officiel* Gouraud was actually named as "interim" Resident-General. To Lyautey, however, who did not see the official gazette, it looked as if there were a desire to supplant him, contrary to what had been agreed upon. But a new feature, much more serious in his view, was the dismembering of the War Ministry, from which for the first time one part was detached and entrusted to Herriot, another to Albert Thomas, whilst Transport and Health were handed over to under-secretaries. Lyautey had come back from his tour of the front with the idea that only a general reform and a complete unification of direction could improve the conduct of the war and the situation of the Allies. But here, he felt, things were far from being unified: they were being split up.

He wired to Briand, expressing the utmost surprise at reading the constitution of the Ministry, pointing out the truncation of the Ministry of War which had been offered to him, and that he could no longer envisage its efficaciousness under such conditions. "In the extremity of peril in which our country stands," he went on, "the one glaring ne-

cessity, obvious to all, is to concentrate the unity
of the conduct of the war, whereas this is being
still further watered down. I therefore formally
withhold my acceptance of the War Ministry in
the new and unforeseen conditions under which I
have now to face it, until I have been able to judge
at first hand whether or not I am being given at the
War Ministry the powers and means of action
which circumstances make indispensable. I shall
hand over my functions to Gouraud on Monday,
at Gibraltar."

The Prime Minister replied that the new organization of the command and the Government ac-
corded exactly with the desire expressed by Lyautey "to concentrate the unity of the conduct of
the war. . . . " In Briand's words, "the Government
has made certain of the supreme direction of the war,
and will exercise it through the instrument of a
small Committee of War. This Committee will
have the supreme direction, internally as well as
externally. . . . Having control of the motive instrument, and possessing the extensive powers for
unity of action which your predecessors did not
have in their hands, you will be in a position to render your country the service that she expects of
you." In conclusion M. Briand invited the General to withdraw his reservations, to respond im-

mediately to the Government's appeal, and to weigh in his conscience the consequences of the ministerial crisis which would ensue if he went back upon his acceptance.

Lyautey was in an agonising position. He saw himself setting out along a path which now seemed to lead nowhere. He would have the responsibilities of power without the real means of wielding power. He had accepted the Ministry of War, but not a Ministry with some of its limbs amputated. His name would cover the action of other ministers, excellent men for all he knew (only he did not know them), but men who were not of his choice any more than the new Commander-in-Chief was. He felt at once a vivid and distressing intuition regarding the future, a desire to decline, and a certainty that he could no longer do so. "Now is not the time to argue," he wrote to a friend who was close to power himself. . . . "I shall enter this like a soldier emerging from the trench when his name is called, knowing what awaits him. . . . I had always said that there was one thing which I would not accept—to play the *Wimpfen* or to be summoned as a doctor to a deathbed. And here I am accepting—for that is how things stand."

On December 15th, overwhelmed by a deep

gloom which those about him at the time still remember, he sent a final telegram to the Prime
Minister:

I respond to your appeal. There is no question
at all of my asking for conditions; nothing is farther from my thoughts or from my conception of
duty. But I am concerned with a loyal and practical examination of the exact means of assuring,
in everything for which I shall be responsible, the
maximum of useful and speedy results; and that
is what I confidently count upon doing along with
you on my arrival.

He crossed by submarine to Gibraltar, where
he met Gouraud, with whom he spent twenty-four
hours so as to inform him about the state of affairs in Morocco. There too a very long letter
from Paris awaited him, the letter of an author
well acquainted with political circles.

"General," it said, "I am profoundly glad for
France's sake that you have consented to accept
the War portfolio. Your arrival brings the country something as comforting as a victory. The
situation is worthy of you: it becomes more and
more difficult. . . . You will immediately be asked
to take on liabilities, and attempts will be made
to tie your hands, and you will prefer, I am certain, to keep yourself free in order to study a ter-
rain which never before has seemed so illusory in

its perspectives. . . . The political situation stands
as follows: Briand is hard pressed, straining every
nerve to stand his ground by bringing in new men,
such as Lyautey or Herriot. . . . His opponents
are grieved at the sight of Lyautey in the opposite
camp. . . . Dining last night at the La Tré-
moïlles', Tardieu remarked: "I am attacking the
Ministry to-morrow. It makes me furious to do
so, because of Lyautey. He is the man we need."
You are doing Briand a very great favour, General, in returning to France. This is the long and
the short of the sitting of the Chamber, and of
all the talk.

Lyautey read this with astonished dismay. Yes
—it was just as he feared, just what he held in
inborn horror: questions of personalities and internal feuds, when action, above all else, called for
unity and union. . . . On the journey from Gibraltar to Paris he was in deep gloom, playing
patience in a corner of the carriage, and not saying a word to the officers accompanying him. He
stopped for a few hours in Madrid to see the King
of Spain, and reached Paris on December 22nd.
He declined to go to the Ministry, and stayed at
his private address in order to reserve his freedom
to refuse the portfolio if he deemed the situation
completely unacceptable after an examination on
the spot.

On arrival he had gone to see a certain politician

in whom he had every confidence and to whom he had shown the telegrams that had been passing; he told him of his distress, and his dread of finding neither unity of command nor inter-Allied organization. And he told him how his first reaction had been to decline. The same evening he received a discouraging note from his interlocutor of the morning:

I am very much afraid that you will be smothered with promises, that within a week you will see their hollowness, and that you will then be (in the Parliamentary style) "the General who is stabbing the Cabinet in the back." And I cannot help feeling that first thoughts were best.

Lyautey knew as much. But it was too late to retrace his steps. Instantly, action had caught him up. He arrived just when there was a desire to sidetrack Foch, whom he had always admired, when Joffre, seeing himself tricked, was threatening a spectacular resignation and to tell France how he had been treated. Lyautey intervened. He saved Foch, to whom shortly afterwards he gave the interim command of Castelnau's army when the latter general was sent to Russia; he placated Joffre by reviving in his favour the dignity of Marshal of France. He himself was offered the post of Secretary-in-Chief to the Committee of War, which he was told would restore a unity of command in his own hands. He was touched by the manifest efforts made by the Government to give him satisfaction, and his hopes revived a little. He went and took up his quarters in the Rue Saint-Dominique.

Hardly was he there before he felt certain of misunderstandings. He had come over to be the animator of France as he had been the animator of Morocco. But in Morocco he had found a country with neither framework nor moulds, and he had carved it out in his own image. In Paris he had to take his place in a rigid and twofold system: the framework of parliamentary democracy, and that of the military hierarchy. This great realist had been able to understand and subdue Chinese mandarins and Arab kaids, but there was one single reality which had always been masked to him by events and by passions, and this was just the one thing which now, at this moment of his life, he would urgently have needed to penetrate —the French Parliament.

The sentiments of his youth kept Lyautey aloof from politicians throughout the early part of his life, and service in distant lands had kept him free from them later; the obstacle of Parliament was something which he had long circumvented by mak-

panied by Field-Marshal Robertson; M. Briand took General Lyautey. This Conference strongly confirmed Lyautey's feeling that nothing further could be effected in his Ministry. From the outbreak of war he had insisted on a single command of the Allied armies; now, after almost three years, he saw that command in the hands of an assemblage of civilians and soldiers, a more impotent collection even than a national parliament, because it was powerless to impose its will on any of its members.

In particular he could not reach an understanding with Lloyd George regarding the powers which ought properly to be allotted to General Sarrail, who commanded the Salonika expedition. Before the war Lyautey had been on very bad terms with Sarrail, but as Minister of War he had always given him loyal support. The Conference summoned Sarrail to Rome, and there Lyautey went straight up to him, took his hand, and said: "You can count on me. . . . Here is my principal military secretary. Tell him what you need. . . . I shall do my best." Sarrail's face lit up; he thanked Lyautey cordially and always retained a sense of gratitude towards him for this attitude. "General Lyautey," he noted later in his memoirs, "was a leader, and even a comrade, to me." Sarrail shared

Lyautey's bad opinion of this Conference: "the official communiqués say that there is complete agreement between the Allies. There is no agreement; the decisions taken are non-existent. At bottom, words and nothing but words."

Sarrail was particularly anxious to have more extensive powers to protect himself against the Greek royalists. But the Conference insisted that in the event of the Greek Government not carrying out conditions accepted by it, General Sarrail, before assuming the initiative in any action, should first obtain the approval of the Governments of Britain, France, Italy and Russia. In Lyautey's judgment such restrictions in the course of a campaign would imperil the Salonika forces. He was told in reply that the approval of the Four Powers could be obtained within forty-eight hours. But he was beginning to know the habits of the Four Powers. "It is very possible," he said, "that General Sarrail might have to take an immediate initiative which forty-eight hours would suffice to make impracticable. Besides, this would *certainly not* be given within forty-eight hours. It is enough to remember what discussions have been raised in the past by the most minor measures concerning this army to be convinced that there will ensue a long interchange of correspondence, negotiation and discussion."

In the train on the way back from Rome, on January 9th, 1917, he told his officers: "Really, I don't know what I am doing there any longer." He summoned Wladimir d'Ormesson and dictated to him a note addressed to the President of the Republic and the Prime Minister, a note which he believed would necessitate either his resignation or a total reform of the conduct of the war:

I. In the Rome Conference I have been confronted by the following situation:

In the twenty-eighth month of the war there is a total absence of agreement between the Allies, and almost no possibility of attaining it in general conception or in details, each party advocating unity of action and unity of front, but actually lodging itself obstinately on its own front and claiming in practice autonomy in command. . . .

This state of affairs is particularly flagrant in the Army of the Orient, which is placed in a critical situation and confronted by imminent dangers, and which our Allies formally decline to help, leaving to us the total responsibility.

The reservations which I have been obliged to make, in the clearest and strongest terms, regarding the decision taken by this Conference, contrary to military necessities of the most glaring obviousness, have fallen into the void; and I have had formally to declare that I could not accept any responsibility for the position in which the Commander-in-Chief of the Army of the Orient was being placed, in that he was, on the one hand, being made responsible for the total maintenance of his present front, and, on the other hand, being refused the means of doing so. He has been placed between the horns of a dilemma. The situation must be boldly and directly faced.

II. Further, this Conference has made it clear that any idea of an efficacious inter-Allied organ of action must be put aside, as it is not admitted by anyone, except in the form of Conferences, which have no outcome and merely underline the disagreements, and are a negation of the intensive, immediate and unified direction demanded by such a war. Such a directing force exists amongst our opponents, and therefore a situation of this kind, if it be irremediable, can only lead to defeat.

I have further observed that the decisions made at the Conference were inspired exclusively by political considerations, which dominated military considerations, whereas in time of war the latter ought to be preponderant. Whenever a question has arisen of a decision imposed by the most obvious necessities of war, it has been set aside for purely political reasons.

III. Further, I observe that this practical, effective, immediate directing force does not exist in France any more than elsewhere, and that the organizations at which we have stopped short are its very negation.

The Committee of War, as at present constituted and working, neither represents nor allows of a *higher command of war*.

It is a sequence of conversations and comments upon the situation, admitting neither of definite solutions nor immediate decisions, to be transformed without delay into *orders,* stamping action instantaneously upon every front. Every day it means a waste of valuable time, when not one minute ought to be wasted. It is based upon a continual confusion between political direction and command, in which it constantly intervenes.

This superstructure of national or international Conferences and Committees will never constitute an organ of action. It is materially impossible for such a conception to result in co-ordination of efforts, in an effective result, or in success.

To ask a people who have been unstintedly pouring out their blood for twenty-eight months to continue their self-sacrifice in the void, with neither course nor compass nor pilot, is simply criminal.

Seeing these situations clearly, as I do, the moment may well be near when my conscience will no longer allow me to share in the responsibility.

A civilian War Minister is possibly entitled not to have so clear an awareness of the vices in such a conduct of the war, and he can afterwards return to civilian life without dishonour. A general who has held a post of the highest command, and whose profession teaches him the necessities of command in war conditions, cannot do so. If he does not see the situation, he is incompetent; and if, seeing it, he submits to it one day beyond the day when he realizes that he can do nothing to remedy it, he is criminal.

It was Lyautey's intention to hand this letter on his arrival to M. Poincaré and to M. Briand. But the Prime Minister was met on the platform of the Gare de Lyon by several members of the Cabinet. They brought bad tidings, both from the front and from home. And once again Lyautey felt scruples about slipping out and letting resignation on his part aggravate the difficulties of his colleagues' task. He told Wladimir d'Ormesson to keep that draft letter, and only sent in a technical despatch, drawn up in Rome, in which he formulated his reservations on the situation forced upon the Army of the Orient.

* * * * *

It was not until after the Rome Conference that Lyautey was able at last to obtain the communication of the "Nivelle Plan," of which so many politicians spoke as if it were the first original conception of the war. After long parleys, General Nivelle sent Colonel Renouard, the head of the Third Bureau, to explain it to him. Lyautey knew him well; Renouard had served under him in the southern Oran. It was to Captain Georges Renouard that he had dictated the famous despatch of Tas-el-Aïn. He valued him and held him in high affection. He received him hopefully. At last a competent and intelligent man was going to explain this mysterious plan to him. To his great surprise the General found himself confronted by a man bolted and barred. Unfolding his maps and plans, Colonel Renouard demonstrated the operations in the manner of a disciplined and impersonal officer. Lyautey listened with dumbfounded anxiety. They had always been telling him of a new army, miraculously formed by Nivelle to exploit the success, but he now learned that the component parts of this army were to be drawn, during the actual fighting, from the attacking troops themselves. "But surely, Renouard," he exclaimed, "this is a plan for the Grand Duchess of Gerolstein!" Impassively, almost warningly, Colonel Renouard resumed his exposition. General Nivelle believed that Laon would be reached at the first jump. Lyautey interrupted him: "Renouard, you've got to answer me. I'm not Minister of War now, and you're not Colonel Renouard. We're two Frenchmen, face to face, and it is a question of the safety of France. . . . Now what do you really think yourself about this plan you've brought me?"

"General," said Colonel Renouard, still impassive, "I do not think I am obliged to give you my views. I am here as General Nivelle's subordinate and messenger; I am not entitled to criticize my superior officer."

Lyautey took him by the shoulders and shook him.

"Come, come, my dear Georges," he said, deeply moved. "Look me in the eyes. Just fancy that you're once again my confidential officer at Aïn-Sefra, and tell me the truth. . . . What do you think of it?"

And then, for an instant, the mask dropped from the Colonel's face. Tears came into his eyes.

"General," he said, "I think as you do. . . . It is mad."

Pierrefeu tells how Renouard, before the offensive, salved his conscience by addressing a letter to the Commander-in-Chief. No reply was given.

But Renouard was only an executive officer; Lyautey was outwardly the chief. Could he, as Minister of War, lend his nominal authority to the pursuance of a plan which he condemned? He did not think so. He tried to oppose it. He even had thoughts of replacing Nivelle, and M. Pain-levé, who succeeded him, found written traces of this intention.[1] When Lyautey definitely saw that

---

[1] Painlevé, quoted by Palat, 146.

he would not have satisfaction on this point, his decision was made: either he would obtain wider powers by appealing to public opinion, or else he would resign his portfolio on the first opportunity that would let him do so without compromising the conduct of the war in the eyes of enemy informers.

A motion of interpellation on the air services had been fixed for March 14th. It had been agreed in the Council that the Government would not allow the Chamber to meet for this occasion in Secret Committee. Lyautey had to leave for London, where a new inter-Allied Conference was about to be held. Before leaving, he wrote the speech by which he desired to inform the Chamber, firstly why certain military secrets could not be revealed to a numerous assemblage, but principally, how he himself conceived the work in the light of action. It was a bold text. Worn out by his impotence and by quarrels in the face of the enemy, he wished to apply to Parliament the method which he had so often used successfully in Morocco—frank intercourse, an "opening of the floodgates" in which men tell each other hard truths, but from which, if real men have faced each other, they emerge relieved and ready to act.

What he wished to say to the deputies, as he had once said to the colonists at Casablanca, was this:

I am talking to you face to face, heart to heart; and I should like you to let me say aloud what most of you have come to tell me singly and between ourselves—namely, that we must all of us, without delay, change our methods of working.

Let us say it frankly, on the eve of supreme efforts—this people, the man fighting at the front with such self-sacrifice and confidence, as well as the man who exerts his efforts at home to maintain life and production, this people, I say, is tired of words and thirsting for decisions, for command, for authority.

Those decisions, that authority, it is your task as rulers to assume and to exercise. We can do so only in security of mind, quietude of spirit, and the free disposal of our time, that time which is so precious to us, not one particle of which ought to be lost.

The Government of this country at war are the managers of a factory in full production; I conceived them, I still conceive them, as bending over their maps—I do not say only the map of the front, but the map of the whole country, its agricultural map, its industrial map, its railway map—absorbed solely by the great business, the business of winning, of concentrating every effort towards that single goal, of co-ordinating every means of action, as much to maintain the life of the country as to ensure the forward line its maximum power.

But let me tell you frankly that I see them, on

the contrary, endlessly harassed, with difficulty
snatching an hour here and an hour there for really
effective work, compelled to fulfil the heaviest task
that has ever been laid upon the shoulders of men
whilst endlessly disturbed in a heavy and depressing
atmosphere of inquisition and suspicion.

I see them in the plight of men perpetually accused. And it is under such conditions that the
gravest resolves have to be taken, that decisions
affecting the nation's fate have to be weighed, that
the heaviest responsibilities regarding conscience
and country have to be taken up.

Speaking not long since of a general holding a
high command, I said: "If people are not content
with him, if they do not trust him, let them change
him. But if he is to be left in his post, then let him
be given trust and confidence; let this sniping at
his legs be stopped; let him be assured of security
of mind and serenity, the prime conditions for exer-
cising command."

And I say the same thing as concerning ourselves. If you have not confidence in us, or in myself, then change us. It is quite easy. A scrap of
paper in a ballot-box is enough. But if you keep
us in the places we hold, have the goodness to give
us your trust, and leave us to work for France, and
for you.

It was a fine appeal. It was heartfelt. It might
possibly have been listened to. But the stage and
the moment were unfavourable. Lyautey believed
that confusion and the country's misfortunes had
inspired Parliament with the desire for a leader.

The contrary was the truth: the deputies, who in their respect for General Headquarters at the beginning of the war had then left it an almost absolute authority, were now calling up memories of the representatives attached to the armies of the Convention, and were coming to believe, after all these setbacks, that parliamentary control ought to be strengthened. Lyautey's arrival in France had set ill-wishers talking of Bonaparte's return from Egypt. There were many who pretended to fear the Minister in order to avoid supporting him. He desired, by an impassioned speech, to create a spiritual atmosphere; he encountered mere politics.

He returned from London on the very morning of the interpellation. Admiral Lacaze, who was in London with him, was very sorry to see him go. During this Conference Lyautey had for the first time obtained a real ascendancy over his English colleagues, and had brought them a good way along the path towards a single command, which he had so long regarded as the primary condition of victory. The debate on aviation could have been postponed. But Lyautey expected great things from this speech and from the salutary emotion which he believed it could evoke. He insisted, asked for a destroyer, and left. On reaching Paris at nine o'clock in the morning he learned that in his ab-

sence, and contrary to the assurances given him, the
Government had decided to accept the session in
Secret Committee. This annoyed him, for he
counted strongly on his speech, as an appeal to
public opinion, being made known to the country.
He resolved not to speak during the secret session.
The morning was taken up with a long meeting of
the Council of Ministers. Then, during the debates
in the Chamber, whilst the replies to the interpella-
tions were given by officers appointed as Government spokesmen, Lyautey remained silent on his
bench, with folded arms. In vain did Briand,
Barrès, and even Deschanel, President of the
Chamber, come over to ask him to say a few words.
He took no part in the debates. From time to time
he slashed hurriedly with a blue pencil at the notes
he had prepared. When the public session was resumed he entered the tribune, to the deputies' great
surprise.

Gentlemen [he said], I confess that I first
thought it would be preferable that this debate
should not take place. It did not really seem to
me to be opportune, at the moment when I had just
set up an organization which accords, in principle
at least, with most of your desiderata. I felt that
it would be best to let it take proper roots and bear
its fruits. I believed, and I still believe, that such
debates hold many hidden reefs. I have accepted

this debate because I felt a deep repugnance in apparently shunning it, and because I felt no less strongly that essential things might well be spoken which we should be the first to profit by, and from which I shall obtain greater strength for the reforms which I must still accomplish. But you will allow me to refrain from following you on technical ground, as my officers have had to do, because even in Secret Committee, I consider, in full responsibility, that the National Defence is exposed to risks——"

At this point he was interrupted by protest.

Several members of the Left: "What does that mean?"

Pres. Deschanel: "The words of the Minister of War. . . . Kindly allow me, gentlemen, to say a word. . . ."

M. Raffin-Dugens: "You have only to suppress Parliament!"

Pres. Deschanel: "The words of the Minister of War can only be, I imagine, the justification of the Secret Committee. . . ."

M. Raffin-Dugens: "They go on denying parliamentary action, which has saved this country. . . . It is Parliament that has saved the country!"

M. Jugy: "The Minister's words are nothing less than a provocation."

The din in the amphitheatre was incredible. From the left there was a demand for the speaker

to be called to order. On the right M. Jules Dela-
haye was shouting: "The Germans are at Noyon!"
On the extreme left M. Raffin-Dugens was roaring:
"Parliament cannot be insulted!" Lyautey was
amazed. He could not understand this outcome of
a speech which he had hoped would rally all parties
round him.

The President: "I beg you, gentlemen, in the
name of France. . . . I implore you, gentlemen,
in the name of those who are fighting. . . . I beg
you, in the name of those who are pouring out their
blood at this moment, to keep silence. . . ."

Whereupon a certain number of deputies rose
and cried: "Long live the Republic!"—"Yes, long
live the Republic!" answered Deschanel, and suspended the session.

Lyautey came down from the tribune. In the
private room reserved for ministers he was surrounded by his friends and colleagues. "You must
get up and speak again, General. . . . You must
explain. . . ." Etienne, Barrès and Admiral Bien-
aimé were insistent that he should address the
Chamber again. "I beg you," he said, "not to be
insistent. . . . I have the strongest reasons for
leaving the Ministry. . . . I cannot tell you what
they are, but leave me." But he had been painfully
surprised to find that a speech which he regarded

as one of common sense should have been capable
of producing such results. "I can't understand a
thing about it," he said to Guillaume de Tarde on
returning to the Ministry. "You were quite right,
I have never understood anything of this race. . . .
I'd hardly begun when they started shouting—I
don't even know why. . . ."

Lyautey resigned that same evening, and returned to his own house in the Rue Bonaparte. His
departure moved public opinion deeply; it was the
last straw to an already enfeebled Cabinet. Two
days later the Briand Ministry followed him into
retirement.

M. Ribot, the new Prime Minister, came to call
on Lyautey and asked him rather anxiously: "And
what are your plans now, General?"—"I am quite
knocked up," said Lyautey. "I am suffering from
my liver. I should like to take a cure at Vichy, if
I can. . . . After that, I shall ask for a division at
the front."—"Just so," said M. Ribot. "Go to
Vichy as soon as possible. But afterwards, will you
not resume your government in Morocco?"

Lyautey left for Vichy. There he learned of the
failure of the Nivelle offensive. His successor, M.
Painlevé, had tried, like himself, to prevent it. It
was shattered, as he had foreseen, on the German
defensive systems. So he had been right in his

dread of that gambler's venture, a bloody and useless throw of the dice. Shortly afterwards he returned to Paris to settle some questions of finance and effectives regarding Morocco. He left on May 20th. At Madrid he conferred with the King of Spain and Gouraud. On May 29th he was at Casablanca. He was restored to his kingdom.

XV

NOVEMBER 11th, 1918. The news of the armistice came in the morning, by wireless. Forwarded to the regional commander, it spread that day into the farthest corners of Morocco. Foot-travellers, horsemen, camel-drivers bore it amongst the unsubjected tribes. On the following day, in the streets of Casablanca, Lyautey mingled with the crowds to share in the popular rejoicings.[1]

So, in spite of the most terrible of storms, he had brought into harbour the vessel which had been entrusted to him six years before in an almost hopeless condition. True, the landfall which the man of action believes he is making is an ever-receding mirage. Rebel centres survived; but compared with the vast extent of Morocco their importance was minute. A certain number of colonists, annoyed by monetary fluctuations, were grumbling; but statistics gave irrefutable proof of the country's prosperity. Morocco's trade in 1912 amounted to 177 million francs; in 1919 to 707 million. Merchandise passing through Casablanca in 1911 totalled 130,000 tons; in 1919, 800,000 tons. All

---

[1] Britsch, 225.

over the country the projects of expansion approved on paper by Lyautey at the beginning of the war were becoming real towns. The master-builder saw his creation growing and growing.

It was his own. And never had a work borne closer likeness to its author. In the midst of a world delivered by human folly to misery and destruction, Morocco offered the foreign visitor a miraculous oasis of order and beauty. In all that it contained one could see emerging the action of a unique spirit; and just as in Lyautey's mind the love of action was blended with romantic dreaming, so in this new Morocco the modern towns, humming with machinery, were growing up side by side with native palaces without damage to their peaceful luxury, their sensuous delight, their languor.

In the political sphere Lyautey had succeeded in keeping intact the Protectorate régime. There were many who wished him to profit by victory and the temper of France's allies to give Morocco a direct administration modelled on that of France. That was exactly what he did not wish.

I assure you [Lyautey wrote] that nothing could have less resemblance to the arrondissement of Guingamp or Trévoux than Fez or Marrakesh. . . . The Protectorate régime is not a question of opinion, personal, local, or metropolitan. It is a fact determined by treaties. It is guaranteed by inter-

national agreements which it is not within our
power, nor within that of the French Government,
to modify.

In order to establish permanent contact with
public opinion, notwithstanding the maintenance of
the Protectorate, he had set up a Council which
brought together the representatives of the colonists. It was not a question of an assembly in
parliamentary form, but of a real "administrative
board of the Morocco firm." This Government
Council, which sat every two months, comprised the
chief officials of the administration and the presi-
dents of the Chambers of Commerce and of Agriculture. For seven years it was the essential factor
in administrative activity, and its meetings, nearly
always attended by Lyautey, were like the sittings
of Napoleon I's State Council, alike in the fruitfulness of their work and the directness and simplicity
of their discussions.

The varied range of Lyautey's creations, and the
interest he was capable of taking in any new tech-
nique, often surprised his fellow-workers. Sometimes his boldness startled the specialists. When he
had approved the plans of the harbour for Casablanca, there were many protests. Never, it was
said, would the needs of a country like Morocco
justify the building of a port on so large a scale.

But in 1922 deposits of phosphate were discovered which in quantity and ease of working surpassed those in any part of the world. A small factory was built first at Bou-Jniba, and then, certain that a source of wealth for Morocco had been found, Lyautey set up a Shereefian Phosphates Office, and authorized the construction of model works at Kouriga. In 1925 Kouriga was astonishing American visitors, who held the methods to be superior to those used in their own mines. In 1929 the deposits were yielding two million tons, and the harbour of Casablanca looked as if it might be too small.

Meanwhile, at Rabat as at Fez, the Moors kept their narrow lanes, their blind-fronted houses, their terraces screened from prying eyes. In the *souks* of Marrakesh the throng of negroes, Arabs and Berbers, the neat-footed and submissive little donkeys, the calm horsemen crying *"Balek!"* to the foot-passengers, all remained the image of what they had been five or six centuries before, and on the square of Djem-el-Fna the same story-tellers told the same stories to the same squatting listeners.

* * * * *

In 1920 Lyautey delivered his address on being received as a member of the French Academy, to which he had been elected in 1913. In 1921 he was made a Marshal of France. In the following year M. Millerand, President of the Republic, came to Morocco. During that journey Lyautey secured the principle of an annual conference of the Governors and Resident-Generals of French Northern Africa for common consultation on all economic questions. The first of these conferences took place in 1923 at Algiers, and in the car which was taking him there the Marshal had an attack of liver trouble of such severity that he had to halt, first at Taza and then at Fez. There, in the beautiful palace of Bou-Jeloud, with its courtyards paved with warm tiles and scented with orange-trees, he was examined by the doctors. They considered an operation necessary. "But it will be a dangerous operation," they said. "If the Marshal could recover sufficiently to be taken to Paris, it would be much better. . . . If operation becomes inevitable, we shall operate. . . ."

It was a blazing hot spring in Fez. Lyautey suffered atrociously; he seemed to be dying. The rumour of his illness had spread amongst the natives in the town. One day when Madame Lyautey was receiving some English visitors, she saw a throng of Moors entering the courtyard of Bou-Jeloud. Headed by the Ulemas, the Imans, with

their banners, they ranged themselves under the
windows of the sickroom and recited the Ia-el-
Attif, the prayer which is spoken only when a great
peril hangs over Islam.

Madame Lyautey went to tell the Marshal what
was happening, and he allowed the Iman of Mulai-
Idriss to be brought beside his bed. He had
brought with him a flask of water from Mulai-Idriss
and two candles, which he placed beside the
Marshal's bed. "We know that you will recover,"
he said to Lyautey, "because the people of Morocco
have asked us to take two candles for you at the
sarcophagus of Mulai-Idriss." Lyautey thanked
him, hardly able to speak. Next day his condition
was a little better, and when the inhabitants of Fez
heard this they attributed the miracle to the candles
of Mulai-Idriss. His progress was maintained,
and after some days the Marshal was allowed to go
out for a drive. The Imans requested that his first
visit should be to the mosque of Mulai-Idriss. "No,
no," said Lyautey; "I shall go first to my church."
The Moslems approved. When he came out a
great crowd escorted his carriage, and as it passed
before the mosque the Imans invited Lyautey to
enter. "Be careful," he said to them. "I have always forbidden Europeans to enter your mosques;
do not make me break the rule I have established

myself. . . . In time you would be led to do for others what you have done for me. . . . You would be sorry for it. . . ." Then, as they insisted, he consented just to set foot inside the mosque.

At last it was possible to have him taken to France and operated on by Dr. Gosset. The operation was successful, but Lyautey felt greatly enfeebled and retained a wound in his side which had to be dressed daily. He saw M. Millerand, and said to him: "I must be replaced. . . . You can see the state I am in. If I go back to Morocco, it will be the end of me."—"Well," said Millerand, "leave your bones in Morocco—that would be the right thing." Lyautey went back again. The country had been administered in his absence by M. Urbain Blanc, his delegate, with whom he had always lived in perfect agreement, a delightful specimen of the cultured high official, brimming with poetry, humour and common sense. That year the North African Conference was held at Rabat, and included the Marshal, M. Steeg, Governor of Algeria, and M. Saint, Governor of Tunis.

In 1924 Lyautey had to come to Paris for a second operation. He was there during the May elections of that year, which left his friends stripped of power, and he saw with anguished feelings the departure of Millerand, who had made him Resident-General in 1912, and had always supported him. Henceforward he had an increasing number of reasons for leaving Morocco. Not only did his health remain frail, but despite his friendly personal relations with Herriot he no longer felt himself in harmony with the men who were going to hold power. He remarked to M. Saint, who had come to see him off at the Gare de Lyon: "I am only returning to Rabat to pack my trunks." And when M. Saint protested, he said: "No, no. . . . These elections. . . . My health. . . . It's the end of things. . . . In any case, no protests: I shall name you to Herriot as my successor."

He arrived in Morocco on June 18th, 1924, with the intention of staying there only a few days. "I've come," he said once again, to his fellow-workers at Casablanca. "But it is only to pack up." At Rabat he was informed of disquieting changes in the military situation. In the borderland district between the French and Spanish zones, to the north of Fez, Lyautey had never made any move that was not extremely cautious. He insisted that wherever France established a post it should be matched by a correspondingly placed post on the Spanish side. But after the Anoual disaster General Primo de Rivera had suddenly abolished these Spanish posts and withdrawn his troops on to the coast-line. This withdrawal left the French posts in the air, confronting the rebel Berbers of the Riff, a warlike population excited by victory. It was a dangerous state of affairs. Lyautey felt anxious, and prepared a telegram for the information of the Government. When his Chief-of-Staff read this message, he nodded: "Yes, Marshal. This means that you will not be leaving." And he was right. Once again the Government held that Lyautey's presence was indispensable and asked him to remain. Once again Lyautey yielded; and for a few months longer his enthusiasm animated the efforts of those for whom he still remained "the Chief."

*   *   *   *   *

April 1925. Casablanca. The Marshal had invited a few writers and engineers for the inauguration of the Casablanca-Rabat broad-gauge railway, and he came in person to meet his guests on the quay.

"Would you like to come back with me on foot? I should enjoy showing you the town."

"Certainly, Marshal."

"Well, then . . ."

A wide sweep of his cane takes in the vast white quarter, the cubes of the rough-cast houses, smothered by the pink waves of geraniums, the light-blue pergolas, the large violet flowers of the bougainvilleas climbing up towards the Arab terraces.

"All that was encampments," said the Marshal. "And here"—(he jumped with a bound on to the plinth of a monument)—"here I wanted to make something like the Palais-Royal. You see it? A flowery square, framed within long symmetrical buildings. . . . It's very fine, the Palais-Royal. . . . But when I was ill, very ill, and away for two years, they spoilt the whole thing. . . . I got angry, terribly angry. . . . But what's the good? It was done. . . . I'm a man who always accepts the irreparable. . . . I'll find a way out. We'll get the symmetry of the square again. . . . Over there, we shall have the town hall. . . . And over here . . ."

The cane rose slowly, like a magic wand. In that hot, quivering air it seemed as if we could see vague shapes rising up. Dryly, abruptly, he broke the spell.

"On we go!"

He jumped down from the base of the monument, which is high. The younger men followed him. The less active section of the escort cautiously made for the steps. We raced across the barracks of the 1st Regiment of Zouaves. . . . The Malakoff flag. . . . The Canrobert medal. . . . We reached the motor-cars again. The chauffeur started off.

"Easy, good heavens! Go slow! Now look at this street; it's the axis of my town. It will run straight to the sea. I want passengers to land right in the middle of things. . . . These ramparts? I'm demolishing those. . . . They're not beautiful. . . . I am keeping this little marabout; it is sacred. . . . They say to me: 'You have low houses on one side and tall houses on the other. . . .' I reply: 'Exactly! On the left is the façade of the native town —an Arab *fondouk*. And on the right, the façade of the European town, great buildings in the French style. . . . It's just right.' And then to the chauffeur: "On you go."

He arranged to meet us on the breakwater. We were punctual, but in the distance we saw the tall, slim, blue silhouette surrounded by the engineer's jackets.

"Come along. . . . Heavens! How slowly you walk! Time is everything, in action. . . . At last. . . . Are you ready? Well, then . . . M. Delandre, the harbour engineer, will explain the state of the works to you. . . . Now, Delandre, be sure to tell us everything in logical order. . . ."

M. Delandre explained very well. He told us how the harbour of Casablanca was closed by a bar, and the breakwater had therefore to be pushed far enough to break the bar; he explained the equipment to be provided for the export of phosphates, how Casablanca is now one of the greatest of French ports, and how it can be expanded if the development of the country calls for it.

"Good. . . . Now I'll explain the philosophy of the matter myself. . . . When I began this harbour every one said: 'Lyautey sees everything too big. He's mad. . . .' But it made no difference to me. I thought to myself: 'This country is a big country. . . . Needs will turn up: I must be ready! Good. . . . You know that at Kouriga, near here, they have discovered phosphate deposits that are the best in the world. This year we shall produce 600,000 tons; next year we'll touch the million. . . . Well, these phosphates alone would justify the scale of the harbour. . . . There. . . . But you'll ask me: 'What if there hadn't been phosphates? . . .' Well, my answer is that there are always phosphates. . . . When you do something you must have confidence in what you are doing. . . . Talking about that, Delandre, where is the factory of the super-phosphates?"

"It started work this morning, Marshal."

"Heavens! And I haven't seen it. . . . Let's go there at once."

The direct road was strewn with huge ashlars and packing cases; the car bumped over rails; the springs screamed; the chauffeur hesitated and turned.

"Go on, go on! Get along. . . ."

An Arab labourer stopped his barrow, saluted the familiar silhouette, and with a smile of affectionate amusement called to the occupants of the next car, as they too were bumping and grimacing:

"The General is great master!"

An astonished manager emerged from the superphosphates factory, a creation of cylinders and cones.

"Good day! What is your name?"

"My name is Césard, Marshal."

"Oh yes, of course. . . . Césard. . . . Heavens, but I knew your parents in Nancy when I was a child. Good day, Césard. . . . Now you are going to explain your factory, my friend. And mind, in logical order. . . . In what form do you receive your phosphates? . . . Good! Where do they arrive? Let's go there."

Small iron staircases. Galleries along the crushing-machines. Preparation of sulphuric acid. More iron staircases. Fine dust of phosphates. Long cement corridor. Galleries. At racing speed. . . .

LYAUTEY

At Rabat, a visit to the Sultan. A negro guard dressed in red, playing Poulenc and Stravinsky on melancholy flutes and intoxicating drums; Arabian Nights slaves, sinking to the ground along the white staircases; viziers in a frieze along the walls, as in some palace of Susa.

"Wait," said the Chief on coming out. "I am going to show you my offices."

Round us stretched the white, perfect town amidst the flowers. The traditions of Moslem art had been judiciously preserved, adapted to the new materials. Disciplined ornament kept its modest place, subservient to line. Sudden halt. Flourish of cane.

"Well, here we are. . . . I shall explain the philosophy of the thing. . . . The whole grouping of the buildings forms a fan. . . . In the fan's centre are the head offices. Behind them, in the wider hinterland, the departments are ranged in a logical order. . . . You understand? Here, for example, are Public Works; behind that, Bridges and Roadways, and Mines. . . . Behind Agriculture are the Forests. . . . Here is the Finance site. . . . The building is not up yet, but it will fit into its logical place. . . .

"And what is this kiosk, Marshal?"

"That's for the sale of maps to the public. In

France the State departments make admirable maps, and the public are supplied by private enterprise. . . . Why should that be? Because anyone who wants to buy the State maps must clamber up five flights of stairs in a Ministry, and ask for them from a sergeant who treats you like an intruder. . . . I don't want any of that sort of thing. A commercial department ought to be organized like a commercial house. . . . I have salesmen whose job it is to make my maps sell, and who get a percentage on the takings. . . . Here is the civilian and military Health Department. . . . Both together. . . . I've always said there are not two things, civil medicine and military medicine. There is just medicine. One point, that's all."

And we entered the Forests building, bewitched by the delicate scent of cedarwood.

In the evening, dinner at the New Residency. Cavalrymen in red cloaks lined the staircase, two friezes of gleaming, barbaric, alert figures. The Marshal had just been presiding at a Council. He would resume it at ten o'clock. During the meal he wanted relaxation. He talked to us of his young days, and of the masters who moulded him: "I shall always remember the day when I discovered Descartes. It was at the lycée in Dijon, and I was starting in the philosophy class. That morning we

had been given the *Discourse on Method* in a little
school edition. I kept it for years. . . . Since the
war I haven't been able to find it again, to my endless regret. . . . I was very fond of that little
Descartes of mine. . . . Well, I started reading
this new book in bed that night. . . . And, how
dazzled I was! The clearness, the order. . . . Admirable! The first part, because the rest . . ."

I murmured to my neighbour:

"I'm glad the Proconsul mourns his school-book
Descartes. . . . That *'alors, voilà . . .'* of his represents the clean slate, the method of philosophical
doubt which is the starting-point of a reconstruction. . . . And when he says 'tell us in the logical
order,' he is saying 'to conduct one's thoughts in
due order, proceeding from the simple to the complex. . . .' "

"Did you know Charles Guérin, the poet?" said
the Marshal. . . .

*　　*　　*　　*　　*

Some travellers wondered whether this trium-
phant achievement, so marvellous in their eyes,
seemed so in those of the natives. They questioned
colonists and officers. "It is complicated," they
were told. "When they see a thing for the first
time they are astounded, but their astonishment

does not last. The first aeroplane was a source of wonder, and then, when it landed and they could examine it, they just said: 'There's no harm in that; it has a machine.'—'Yes, of course. But all the same, it is we, Christians, who invented it.'—'It was the will of Allah that you should invent it. If he had willed that it should be we . . .' "

"Once they've understood the possible uses of something they immediately adopt it. On the roads you will find aged Arabs and Berber women unconcernedly turning from their little asses to the motor omnibus. The Kaid of Mulai-Idriss, a sacred village almost forbidden to Infidels, has the telephone, and uses it. The railways have native engineers, who drive their engine and understand it. In the drying room of the Kouriga factories the furnaces are controlled by Arabs who watch their gauges. . . ."

"Yes, but are they any happier? Do they regret the days before we came here?"

"Possibly. But they bear us no grudge for being their conquerors. The Moslem's mental outlook is not that of a European. . . . 'Until such time as Allah judges between us I shall fight you bravely,' they think; 'but if you are the victor, it is because Allah has so willed it, and I can serve you without disgrace.' Many of these chiefs who have rallied to France have done so in all sincerity. . . . As for the humble folk, and the sedentary people especially, they are certainly happier than in the old days. Not because they are provided with railways and roads and motor-cars, but because they are less the victims of oppression and robbery. . . . Naturally, the warrior tribes have their regrets.

"One day the Marshal paid a call upon a friendly and powerful Kaid, who spoke enthusiastically of the new order and of the tranquillity that reigned everywhere in the occupied zones. 'Nowadays,' said the Kaid, 'the tribes can till their land without fear of the raiders, the *razzia;* nowadays the herds, the camels, the horses can all live in safety.' When the Marshal took his leave he was accompanied to the gates by his host, escorted by slave lantern-bearers. It was a lovely moonless night; the stars diffused a vague light. On the threshold the Kaid stood looking for a moment over the shadowy plain. With a sigh of regret he spoke. 'All the same,' he said 'if you weren't there, what a fine night for horse-stealing!' "

*   *   *   *   *

Fez. April 25th, 1925. For all the mysterious beauty of the town, for all the orange-trees in the courtyards of the welcoming palaces, and for all the warmth of the welcome, the visitors could detect uneasiness in the air. General de Chambrun took them on endless expeditions through the *souks,* where the brass, the leather and the cloth gleamed in the narrow sunless streets; in the twilight they were taken up the hills to watch the darkness falling over the white terraces, and the shadows pass singing along them. But at night, in the General's quarters, the visitors saw a group forming at the other end of the room, looking anxiously in their direction. They caught a few words: "Will that post hold . . . ? If the Tsouls break out . . ." At dinner-time General Heusch, the Marshal's Chief-of-Staff, arrived in Fez. Throughout the meal he was extremely cheerful; he told anecdotes, and of how he passed his *baccalauréat* in spite of his complete ignorance of the Treaty of Cateau-Cambrésis. But after dinner he was closeted with General de Chambrun. The visitors took their leave, and went off towards their cedarwood bedrooms through the streets with their passing patrols. They were roused at three in the morning.

"The General requests you to leave at once. The car is waiting for you at the door."

"But why? What is wrong?"

"Nothing serious," said the soldier, "but the General would prefer you to travel by night. He has had rifles put in the car."

At daybreak the car was driving along beneath the ridges of the Tsouls. On either hand, amidst the high white sandhills, handsome Arabs were galloping with their long rifles slung on their backs. The travellers admiring them were far from suspecting that they were tribesmen, loyal until yesterday, setting off for the Holy War, and that the evening before, whilst General Heusch spoke so gaily about Cateau-Cambrésis, he was wondering whether Fez was not lost.

XVI

AND what had happened in this apparently calm and contented country? How could the security of Morocco be endangered, after thirteen years of peace and prosperity, by the rising of a few tribes, when that security had been kept safe in 1912 and 1914 in circumstances which seemed far graver? To answer these questions it is perhaps necessary to recall certain features of the political formation of the country.

Firstly: Before the French occupation, Morocco had never been a homogeneous and stable state. The most powerful Sultans had always encountered the resistance of independent tribes who did not pay tribute and would not allow the passage of Maghzen officials over their territory. Lyautey had overcome most of these rebels, one after the other, and had extended the safety-zone far beyond its historic limits. When he left for his operation in 1924 the pacification of "useful" Morocco was very nearly complete. The sole remaining rebels were the tribes of the Spanish frontier, to the north of Fez, a few tribes in the mountains south of Marrakesh, and, to the east, the tribes of the

Taza region within the narrow compass of an islet of hill country.

Secondly: This pacification of Morocco had been achieved as much by persuasion and moral conquest as by force. The tribes had not been disarmed; they had retained their chiefs and their autonomous outlook. It was a remarkable success for the policy of penetration. But was it not within the bounds of possibility that these large units might be brought, by unforeseeable circumstances, to turn against the French, to rise in the mass as they had submitted in the mass? If such a movement ran through the neighbouring tribes (and in Islam contagion is speedy), might not a tidal wave carry off the admirable, but as yet unsubstantial, structure? Lyautey had long feared that wave. One after another, agitators like El Hiba or Abdul Malek had foundered. Their failures were reassuring. But hitherto they had all been badly equipped and badly advised. What would happen if a really "modern" Moslem should become the core of crystallization for a movement hostile to France?

Thirdly: Just such a leader, who could not have gathered strength and arms in French Morocco without encountering immediate French opposition, had appeared in the Riff, that mountainous, chaotic and poverty-stricken province bordering the

Spanish zone. It was inhabited by about a dozen Berber tribes who, under the former Sultans, had always lived in a state of semi-independence, recognizing the sway of the Maghzen only when it had the strength to impose its authority. About 1905 the Kaid of one of these tribes, the Beni Uryaghel, had entered into negotiations with certain German industrialists, the Mannesmanns, and in 1913 had allowed them to survey the numerous rich mineral deposits lying within the Riff. The Mannesmanns, men of bold temper who dreamed of combining political with economic action, had made an offer to the Spaniards to take a lease for the exploitation of their zone and carrying out a policy of pacification and organization therein.[1] The Spaniards had refused.

Negotiations were still in progress when the European war broke out. This put an end to them. But the Kaid of the Beni Uryaghel, by long contact with the German industrialists, had acquired a certain knowledge of Europeans, a liking for their methods, and a little money. His son, Abdul Krim, had been educated at the Moslem university of Fez, and had then entered the service of the Christians. The Spanish command at first gave a cordial welcome to this intelligent and cultivated young man,

[1] Ladreit de Lacharrière, *Revue Hebdomadaire*, August, 1925.

who in their eyes was "not only a sort of link with the native population, but also a kind of hostage." Abdul Krim became the Kaid of Melilla, where he gathered information about world politics and the rivalries of the Christians. During the war he was the witness of the number of rebellions in this region, particularly that of Abdul Malek, the grandson of Abdul Kader. He himself was maltreated and kept in confinement by the Spanish General Silvestre, a fact which kindled him with a natural desire for revenge.

On the death of his father, Abdul Krim succeeded as the Kaid of his tribe. His long sojourn amongst Spaniards had shown him the weakness of their position, and he undertook the task of showing the warriors of the Riff tribes that if they would temporarily forget their local quarrels, they could achieve a great victory and gain a magnificent booty. The Berbers, quick to recognize his intelligence and competence, rallied round him. In 1921, after the despatch of an ultimatum, he inflicted a defeat on General Silvestre at Anoual and became sole master of the Riff.

This victory left in Abdul Krim's hands 120 guns, thousands of rifles, and millions of cartridges. He was now to become the redoubtable type of Berber partisan furnished with modern weapons.

In a very short time he had ten or fifteen thousand men in the Riff provided with quick-firing rifles, machine-guns; outposts linked by telephone to his headquarters, and depots of stores and munitions. He built roads and bridges, and with the four million pesetas paid by the Spaniards as ransom for prisoners he provided himself with the assistance of European officers.

At the beginning of 1924 he was absolute sovereign of the Riff, exerising a genuine military dictatorship, and his ambition was to extend his sway still farther, especially towards the south, in order to draw nearer to Fez, the riches of which had always been a lure to the mountain tribes. Pushing forward on that side, he came into contact with the Djebala tribes of the south, who almost all lived within the French zone and had hitherto been left by Lyautey in a state of tolerated independence. Must the Riff tribesmen be allowed to permeate tribe after tribe, as far as the Vergha river? That would have been highly dangerous. The tribes along the river served as a shield both to Fez and to the Fez-Taza railway, the sole line of communication with Algeria. It was essential to be sure of their loyalty.

General de Chambrun was entrusted with the establishment of a line of posts north of the Vergha.

The Djebala tribes allowed the expedition to advance without resistance, and the great tribe of the Beni Zeroual, numbering 24,000 souls, came under French authority. At the end of December, 1924, Marshal Lyautey addressed a despatch on the situation to the French Government. He pointed out that the French effectives in Morocco had been decreased from 95,000 men in 1921 to 64,000 in 1923. This reduction he had accepted on account of the difficult financial situation in France at that time. But he drew attention to the fact that, in consequence of the evacuation of a great part of the Spanish zone, the enhanced prestige of Abdul Krim, and the vast residue of munitions, guns and machine-guns acquired by his victories, the peril was growing greater and that urgent action was becoming necessary. If the rich Vergha valley and the peaceable agricultural tribes inhabiting it were allowed to fall into the hands of the Riffis, Fez would be in danger. Although Abdul Krim, for propaganda purposes, had given the style of Republic to his state, he openly spoke of setting himself up as Sultan in Fez, for, in his own words, "Mulai-Yussef is merely a puppet in Lyautey's hands." Already prayers were being said in his name in the Riff—a thing that had not happened in Morocco for a very long time. When asked what his frontier was, he would answer: "War will decide." He no longer concealed his determination to follow up his attack on the Spaniards with an attack on the French.

Could an understanding be reached with the Riffis? Would it be possible to make a successful trial, amongst the mountain tribes, of the Lyautey-Galliéni policy? "For the moment, no," was the Marshal's answer. "They are intoxicated, suffering from extreme megalomania and from xenophobia. They are openly preparing the change of front against us. Opposite our posts they have set up a whole system of symmetrical posts, manned by picked chiefs armed with machine-guns. They are arranging roads and telegraph lines." Abdul Krim was aware of the weakness of the French effectives. He counted on the desertion of the Foreign Legion, as also on his secret relations with the chiefs of rebel tribes in the French zone and with the young intellectuals of Fez. "I recognize," he said, "that the French have given Morocco order, security, and economic prosperity; but I shall bring the same benefits, with the further advantage that I am a Moslem, and so it will be from a leader of their own faith, not from an Infidel, that the Moors will receive these blessings." In Asia Minor they were already selling coloured lithographs showing Abdul Krim laying low the armies of the Christians. Here was a menace of the utmost gravity, not only for Morocco, but for all Northern Africa.

Not that the Marshal feared a rising of the whole of Morocco in sympathy with Abdul Krim. In the eyes of the citizens of Fez he was an adventurer and a usurper. The young Moors with advanced ideas did not desire his victory. Their desire was not to go and live in a primitive capital at Ajdir, but to go and work in Paris at the schools of Political Science or Fine Arts. When Lyautey questioned them about their feelings, one of them answered him: "Abdul Krim's modernism is stuff-and-nonsense. Our fathers had experience in their day of a modernist Sultan—Abdul Aziz and his friends. We know what he cost us. He ruined Morocco."

But although Lyautey could feel sure, and rightly so, of the majority of the Moors, he did not encourage excessive optimism. Gusts of fanaticism and xenophobia could blow across the country very quickly. Morocco might be in no grave peril, but that was only conditional on certain measures being taken. First, political action must make sure of the tribes, and of the Beni Zeroual in particular. Then, not one step should be taken over the Riff border, a wasps' nest where there was everything to lose and nothing to win. Abdul Krim must not be provoked, but enough men must be held to secure the loyalty of the Sultan of a population which only asked to remain in that loyalty.

Marshal Lyautey pointed out what reinforcements were necessary, and had reduced his demands to the lowest possible figure. The General Army Staff had told him that he could not be provided with more than eleven battalions; he accordingly asked for eleven battalions. "If I have obliged myself to ask only a minimum, it is because I am deeply conscious of the difficulties which France might have in providing more." Naturally, this report could set forth no more than the situation on December 20th, 1924, and Lyautey concluded, with his customary respect for the fluid character of truth where action is concerned, in these terms: "It is possible that my proposals will no longer accord with the situation to-morrow or the day after to-morrow. We are not reasoning about inert matter; we are confronting a living reality which is evolving day by day."

*   *   *   *   *

The first attack by the Riffis in 1925 took place against the "buffer" tribe of the Beni Zeroual, and began on April 13th. By April 16th this great tribe was vanquished. Villages were burnt and sacked; countless hostages were sent back into the Riff; and the Beni Zeroual tribesmen, closed in on all sides by the Riffis, found themselves constrained to take up arms against the French. Their rapid collapse made a deep impression on the neighbouring tribes, who, under threats from the Riffis, forsook their allegiance one after the other between April 23rd and 28th. At the moment described in the preceding chapter—that is to say, at the end of April—the situation had already became serious. The stampede of a few tribes might well mean the sudden uncovering of Fez, and all the troops that the French had were the six battalions holding the posts and nine battalions in reserve.

The defence of Fez was provided for, under General de Chambrun, by two main bodies blocking both of the chief arteries leading to the town, and Abdul Krim's southward progress was checked. Unfortunately, many small posts in the Vergha valley fell. Nevertheless, by the end of May, the Riffis were forced to realize that it would be difficult for them to cross the river, and in June, as Abdul Krim had been unable to break the front by a direct attack, he tried an outflanking movement. This was stopped by General Freydenberg. For a moment it seemed that everything had been saved. Harvest-time was drawing near, and this would doubtless deprive the Riffis of a large part of their forces. Lyautey considered that the moment for an offensive had come. M. Painlevé, the Prime Minister, had come over to Morocco by aeroplane, and the Marshal sent him a letter concluding with these words:

An offensive is the absolute essential to restore the situation. It cannot at present be envisaged on the northern front, and failing this it must be envisaged elsewhere. Where? There is only one single point: that is, Ajdir, with Franco-Spanish, and if possible British, co-operation. Therefore, Ajdir—and at the earliest possible moment.

Ajdir lay near the Mediterranean coast within the Spanish zone, and a landing of troops carried out there would have reversed the position of the Riffis. But for this an agreement with the Spaniards was necessary, and was only effectually realized later.

Towards the end of June a fresh and very violent attack was made in the Taza region, and all new projects had to be suspended in order to cope with the most urgent. Certain loyal tribes, the Tsouls and the Branes, attacked by five thousand Riffis, had partially deserted. This was serious. If other tribes did likewise, it might mean the loss of Taza, a conflagration in the Atlas, a threat to Fez both east and south, a fifty-mile front to be held with fifteen battalions which had suffered both physically and in morale, in a country in full insurrection. Lyautey came to Fez. Once again he had to take a decision on which the fate of Morocco depended. Was it possible to hold on to Taza? Many considered that it was not, and advised evacuating the town. On July 4th the liaison officers despatched to Taza came back with the report that the situation was desperate. The only reserves left in the sector were two battalions, and no reinforcements from France were expected. After a night's reflection, the Marshal reached his decision, on July 5th: "I am not bound to accept everything I am told," he said. "To evacuate Taza would be foolish and absurd." He therefore gave orders to hold on, and, if withdrawal became necessary, not to evacuate Taza, which would remain defended by six battalions. The remainder of the troops in the sector would fall back upon Fez. He wired to Paris:

To abandon a French town to the hands of the enemy at the present moment, without resistance, would compromise us in the eyes of the Moorish Moslems and of our opponent in such a way that I still prefer to run all the risks of the steps I propose.

345

On that very day this attitude was justified by two successes. After the 6th the Marshal was able to regard the crisis as over. It had marked the most critical moment of the campaign. Reinforcements from France and Algeria were beginning to arrive, and above all, it was reassuring to note that the submissive tribes, although worked upon by Abdul Krim, were showing a calmness and loyalty which were the crowning result of Lyautey's internal policy. The frontier tribes were alone in their desertion, and it is right to mention also that the Tsouls and Branes themselves had fought on the French side for two months before breaking away. As for Abdul Krim, he had certainly shown himself a true leader during this time. His strategy had been prudent; he had attempted first a breakthrough by sheer force in a surprise attack towards Fez, and then flanking movements, in accordance with all the rules of military science. Falling back into his mountains, he was to put up a resistance for nine months longer.

But from July onwards the command of operations passed into the hands of General Naulin, and then of Marshal Pétain. Marshal Lyautey had himself requested to be relieved of a responsibility that was truly overwhelming, as he was obliged to command troops on active service and at the same time to administer a great country. But it is clear that he did not relish this duality of control in a country where he had so long been the sole ruler. On September 24th he resigned.

Lyautey, Marshal of France, Commissioner Resident-General of the French Republic in Morocco, to His Excellency the Minister of Foreign Affairs, Paris.

Recent military operations have brought about a recovery of the situation which leaves us practically on the line which we held before the attacks from the Riff.

The Protectorate is now restored to the position which it held in April, that is to say, to the point which it had reached after thirteen years of continued progress. I think I am entitled to say that my task, as entrusted to me in 1912, has been accomplished.

So long as Morocco was in danger I refrain from renewing my request to be replaced, which I presented to the Government in 1923 and 1924, a request based upon a serious failure of health, and the need for a repose to which my thirty years of colonial activity have properly entitled me.

From the day when the Riff menace, to which I drew attention with increasing anxiety, came to a head, and did so at the time when my reports had anticipated, my sole consideration has been to withstand the blow with the diminished means at first at my disposal, and to save the situation.

To-day it can be sincerely affirmed that the danger has been averted, and that, in view of the important effectives close at hand, the future can be viewed with confidence.

It is, then, with a perfectly free conscience that I request to be relieved of my functions as Commissioner Resident-General in Morocco.

My succesor will be faced by new problems raised by the Riff question, as I explain in the confidential letter herewith, recalling what has been achieved since the Riff attack.

These fresh problems require to be faced and dealt with on lines of continuity, and call for a new man in the prime of his strength, backed by the confidence of the Government.

I therefore request that my successor should be appointed without delay.

I shall hold myself at his disposal to advise him, should he consider that my experience of the country could be of service to him.

LYAUTEY.

He could not without a wrench have left the country to which he had given all his strength and all his thoughts for thirteen years. On October 5th he said farewell to the Government Council, and after its meeting he received the notables at the Residency. For the last time the spahis in their red and white burnouses, holding their lances with the tricolour pennants, saw their chief. When the tribes learned of Lyautey's departure they showed anxiety. "Lyautey is being taken from us," said one Kaid; "at least they'll leave his family, will they not?"

A large number of them assembled spontaneously to send the Marshal an address of farewell, couched in the rich Arab style:

Praise be to Allah! There is naught enduring but His empire! The tribes herein named have but one eloquence and one unanimous voice to proffer their gratitude to that man so full of solicitude who, by his great and splendid work, makes benevolence to rise in the firmament of humanity, spreads everywhere the mantle of order, cast down the citadels of anarchy, and whose care it is that never does there arise there any conflict between civilization and the ancient customs of the country. By following these ways, this man has taken, in the hearts of all the peoples hereabove named, the place which a loving father should hold in the hearts of loyal children filled with filial piety towards him.

One leader of a religious confraternity came to address him in the name of the Moslems of Fez:

Over the lives of our fathers hovered the great figure of Mulai-Idriss. For us that will remain the Protector of the City and the symbol of our religious integrity. But our sons will date their history from Lyautey.

The Marshal embarked on the liner *Anfa* at Casablanca. He took a last meal at the Residency.

M. Charles Reibel, the deputy, was visiting Morocco and sat beside him. Lyautey did not speak. He was absorbed in his thoughts. Suddenly he leaned towards his neighbour, and said, in his abrupt, indistinct voice: "You know, Reibel, there's one thing that annoys me very much. . . . I shan't be building any more towns. . . ."[1]

From the Residency to the harbour the journey was one "of triumph and mourning." No orders had been issued, but a great country was spontaneously crying out its gratitude to its creator. The jetty was thronged with Frenchmen and Moors. Kaids had come from the most distant tribes. For over an hour Lyautey moved amongst these groups, finding direct and deeply felt remarks for all. At last he set foot on the gangway and gave a last sign of farewell. On the quay many spectators had tears in their eyes. When the Marshal turned towards the boat, the officers were startled by his ravaged expression. With old Captain Juliani of the *Anfa* he went below to the saloon. "Now," he said, "I don't wish to see anyone. . . ." The gangway was drawn in. When the ship moved off from the quay, all the sirens and whistles in the harbour shrieked out. From every side came tugs, motor-boats, and native craft, eager

---

[1] Wladimir d'Ormesson, *Revue de Paris*, April 15th, 1931.

to escort Morocco's Chief as long as possible. It was a fine race, and a perilous one, amongst the waves. Then the smaller craft were outdistanced, and the silence was broken only by the beat of the propellors and the plash of waves.

At Gibraltar two British torpedo-boats, by Admiralty orders, were awaiting the *Anfa* at the entrance to the Straits, and escorted her through to the Mediterranean, their massed crews cheering on deck.

Wladimir d'Ormesson was an eyewitness of the return to Marseilles, and has described it: "A few close friends of the Marshal—Félix de Vogüé, Pierre Viénot and myself—had decided to go to Marseilles to greet the Marshal and Madame Lyautey on their arrival. On October 13th, about two o'clock in the afternoon, we were on the pier where the vessel was to moor. We looked round for the troops who would doubtless be there to honour the great commander. We looked for the official personages invited by the Government to greet, on his final return to his native soil, one of the supreme builders of French greatness. Had we made a mistake? How? Was it the day? The time? There was no sign of any assemblage. Not a man. Not a flag. The Préfet? Absent. The General commanding the Fifteenth Corps? Absent. The Mayor? Absent. The representatives of the Department? Absent. Nobody. Well, we must have been misinformed. That ship coming was not, could not be, the *Anfa!* But it was. We had not been misled. For there was the Marshal on deck; he had seen us and was waving his hand. . . . We were a handful of friends—the Pasha of Marrakesh amongst us—and in silence we took off our hats. . . . The *Anfa* was moored. A gangway was put across. Half an hour dragged by, a dreary, cruel half-hour, during which we were stuck there, the Marshal on deck, ourselves on the pier unable to join him because "nobody was to go on board." The port doctor was late. . . . We had to await his pleasure. . . . Then, when the formalities were at last completed, a Brigade General arrived in a hurry to offer the apologies of the Corps Commander, "who was extremely busy." An official in a soft collar came down to offer the apologies of the Préfet, who also "was very busy." A few gentlemen representing business groups in Marseilles, two or three local journalists, came along. . . . And that was all. . . . Lyautey, the greatest of France's colonial soldiers, the man who had rounded off in Northern Africa the work of Charles X, Bugeaud and Ferry, the man who had organized and defended the Protectorate of the Re-

public in Morocco, the man who saved the whole
of the French African empire, and was now returning to France to enjoy a well-earned retirement—
Lyautey landed. . . . And the only official communication awaiting him at his home in Paris was
a letter from the revenue authorities, requesting
him to settle his outstanding taxes without delay."

XVII

NINETEEN TWENTY-NINE. Thorey.
A Lorraine village, a simple place, overlooked by the high, wide table of the Colline de
Sion. That is where Lyautey lives to-day. He
did not feel inclined to rebuild Crévic. At Thorey
he was the owner of an old house which had belonged to the charming Berthe de Villemotte, who
read her Saint Teresa in fine editions. This house
he had added to and transformed, patiently striving
to revive around him the memories to which he is
faithful.

So painful to him was the ruin of Crévic that he
has sought, in memory at least, to reconstruct the
"house that is dead." In a notebook penned in his
own hand he has drawn it forth from the ashes of
oblivion, room by room, book after book:

Our two rooms were adjacent, with a common
balcony facing westward. Oh, the view from that
balcony in the dawn! The faint mist over the park,
to the left towards the pond, where the Chinese
kiosk perched on its artificial rocks (a whimsy of
1825), and the park, hampered by no enclosure,
stretching across the countryside to the hillsides
fringed with the poplars of the high-road from
Nancy to Strasbourg. Opposite, against two great

clumps of firs, stood out the white shapes of two old Louis XVI vases, and the portico of the swing and trapez. . . . Beyond that, the slopes on the right bank of the Sanon, then the factory smoke of Dombasle, and at night-time the great glow of Nancy. Further to the right, standing out against the copses, the charming statuary of Guibal's "Four Seasons," the jewel of Crévic. . . .

The objects lost at Crévic were irreplaceable, but Lyautey has assembled whatever could recall them. Once again at Thorey he has surrounded himself with his Lorraine *lares:* the portrait of "his Dukes," the yellow and red flag, the engravings showing the funeral procession of Charles III. Standing on the furniture or hanging on the walls are grouped the portraits of all who have worked or battled with him, comrades or superiors of Tonking, Madagascar, and Morocco. Methodically classified in stout files stands the panorama of his crowded life. On the grey canvas backs one reads: *"Family. . . . Social Action. . . . Italy. . . . Southern Oran . . . . Correspondence with Vogüé. . . ."* In a Lorraine granary at the top of the house he has made a Moorish hall. The floor is covered with fine Moorish rugs, and seated on the divan he can still fancy himself at Fez or Marrakesh or Rabat. For a long time he forbade conversation about Morocco. "I don't know that country," he would say. Now the wound is almost healed. There remains the memory of a work that was great, of an empire which he drew forth from the void.

In his village, in the whole of Lorraine, he carries on the regional politics which were already his delight at sixteen. After luncheon on Sundays the Thorey farmers come for coffee and to discuss the affairs of the province. One particular afternoon he had brought over from Nancy a team of students to play against the young men of the village. He enjoys making contacts between intellectuals and peasants, the two classes he has always liked. After the game he took his guests as far as the *"Colline Inspirée"* to visit the monastery. He was welcomed by a cheerful group of novices, sturdy lads in cassocks, mostly Bretons or Alsatians. "I am tired of Paris," he told them, "tired of men, tired of myself. I should like to settle down in your midst to make a retreat from work." They clapped their hands. "Come, Marshal, come! Come along!"—"I shall come. . . . But I want to live your life, and eat the same dishes as you do, and obey your Rule."—I can easily see him ending up as Tolstoy did, with a flight to a monastery. But he would instantly be the superior, the prior, the abbot. He would rebuild and transform and issue orders.

For a moment longer, on the edge of the plateau, he looked over the plains of Lorraine. On that autumnal day the colours of the country had an exquisite subtlety and softness. He leapt into his car: "Drive on . . ." he cried. (*Casablanca, the white walls, the harbour. . . .*) "Good heavens, go easy! Take the little road. . . ." (*Césard, show us your factory . . . and mind, in the logical order. . . .*) "Gently. . . . Go at a walking-pace. . . . Stop at the top of the garden. . . ." He had just purchased up there a few acres of meadowland to round off his park. The land was bare, but planted with stakes that sketched a still invisible wood. Here and there one noticed a bench or a statue, facing in unexpected directions and surprising by their apparent planlessness. The Marshal stopped and took my arm. "Now, look here. . . . What I want is a garden in the French style. . . . The benches and statues indicate the perspectives of the avenues. . . . The benches are Lorraine chimney-pieces turned round and orna-mented with Moorish *zelliges*. . . . Come forward a little. . . . A star, just here. . . ." His cane sketched out its points, and sure enough I saw that the point where we stood was the centre of the circle outlined by the statuary. He gazed on the horizon far away towards a clump of trees. "Those are in

the axis of my central avenue. . . . It will be very
fine. . . . They must not be cut down. . . . Come
along. . . ."

To reach the house we crossed a flooded meadow.
The road-builder has laid across it a pathway of
large flat stones. He turned to me: "When I was
a child, I played at 'countries.' I laid out towns
and roads and rivers in my sand-pile. . . . Later
on they gave me real countries, first, in Tonking,
then in Madagascar, then in Africa. . . . I continued my game. . . . There are more than twenty
towns in the world of my own building. . . . Then
they left me only with this—a park, a village. . . .
All the same to me . . . questions of scale don't
count. . . ."

1930. An autumn evening. (*Do you remember,
Daniel Halévy?*) After dinner, in the light oak
library, he remained silent for a long time. A great
wood fire was burning. Madame Lyautey was
working beside the yellow gleam of a lamp. I
looked at a portrait on the wall, that of Otto, the
eldest son of the Empress of Austria, the last Duke
of Lorraine. I turned over some books. . . . An
inscription from the Princess Bibesco. . . . "To
the royalist who has given an empire to the Republic. . . ." Suddenly the Marshal rose and went
to fetch a file. It was the Aïn-Sefra file. . . .

"Heavens! How could I stop my cavalry at an ideal line traced across desert sand by the imagination of the Paris functionaries . . . ?" Until two in the morning he read. When we left him I heard him summoning one of his officers: "Let's work. . . ."

And next day he took me up to the top of the garden to show me his stripling avenues. On the site which two years earlier I had seen planted with sapless stakes, those white statues, then the sentinels of an imaginary plan, now marked off the visible perspectives of a leafy and living star.

INDEX

INDEX

INDEX

INDEX

El-Mungar, 105, 107, 112
England, 79, 102, 255, 298; still unfriendly, 119; now friendly, 161; their coöperation needed, 344
Epinal, 37
Etienne, Deputy, 151, 311; letter to, 162-154
Eu, 37

Fallières M., 192
Family discipline, in French provinces, 1 *et seq.*
Fashoda, 56
Ferdinand, Archduke, 237
Ferry, Jules, and reverses in Tonking, 119*n.*, 352
Fez, 116, 121, 132, 161, 166, 188, 189, 191, 192, 194, 195, 196, 199, 203, 204, 205, 207, 214, 218, 226, 228, 232, 239, 241, 245, 246, 255, 257, 258, 262, 275, 277, 315, 317, 319, 321, 331, 333, 334, 336, 338, 339, 340, 343, 345, 346, 355
Fianarautsoa, 95,
Figig, the palm trees of, 102, 112, 131, 134, 149
Flanders, 152
Foch, General, 284, 296; saved by Lyautey, 291
Fontaine, Arthur, 48
Fortassa, 149
Fort-Dauphin, 112
Fortoul, Captain, 241
Fortoul, Madame. *See* Madame Lyautey.
Fourtou, M., 27
Franche-Comté, 14, 219
Freydenberg, General, 343
Fromentin, 143

Gaillard, M., 205, 219
Gallibray, Marshal de, 159
Galliéni, Colonel, 75, 77-86, 91, 92, 94, 99, 104, 106, 108, 110, 113, 127, 128, 138, 201, 221,

Galliéni, *continued*
252, 268, 340; described, 62-64; a tour of inspection, 66*ff.*
Gallifet, General, 127
Gallipoli, 249
Garnier, 55
Gautier, E. G., his *Le Sahara*, 124*n.*
George, Lloyd, 284, 296, 297
Germany, 79, 184, 255, 275, 276; jealous of French colonies, 119; new naval policy, 161; policy at Morocco, 162 *et seq.;* beaten at the Conference, 164; threatening clouds, 187, 188
Géryville, 143
Gibraltar, 115, 162, 287, 289, 290, 351; key position for England, 119
Glaoui, a chief, 206
Godard, M., 285
Goethe, 131
Gorizia, 30, 34, 37
Gosset, Dr., operates, 320
Gourand, Colonel, 195, 198, 203, 205, 232, 234, 235, 242, 244, 246, 285, 286, 287, 289, 313; a man to "count on," 226, 227; succeeds Lyautey, 279 *et seq.*
Grande-Chartreaux, the, 24
Gray, 50
Great Wall of China, 182
Greece, 74, 278, 283
Guérin, Charles, poet, 329
Guibal, 355
Guillaume, an officer, 199
Guillaumet, 143
Guingamp, 315
Guynemer, receives Croix de Saint Georges, 296

Halévy, Daniel, 358
Hamou, Zaïan chief, 251
Hamyan tribes, 135
Hanoi, 55, 57, 59, 67, 73
Haouz, 205
Hartley, Sir Charles, 261
Haut-Guir, 183

INDEX

365

INDEX

INDEX

INDEX

INDEX

(1)